"Growing up on the upper West Side of New York City, spending his teen years in Dallas, becoming a lawyer, losing his older sister to suicide, Philip Uninsky has wrestled with his family dynamics and now, in his seventh decade, written about his experiences. This unique memoir by the child of Holocaust survivors, including an enormously gifted mercurial concert pianist father, and a mother who held the family together through the continued reverberations of loss and death into the next generation, is a meditation on the legacy of the Holocaust plus the dislocations, othering and adaptations affecting immigrant parents and their children as they sought to adjust to life in this country. Philip's meditation on the effects of his intense upbringing reflects the realities of resilience and persistence in a society whose ambivalence to immigrants increasingly challenges efforts at assimilation. It is especially compelling in our current circumstances."

—Rochelle Ruthchild, Center Associate, Davis Center for Russian & Eurasian Studies, Harvard University

"This remarkable book challenges received wisdom about memory, trauma, and narrative. Rejecting binary and reductive approaches to the veracity of autobiographical memory, Invented Lives from Troubled Times explores the scattered and elusive history of a family torn apart by the unspeakable horrors of the twentieth century. Uninsky does not simply winnow the wheat of truth from the chaff of confabulation, but takes on the messy, creative, costly, and ultimately human strategies for managing loss and for building a future for the next generation. Conventional explanations for silences and inconsistencies about the past, such as denial and repression, can be relatively inert or reactive ways of approaching trauma. Instead, this book paints a picture of playfulness, creativity, and adaptability that helps to explain how its subjects 'managed to persist despite it all.' The result is a compelling and moving intertwining of personal, psychological, and historical ways of thinking through memory, trauma, and resilience."

—Evelyn Byrd Tribble, Professor of English, University of Connecticut

"Philip Uninsky's gripping memoir plunges us into the stories of his parents' generation—fantasies, romances, and sagas of survival, despair, and hope from those marked forever by displacement and war. Extraordinary people find ways to protect the next generation from the horrors of the past, in music and art, through black humor, or by shifting identities. Uninsky's quest for the truths behind the tales, testing family lore against the record, brings a powerful sense of the limits of memory, as omissions, revisions, and constructed versions help carry, manage, and share intense emotions. The twentieth century's extreme events come alive in this riveting book about a unique family and its remarkable stories."

—John Sutton, Centre for the Sciences of Place and Memory, University of Stirling

Invented Lives from Troubled Times

A Jewish Family's Forms of Resilience after Surviving Pogroms, Revolution, and the Holocaust

Cherry
Orchard
Books

Invented Lives from Troubled Times

A Jewish Family's Forms of Resilience after Surviving Pogroms, Revolution, and the Holocaust

Philip B. Uninsky

Library of Congress Cataloging-in-Publication Data

Names: Uninsky, Philip Boris, 1952- author

Title: Invented lives from troubled times : a Jewish family's forms of resilience after surviving pogroms, revolution, and the Holocaust / Philip Boris Uninsky.

Description: Boston : Cherry Orchard Books, 2025.

Identifiers: LCCN 2025020147 (print) | LCCN 2025020148 (ebook) | ISBN 9798887198477 (hardback) | ISBN 9798887198484 (paperback) | ISBN 9798887198491 (adobe pdf) | ISBN 9798887198507 (epub)

Subjects: LCSH: Uninsky, Philip Boris, 1952---Family | Uninsky, Philip Boris, 1952- ‡x Childhood and youth | Jewish men ‡z United States ‡v Biography

Classification: LCC E184.37.U46‡b A3 2025 (print) | LCC E184.37.U46‡b A3 2025 (ebook) | DDC 940.53/18092 $a B--dc23/eng/20250714

LC record available at https://lccn.loc.gov/2025020147
LC ebook record available at https://lccn.loc.gov/2025020148

ISBN 9798887198477 (hardback)
ISBN 9798887198484 (paperback)
ISBN 9798887198491 (adobe pdf)
ISBN 9798887198507 (epub)

Book design by Kryon Publishing Services.
Cover design by Ivan Grave.

Published by Cherry Orchard Books, an imprint of
Academic Studies Press
1007 Chestnut Street
Newton, MA 02464, USA
press@academicstudiespress.com
www.academicstudiespress.com

Contents

Acknowledgments

I am indebted to all the survivors who shared their narratives over the course of decades and who allowed repeated entry into lives that were bright lights of vivacity, resilience, creativity, and profound humanity, despite it all. And for the stalwart encouragement and historical insights of Kira Stevens, my partner and colleague, who shared much of my journey through this memory palace, no thanks are sufficient.

CHAPTER 1

Memories of Memories

My family maneuvered in piles of secrets, clothing their past with inventive confabulations, half-truths, and comic misdirection. In retrospect, their memories were marked as much by what they excluded as by what they conveyed. When I was young, my family rarely dwelled on their backgrounds and upbringing, and they avoided any detail about the deep and recurring traumas that marked their families' lives, which included World War I, the 1917 Revolution in Russia, the 1919 pogrom in Kyiv, the Ukrainian War of Independence from 1917 to 1921, the Holocaust in France, and the Red Scare in America. Family reminiscences were exclusively conversational, never written; they invariably offered engrossing episodes about their adult lives that ranged from art appreciation to anecdotes highlighting traits they admired, foremost among them cleverness, wit, resilience, empathy, self-sufficiency, and courage. There was never any doubt, from their stories, social life, and self-presentation, that my parents, Alexander and Lucie Uninsky, were secular cosmopolitans who valued talent and clever, literate discourse. Their stories often took the form of droll entertainment that obscured any life lessons they may have contained, as well as any trauma experienced. And whatever theme may have undergirded a particular recollection, it was rarely reinforced in any systematic manner. My family history—my memories of their memories—was discontinuous and certainly unfocused; it was never offered as part of a seamless chronology; it was more akin to a rich archeological dig, my parents' memories providing glimpses of their past, gleaming shards from fractured lives.

Any careful examination of this family narrative must begin with my childhood in New York City. We lived in an apartment overlooking Central Park in an Upper West Side rent-controlled building that was a symbiotic ecosystem of artists and psychoanalysts. With my father, a renowned pianist, away on tour most of the year, it seemed an ideal situation for Lucie. My mother was enveloped in a supportive community, many of whom had left Europe to escape persecution, particularly from the bloodlands of Eastern Europe. To me, as a child in Manhattan in the 1950s and early '60s, Lucie revealed elements of the family history in brief vignettes, snapshots that shuttled by in no particular order, like images on my prized View-Master. Perhaps because my sister and I asked for them, Lucie would occasionally tell stories about the circumstances that brought them to New York during World War II. Infrequently autobiographical, they were typically tales of my father's heroism, dwelling on his quick presence of mind at a time of enormous, but only vaguely described disorder, and his travels across many borders. To a boy fascinated by warfare, these were eminently believable and engrossing tales. They were also romanticized, no doubt partially accurate, glimpses of the past that were sanitized for a young listener, with only glancing mentions of the Holocaust and devoid of explicit violence of any kind; fear played no role. These reminiscences were brief stories that, once assembled, were not far removed from a fairy tale, with clear demarcations of good and evil, heroic readiness to act with wiliness under duress, and fortuitous interventions of magical good fortune. This is a brief composite of those stories:

> *When World War II was imminent, Alexander, age twenty-nine, cancelled the remaining concerts in his tour of the Middle East, returned to France from Cairo, and enlisted to fight for his adopted country, as did his older brother, a painter—two artists taking up arms. The army, knowing my father was a great pianist, decided to protect his hands (was it ever so?) and placed him in a truck supply detail along the Maginot Line.*
>
> *In the spring of 1940, Nazi Panzer divisions overran the French army. Alexander evaded capture, eventually making it back to Paris, but only after German troops had entered the city. He soon learned that the Nazis had ordered his arrest, and for seven months he evaded capture, moving nearly daily among friends, practicing whenever he could. He was a marked man, a celebrity Jewish pianist who, with his best friend Monio (Lucie's brother), had actively supported the Popular Front of Léon Blum (the first socialist and the first Jewish prime minister of France) and had raised funds to support the Republicans in the Spanish Civil War. My father escaped France by bicycle, riding south, nearly eight hundred miles, to Madrid, where he was identified, having performed to great acclaim the year before, and arrested as an undesirable.*

> *In short order, Alexander managed to free himself by bribing a guard, left Spain, again by bicycle, riding to neutral Portugal, where he found Monio and Lucie. In 1941, he boarded a passenger ship to Argentina, and for the next year performed throughout South and Central America, sending funds to support family and friends in Portugal and France. In mid-1942, he arrived in New York and made his debut at Carnegie Hall. Soon after, he was reunited with Lucie who accompanied him as he performed across North America. They married during their wartime travels, a victory of love and art amid the ruins of war.*

As I neared my teen years, I began to suspect that my mother's wartime reminiscences had a mythic, embellished quality, but they were believable nonetheless, or at least, admiring my father, I wanted them to be true. They followed a pattern typical of many of my family's recollections. Weaving stories together, they constricted time, alternated periods of triumph and great loss without bemoaning misfortune, linked appreciation of art and beauty with the determination and ability to survive, traveled across great distances with relative ease, and stressed the importance of being evasive, quick on your feet, and multilingual.

These memories also were often without a well-developed context and were profoundly depersonalized. When asked why his family left Kyiv, my father routinely demurred, never revealing his parents' motives. He would then launch into a tale, remembering, one day, leaving *schul* quickly, slipping out as the rabbi had fallen asleep and because his older brother,

Evsey, had affixed the teacher's beard to the table. Following the sounds of battle to the Dnieper River, the brothers watched in awe as the Red Army on one bank and the Polish and Ukrainian allied forces on the other, exchanged fire across the Dnieper. If the story of two children gazing at battling armies were true, it most probably occurred in 1920, when Alexander was ten and Evsey twelve.

It was their mischievous pranks, their indifference to organized religion, and their fascination with watching warfare that mattered, but Alexander, in the telling, was not interested in discussing why the forces were fighting, detailing what warfare looked like, or divulging how frightening and brutal it must have been. And if Kyiv as a battleground precipitated the Uninsky family's departure from Ukraine, it was never discussed. While nothing was said about their reasons for leaving for Paris in 1924, my grandparents must have had many reasons to emigrate to Paris beyond the Ukrainian War for Independence, including chronic political unrest in Kyiv as different factions jockeyed for power, the pogroms of 1918–1921 in Kyiv and elsewhere in Ukraine, severe economic hardship, and declining opportunities for Alexander to continue his piano studies.

I remember sharing Lucie's war stories with my friends on the Upper West Side. These tales, including heroic escapes, persistence, survival, and triumphant relocation to a new society, all largely stripped of references to the savagery of war, were components of parental memories in common currency among my New York cohort. Many of my friends had family who were either US veterans or wartime refugees, and they could reciprocate with wartime stories of their own. In the 1950s and early 1960s, we were participating in a popular culture of war remembrance, one that ignored the Holocaust and celebrated military victories on television without graphic violence—*Combat!* and *You Are There*—or replaced death and confinement with laugh tracks on programs such as *McHale's Navy* and *Hogan's Heroes.* My family's stories about the war differed from the popular culture in certain important respects, particularly by avoiding humor in discussions of World War II and by never glorifying the military, even to the extent that made joining the Cub Scouts unthinkable because they were a paramilitary organization requiring a uniform and salutes.

When Alexander was on tour, often for nine months at a time, without any word home other than an occasional telegram, I would imagine he might be something more than a famous pianist, this brave man who had survived so much turbulence. In the early 1960s, I even imagined he might be part of a protective society, perhaps even in the Undzer Shtik (Yiddish for Cosa Nostra). Childhood fantasies of a dangerous, hidden side to my father, in retrospect, seem clear in their origins—it was a time of headlines about gangs roaming the city, of *West Side Story* without Romeo and Juliet.

When he was home, Alexander would assure us that we were safe even when he was abroad. But it did not often seem so. Near our apartment, the turmoil caused by urban renewal on the Upper West Side, which began in 1962, was becoming violent, with gunshots heard at night. This was caused by displacement of the heterogeneous working-class community who lived nearby in apartments and rooming houses to make way for lodgings intended for a wealthier class of renters in the area's sought-after brownstones. I remember my six-block trip to and from our apartment on Ninety-First Street and Central

Park West to school, PS 163 Alfred E Smith "Happy Warrior" Elementary on Ninety-Seventh Street, as a daily adventure, navigating real and imaginary threats.

Beyond this background of turmoil, my childhood suspicions that Alexander was capable of engaging in nefarious activities became all the more vivid when I learned he was spending much of his time in France with the family's most dangerous and heroic member, Anatole, his younger brother. A Resistance hero, Anatole had become a resolute risk-taker who remained on the margins of society.

The family narrative was particularly embellished during the summers in the 1950s and early '60s, when Alexander lived with us, working incessantly to prepare the next year's tour, and occasionally participating in summer festivals. During those months, idyllic times in Aspen, Cape Cod, Fire Island, Nantucket, and elsewhere, my father was at once a glittering and distant parent, always hard at work during the day, communicating with his children only occasionally, often as a comedic dinnertime storyteller, an intellectual borscht belt raconteur, other times as a guardian of the family history, using it to entertain and instruct about music and art with anecdotes that recalled his interactions with the famous. Prokofiev discussed music with him over a chessboard, and they performed piano duets together during late nights. He recalled using his gift of musical mimicry when he was a teen, learning how to play jazz in late 1920s Paris by going out at night to hear Josephine Baker and Django Reinhardt. His proficiency at improvisation brought him work accompanying silent films, one of many examples of how his gift was an essential component of resilience, here providing necessary income for his penurious family. Performance was always associated with the expression of great joy and satisfaction, but in the retelling, occasionally a source of amusement. His account of playing with the Israel Philharmonic Orchestra in 1951, for example, would be followed by a playful critique of the strong-willed musician-survivors who accompanied him, all of whom believed themselves to be the true conductor.

When he was disposed to discuss his family at all during my childhood, Alexander usually focused on his younger brother, Anatole. In each telling, my uncle's mythic qualities grew, offering me a character of bravery, humor, and invincibility, who also had a norm-busting, anarchic, and criminal side. He underwent a nearly hallucinatory kaleidoscope of transformations, emerging from his prewar chrysalis of proto-bohemianism into a guerrilla warrior of the Resistance, who then enforced a brand of postwar justice on *collabos* when the government sought reconciliation. In later years he allegedly supported the Algerian struggle for independence and then embarked on a varied career as *roué*. A charming grifter who reportedly drank heavily and ran up enormous gambling losses, he apparently had an uncommon skill at convincing marks to act against their financial interests. In postwar France, Alexander's little brother lived in a state of constant struggle and disruption, seizing the wealth of others, thumbing his nose at the laws of private property, and, my father would say with evident pride, finding ways to undermine Charles de Gaulle's government for its forgiveness of traitors and colonial brutality.

My father's affection for Anatole was strong, unshakeable, and, he would say, costly, as he routinely paid off his brother's debts. It was easy to believe that Alexander's fierce and generous loyalty was because the younger brother, his flaws notwithstanding, had done something Alexander had not. Anatole stayed behind through the war years, resisted and sought revenge for the French deportations of Jews to death camps. Alexander's particularly strong ties to Anatole, more than to his other siblings, may also explain why he, quite like his brother, would occasionally adopt the role of trickster when I was young, a sometime con artist, but in his case one who did not relieve others of their possessions. His game was to pretend to be something he was not. This curious role-playing intensified during our time in Texas, particularly after the mid-1960s, and revealed, or perhaps crystallized, an occasionally evident dissonance in Alexander's behavior—a well-demonstrated capacity to sustain his ebullient resilience that was becoming tinged with fleeting signs of melancholy.

During the years we lived in New York City, no extended family members ever came to visit. The exception to this familial insularity was my one grandparent who survived the war, my maternal grandmother, and we never spoke of her at home. Although she lived nearby in the city, we saw her rarely and, on those occasions, she was uncommunicative and brusque. Lucie rarely spoke of her father, deflecting most discussions about him, even to the point of never telling us his first name; nothing was ever said of what happened to him during the war. There were no stories of family activities, no photographs shown to fill in Lucie's silence, and with one exception related to her older brother Monio, no remnants of the past that revealed much about her life before coming to the US. Lucie would occasionally reflect, in tangential asides, about the remote and judgmental environment of her youth created by her parents, particularly their disinterest in her education and the unfavorable comparisons they made between her and Monio. He was the family's polymath and everyman, who, so it went, boxed, had a law degree, was a passionate advocate for prison reforms, and was pursuing an advanced degree in philosophy at the Sorbonne when he fled Paris in 1940, all before the age of twenty-four.

Curiously, during her life, Lucie shared only one tangible possession from her prewar life with me, when I was eight years old—a pair of horsehair-filled leather boxing gloves that she claimed had belonged to Monio. During her flight from Paris in late May 1940, through Spain, followed by several months in Porto, then in 1942, obtaining transit to the United States, Lucie somehow held onto the gloves. It then seemed as incredible as it does now. If Lucie somehow kept them in her flight from Paris and through to New York, perhaps they served as a talisman during her times of great peril, as well as reminders of a brother who, I sensed, may have protected her from unloving parents. Or they were merely a tangible expression of an invented narrative, to lend, however implausibly, credibility to a version of the past. This was not the first time that magical thinking infused the family narrative, this time a boxer's instruments appearing from nowhere, emblems of fearlessness and strength.

This and subsequent iterations of the family narrative left me with even fewer memories about my paternal than my maternal grandparents. They too were never referred to by name, and lived in a world without specificity, devoid of any details about their personal preferences, livelihood, religiosity, political beliefs, or activities in Kyiv and Paris. At times, Alexander would mention, in an offhanded manner that paradoxically lent great meaning to the words of one who often spoke outlandishly, that there were cantors among our ancestors who sang in the Great Choral Synagogue of Kyiv. This may have reflected one of Alexander's two principal theories of musical talent—that it was inherited, typically skipping generations. The other theory was the quirky notion that great musical talents had curiously shaped ears. Or it may have been a deliberately enigmatic, even misleading, pleasantry, like many of my father's reminiscences, to place the family origins of his musicianship in a Kyivan building constructed to disguise its true purpose, an Aesopian synagogue. Even our family name was blurred by a convoluted story involving switched identities in the early nineteenth century, a mythologizing fog, I suspect, meant to explain why Uninsky was not a Jewish name, which it may, or may not, be.

As a child, it was easy to imagine Alexander, who was so often physically remote through much of my childhood, as harboring an aggrieved side, privately ranting at the injustice of it all, a troubled artist who could effectively disguise his torment. I had already absorbed the stereotype that all great artists were tortured souls, the image we learned of Van Gogh on our trips to MOMA, and what I learned about Lenny Bruce, a favorite of my father's. When I raised this image of Alexander's art being informed by suffering, my mother would partly affirm my suspicions by repeatedly asserting that my father was only truly at peace when he was performing. Even when he was with the family, Alexander kept his distance, practicing long hours, sleeping little. I could hear music through the summer nights, with seemingly endless repetition of passages until he was satisfied, a nightly reminder of this rather unapproachable man's relentless pursuit of a form of musical perfection. When I was young, it was clear that my father's artistic commitment came with a rigid insistence on self-sufficiency and hard work, and, although he could be affectionate, supportive, and ebullient in conversations with his children, he clearly expected us to follow his example. It seemed, to a child, to be a sink or swim view of the world, burned into my memory by lessons in the ocean which involved a sudden and unexpected release from the back of this strong swimmer.

Any feelings of disquiet and confusion about a potential darkness that might exist in my family were tamped down by my own, perhaps ill-informed conclusions, that my parents and those grandparents I never met were exceptionally heroic and resilient folk, all indomitable forces of nature. During and after World War I and through the mid-1920s, so the narrative went, my grandparents and many of their relatives in Eastern Europe were part of an arduous and perilous diaspora to France, Cuba, Argentina, and the US. Once World War II ended and US citizenship was obtained, Lucie and Alexander returned to France in 1948 to rebuild Alexander's career. For many reasons, including more frequent bookings in North and South America, they settled in New York City in 1952, and in a matter of months, Alexander was blacklisted, which included a revocation of his passport, precipitating a suspension of his performing career. The family quickly departed to Toronto for two years until his passport was restored by court order.

This history of persecution and repeated, involuntary migration and career setbacks included cycles of wealth and social status lost, regained, and lost again. Whenever this history was discussed, it was done with a carefully cultivated nonchalance, a shrug to imply the strength of their resilience and their indifference about that which could never be restored. In addition to this astonishing ability to survive chronic misfortune, the family history included those whose powers of endurance seemed folkloric, the family super-mensches. Avram Uninsky, for example, reputedly made it to Cuba from Kyiv in the 1920s and was known, my father would insist, as "Avi der Ligner" (Avi the Liar) because he insisted his age was seventy even when he had reached one hundred. This was all that was said of Avram, leaving me to imagine a survivor with nearly supernatural vigor and, like my parents, a capacity to find humor in survival.

Although I was part of a community of children whose parents were profoundly affected by war, I also came to understand that much of what I understood about my family did not conform to what I could readily observe as a child in Manhattan and, even less, as a teenager in Dallas, where my father became an artist in residence at Southern Methodist University in 1962. Although several of my friends in New York City were also children of Shoah refugees or of blacklisted artists, no one I knew had one parent gone most of the year, none imagined their father to be a secret mobster, and few had parents who could or would frequently drop names like mine did. Lucie and Alexander made little secret of their friendships with many of the inter- and post-war artistic glitterati and the near famous, including the composers Prokofiev,

Ravel, Stravinsky, and Bernstein, painters Diego Rivera, Jean Hélion, and Emmanuel Mané-Katz, and innumerable classical and jazz musicians, from Isaac Stern to Billy Taylor. In retrospect, I recognize these associations with artistic greatness served many purposes, to inflate their children's pride and sustain theirs, to educate us about the vitality of arts, and to set us apart.

This sense of being different, of being the child of parents whose tumultuous and unusual life experiences militated against ready assimilation to American life, produced a deep ambivalence about my place in the family, and led, particularly in my early teens, to a posture of disinterest in the family history that occasionally bordered on alienation. I preferred to fit in with my peers and at times felt more in common with my friends who dreamed of pitching for the Dodgers or the Yankees than with my own family. This distancing from parents and their version of the past and a desire to feel assimilated was magnified by a persistent sense that I somehow was genetically distinct, adopted, or perhaps the child of an affair. By age twelve, I was a head taller than anyone else in my family. I was also, at that age, blond when everyone else in the family was dark-haired, which my parents joked was an anti-Aryan defense mechanism. And my sister was a violin prodigy, appearing in *Life* magazine when she was seven, clearly her father's daughter, while I struggled mightily with my mediocre journey from piano to cello to clarinet to a clumsy baseball player in Central Park and the dusty, hot fields of Dallas.

Like many of the families I grew up with in New York's Upper West Side in the 1950s, English did not come naturally to my parents. They usually preferred French when they spoke with us at home. Even when English was spoken, it was a heavily accented stew enriched with words from several other languages. In retrospect, living with this polyglot family was an ongoing linguistic challenge, as my sister and I worked at deciphering how language clothed our parents' thoughts and consequently disguised them. English was my father's last language learned after at least a dozen others, and it was my mother's fourth or fifth. In our small family, language occasionally created a fog of incomprehensibility, where English and French conversations were infused with Yiddish, Hebrew, Russian, Spanish, and Portuguese. Language shifting served a wide range of purposes. It could establish privacy between adults in the presence of their children; it was also used for emphasis, irony, humor, drama, to establish authenticity, and, on rare instances, to expand our vocabulary. My sister and I tried to translate covertly when our parents were trying to exclude us, but after French, the use of other languages was too intermittent and occurred unpredictably. This meant that some of the family history was enveloped in a linguistic haze, with portions unintelligible, until I finally managed, after years of trying, to interrupt successfully for translations, which were usually, but reluctantly, offered.

Much of Alexander's multilingualism was a form of performance art, often intended to prompt laughter about life's absurdity by punctuating a conclusion or punchline with a Yiddish expletive or a Russian obscenity. Over time, vulgarity propelled family humor, but also served other purposes. It was used, in some instances, to emphasize a strongly held sentiment. He loathed Americans' fixation on shopping, and particularly detested malls, referring to them as "zhopping centers," offered with a heavy Russian accent to ensure we remembered that the word *zhoppa* meant ass. Many of my friends, when visiting, would hear my father swear with great imagination and fervor. He took pleasure in translating vulgar oaths for them into many languages. Alexander also took vulgarity to a higher ground, insisting that it was in homage to Lenny Bruce, who was routinely arrested for violating laws against obscenity. He admired Bruce for insisting on the importance of distinguishing vulgarities from immoral obscenities, which were violence, intolerance, and hatred. But truth be told, Alexander just loved swearing, and it could be a sword as much as a shield, puncturing foolishness and terminating unpleasant or irritating conversations. But when talking about their past, neither parent accepted my entreaties to tell me more about the "real" obscenities they experienced—pogroms in Kyiv, the Russian Civil War, the Shoah in France, McCarthyism.

As my sister and I grew older, there was an unresolved tension between parental memories, that either veiled or entirely omitted discussion of their trauma, and our emerging suspicions that their traumatic experiences, which we knew well had occurred decades ago, might somehow be affecting their recollections and behavior. Eliane and I became more aware that our parents' efforts to establish a semblance of normality were unsuccessful at masking certain discordant signs. These were rare but noteworthy and included fluctuating explanations of the past that were evident confabulations, incidents of jovial tricksterism, sudden histrionic displays of empathy for the less fortunate, and occasional tirades about various form of American injustice and intolerance.

As a teen, my curiosity about trauma's impact on my parents' equanimity and transparency deepened, particularly when disturbing reminders of their troubled past suddenly became apparent. One incident, in particular, stands out. In 1971, Anatole, who I still had not met, apparently wrote my father, informing him of his intention to murder a French collaborator scheduled for release from prison by President Georges Pompidou. I cannot be certain if my uncle really intended this assassination, or even if my father had actually been contacted by his brother, but with the news of the impending release, my father become uncharacteristically somber and withdrawn. For the first time, we discussed the impact of collaborators with some specificity. He referred to cousins in the South of France who were betrayed and sent to death camps. This was a passing moment. Alexander claimed he was calmed when I offered to write a letter of protest to *Time* magazine in his name. Perhaps he was feigning a sense of resolution.

This family crisis occurred during a time, beginning in 1969, when Alexander was exhibiting an increasingly prickly and tempestuous behavior, largely the result of an intensifying struggle with the arthritic deformation of his hands and his displeasure with living in Dallas, particularly his position as artist in residence at Southern Methodist University. In recent years his concert tours were shorter and recording sessions fewer, in part, I surmised, because he had also managed to alienate a succession of managers. This was also a time, when I returned home from college, that we would talk as never before. I asked him to teach me Russian, planning on somehow getting to the Soviet Union, and asked more directly about his past. Not that the opportunity of extended conversations made his version of the family history any more believable. I knew that the sense of humor and the inventiveness of this pianist of the Romantic repertoire were quite baroque. His stories were, as they had always been, theatrical, entertaining, and heavily ornamented. His inventiveness was more on display, much of which wobbled between silliness and mockery of American gullibility and limited sophistication.

Questioning the candor and veracity of my family's narrative did not come easily. I can see now that it came in four stages. The first, as I have described, began as a young teenager, wanting to assimilate and recognizing the odd dissonance of my parents, a feeling which deepened when I went to college. It involved the gradual acceptance that they were not who they seemed to be and were, in some ways, unknowable. I remember, particularly on hot summer days in Dallas, listening to Alexander practice and reading the biographical snippets on the back of his many album covers. I could plainly see that factual consistency was not one of their principal features. Had my father and mother been intentionally deceptive? Were they being theatrically protective? Or was this pathological behavior?

Stage two occurred after college, when my first opportunities to explore the family narrative met with continual disappointment. In 1973 the Thomas J. Watson Foundation funded my proposal to examine the intensifying efforts of Soviet Jews to emigrate. The project was designed at the very moment my curiosity about my family's past had deepened, particularly about my father's Kyivan roots, the secular world views of both parents raised in religious households, and the migration of their families to Paris in the early 1920s. In October

I arrived in the Soviet Union, intent on exploring the first wave of migration to Israel and subsequent transitions to France and other Western European nations. Traveling through Russia in late 1973, two years after a US-Soviet détente had begun, I interviewed refuseniks (those denied permission to emigrate), Jews planning to emigrate, and anyone willing to speak about signs of dissidence. Particularly in Leningrad and Moscow, détente was leading to a new openness. In Kyiv, however, respondents were rare and uncommunicative, and I encountered a determined unresponsiveness from members of the Jewish community and staff at the National Music Academy of Ukraine, formerly the Kyiv Conservatory where my father's musical education began. All my attempts to locate relatives in Ukraine, if any remained, amounted to nothing. After several months in the USSR I learned much about a yearning of Jews to emigrate, but next to nothing about the Uninsky family.

When I finally met them in 1974, my father's siblings, Evsey, Anatole, and Elisabeth, all confirmed a familial pattern, a firmly entrenched reluctance to reveal even a little about their parents, their family's migration from Kyiv to Paris, and most particularly about the Shoah. Evsey, in recompense for his military service, or so the story went, was provided a bistro in the tiny village of St. Rémy-sur-Avre, forty-eight kilometers from Chartres. A confirmed bachelor before the war, he was now correcting his error, happily married, he would say, with a twinkle in his eye, to the *fille du boulanger* (baker's daughter), mother of his six children. When asked about his experiences in the 1930s and '40s, he would deftly deflect to the present. This wariness about the past made him, in my eyes, a pretender in many regards. If he retained a sense of his Jewishness, it was entirely internal, and, he told me, in a private aside, no one in the village knew of his past as an artist in Paris or the fame of his younger brother, the pianist. During my occasional visits to Saint-Rémy-sur-Avre in the 1970s and early 1980s, Evsey occupied, it always seemed effortlessly, the role of a simple tavern owner, at sunrise pouring large glasses of wine in *ballons* to local farmers on their way to the fields and selling hunting and fishing licenses.

Evsey's few contributions to the family narrative were highly circumscribed, limited nearly exclusively to what seemed candid depictions of his postwar life. By contrast, the youngest Uninsky brother, Anatole, was never a person who resorted to candor about either the past or present. Often on the run, he was, as it turned out, everything my parents had described—a charming con man and a gambler running up debts and hiding from creditors. According to my parents' version of the family history, it seemed evident why the past was kept so well sealed by Alexander's brothers. They had suffered mightily during the war, Evsey as a prisoner of war who managed to survive during five years of captivity in a German prisoner-of-war camp, and Anatole, suddenly converted from an aspiring author to Resistance combatant immersed in violence for over three years. Elisabeth, Alexander's younger sister, somehow survived the war in Paris and simply refused to discuss her upbringing, siblings, or parents for reasons she never disclosed.

Stage three occurred in the late 1970s and '80s, when I became a social historian of France and my curiosity about my family's past, as a matter that could be proven, enlarged upon, or dismissed, intensified. In addition to my own research, I attempted to attach family stories to specific times and places, to separate fact from fiction. My interests in following the trail from my memory of family reminiscences to documentary and testamentary confirmation began to dwindle when I became a public interest attorney in the early 1990s. The quest, however, was never fully extinguished, and it rekindled when I became a director of a nonprofit later that decade. Perhaps this was the inevitable result of implementing evidence-based psychological interventions for children and employing dozens of therapists, which turned my attention back to interpreting the family narrative in psycho-social terms. Diagnosis and treatment of pediatric PTSD played a prominent role in therapeutic debates at my agency, and inevitably brought me back to the question of trauma's impacts. It became increasingly clear to me, more absorbed than ever in the work of talk therapists, that establishing verisimilitude in the family history was less important than preserving the created version of their past, that told at night, over dinner, on walks, in everyday interactions.

Stage four was a decade-long period of lessened interest in exploring the family narrative. It began when Kira, my partner, and I took steps to resettle my mother, who no longer could live on her own in Dallas, and helped her move to our small college town. From 2002 until she died, in 2012, Lucie lived in a state of intensifying discomfort, increasingly infirm and unable to adjust to a world that was undeniably devoid of art, music, and fellow travelers. Lucie began increasingly to withdraw from her past, dropping reminiscences from her conversations, with questions about her earlier life often treated as unwelcome intrusions. She enthusiastically and cheerfully adopted the role of doting grandmother, but hints of an undercurrent of melancholy had set in, which understandably became more evident when, in 2006, my sister, Eliane, an accomplished physician who was estranged from Lucie, committed suicide. To my astonishment, Lucie's expressions of grief subsided in a matter of months. However, during her last years, for the first time, occasional feelings of regret and unmooring began to mark her demeanor. In her nineties, she was apart perhaps more dramatically than ever, she would say, with no peers left, a cultural urbanite living in an alien world of small-town New York.

After Lucie's death in 2012, I returned to my notes of family conversations, compiling the memories they conveyed, helped along by a few physical remnants of the past that Lucie had retained but never shared. My parents, who married in the States as wartime refugees, were naturalized as American citizens a few years after VE Day. While they had tried living in Paris again, they decided, a few months before I was born in 1952, to reside permanently in New York City. Immigration to a new country, the decision to become rooted citizens, was clearly a new beginning for Lucie and Alexander, providing fertile ground for a rewritten personal history. This no doubt applies to many immigrants who reframe their lives, attempting to free themselves of parts of a past deemed best forgotten and as a strategy of assimilation. But for my family, and for many others, depiction of who they were and what they remembered or chose to convey as their history was not solely, not even principally, a series of adaptations intended to promote acceptance in new society. I suspected their trauma was so profound, experienced multiple times, resulting in so much loss that they saw themselves as beyond assimilation, as constantly alien, as people who were, in some sense, in a state of continual alertness and readiness to move on. I have come to believe that their memories, told and retold, especially when I was young and most impressionable, was a form of living theater, using laughter, hyperbole, invention, and wit both to entertain and to present a narrative about the past that would help insulate their children from horror and to teach lessons about empathy, courage, love of beauty and creativity, which they believed was critical for survival. It was a playful theater of resilience and protection. Over time, I also began to suspect this performative communication was also a self-directed activity, an often-repeated performance intended to dampen, even displace, what I imagined were their own recollections of horrific experiences, perhaps well hidden, but no doubt present.

Writing about this family narrative rife with invention and playfulness raises many questions about the long-term impacts of trauma on memories retained and shared and on the behaviors of survivors. To paraphrase John Cage, who when asked about the meaning of his innovative compositions using chance form, prepared piano, and, on occasion, silence, famously observed, in essence, that the questions were so good, they should not be spoiled by ready answers. In part, it seems that for my extended family, questions such as these always defied satisfactory responses since they all, my parents and their siblings, rarely provided any details about what they saw, felt, or remembered about the violence they must have witnessed, their repeated flights for survival, and the other grim events in their lives. They must have been deeply traumatized, but in what ways did it affect the ways they remembered, divulged, and behaved?

When we still lived in New York City in the 1950s and early 1960s, Lucie and Alexander offered rare but recurring intimations of the interplay of trauma and their efforts to maintain emotional stability. Once a year my parents provided a glimpse at the intense pain of loss in their lives, and even then, very offhandedly. They would announce that we would be going to a synagogue for Yom Kippur, not as religious observance or to atone for our sins, but rather to hear a talented cellist perform Bruch's *Kol Nidrei.* There was little doubt that this explanation of our family's breach of its adamant avoidance of any religious involvement was a pretext. On those rare occasions, they were melancholic in a restrained manner, which to others must have appeared as a tearless sadness, but in a manner so private and discrete it was impossible to know who, if anyone, they were remembering. Was an open display of grief for lost family and friends too exacting emotionally? Or perhaps trauma had blurred their recall, permitting them to live without so much of their past? Still, such a surgically exact suppression of the past was unlikely to be due to failures of recollection. Lucie's memory and recall were excellent. At age ninety she insisted on providing line-by-line revisions of a recent musical appreciation commemorating the centennial of my father's birth and the bicentennial of Chopin's. The author conceded the accuracy of her biographical revisions and quickly issued a new version, with a more complete discography and compendium of Alexander's performances.[1]

---

1 Lazaros C. Triarhous, *Singing Chopin: The Brilliant Pianism of Alexander Uninsky* (Puurs: UniBook, 2010); Lazaros C. Triarhous, *Singing Chopin: The Brilliant Pianism of Alexander Uninsky* (New York: Corpus Callosum, 2011).

My father's memory was stupefying—he could transpose orchestral scores into piano accompaniments for his students without looking at a score and could remember every card played in a night of bridge. Perhaps the horrors they witnessed and experienced were involuntarily sequestered parts of their memories, or were they consciously compartmentalizing to survive? Or did Lucie and Alexander choose to have their living family exist with an alternate past? Were they deliberately inventing a family history in order to immunize their children, creating a set of mythogenic, entertaining confabulations that were barely rooted in actual experience? And in what ways, if any, were the dissonant behaviors that I began to notice as I grew older related to trauma experienced decades before? Were they perhaps long-delayed consequences, emerging as they aged, or were they intentional if indirect glimpses offered because Lucie and Alexander believed I was old enough and capable of understanding?

For five decades, I have sorted through my memories of their memories, the narratives of my extended family of survivors, trying to unravel the meanings of what was said and unsaid, done and not done. This effort does not dwell on the details of the trauma experienced, partly because the historical record is so well known, and in part because family members provided nothing but veiled hints of the horrors. In one regard, however, it is clear that Lucie, Alexander and their siblings represent a stark counter-narrative to the oft-repeated finding that experiencing intense and repeated trauma serves as a great leveler. This extended family was not flattened by trauma; they were not plagued by evident signs of chronic depression, loss of vitality, or failing resilience and never showed signs of loss of agency. They were quite dissimilar in their patterns of extraordinary persistence, distinct in so many ways, by occupation, interest in the arts, senses of humor, and attachment to place. As I hope will become clear, trauma did not negate their capacity to inventively manage various pathways, their resourceful adaptations toward enduring resilience.

If there is one other widely accepted view of this generation of survivors and refugees, it is that their children are at risk. No doubt Alexander and Lucie were acutely aware of the work emerging in the 1950s on the intergenerational transmission of Holocaust trauma. Many of their closest friends were psychoanalysts who themselves were immersed in this research. Perhaps my parents were persuaded that they needed to insulate their children from the consequences of trauma, and it is now clear to me that they tried. But it is also possible, given their own capacity to survive trauma and reemerge seemingly intact, that they may have harbored some doubts about the research's applicability to their own children. There are good reasons to have such doubts. If one generation's exposure to severe trauma puts the successive generation at risk, it is still poorly understood why some are, for the most part, unaffected, while others are not. Nor are there convincing studies of the relative effects of living in refugee and survivor households compared to other households, where other forms of damaging adversity are legion: to name a few, intense poverty, domestic violence, and chemical addictions. The many efforts to gauge the prevalence of mental health disorders among adult children of Shoah survivors have found an equivalent or perhaps a somewhat higher level than among all adults in the United States. The risk in examining this nexus lies in ascribing causation too readily. The pathways of intergenerational transmission of psychological dysfunctions are many and still beginning to become understood, as is the psychology of resilience. My sister, Eliane, certainly was one who struggled throughout her life. A musical prodigy and a high-functioning physician, from an early age she suffered from increasingly intense mood swings that were ultimately diagnosed as a persistent depressive disorder. She committed suicide at age fifty-eight, but none of her therapists, who allowed me to interview them, believed her upbringing contributed to her mental illness and despair. As the young twig is bent, perhaps so shall grow the tree, but so much more is at play in human development beyond parental nurturing and genetics.

This book is the result of a five-decade quest to satisfy a lifelong psychic itch, a longstanding dissatisfaction that I did not understand how my extended family's past may have shaped their behaviors and what they intended by creating their family narrative. As memories were layered upon memories, a rich, often confusing, brew emerged, revealing highly distinct, individualized decisions to share, omit, and confabulate. My curiosity and confusion became an irresistible motivation to continue the quest. It is my hope that by being more fully remembered, to paraphrase a Russian proverb, their accomplishments cannot be forgotten.

CHAPTER 2

Challenge and Coincidence

Until now, in my seventh decade, I have hesitated to move beyond simply contemplating the often-quixotic formulations of my family's memories, their particular ways of persevering, and how they may have been affected by the traumas they experienced. This was a longstanding reticence to interpret their constructed version of the past and the manner in which they engaged with the present. After years of writing legal documents, evaluation studies, and other turgid, often teleological prose, I suspected that diving into the narrative and behaviors of a family whose lives were so richly packed was beyond my capacities as an author. Or this could have been a simple case of procrastination based on a flimsy belief that a poverty of style would certainly undermine content.

My reluctance to write about my family's recollections and ways of being also stemmed from an inability to find more than faint traces of their lives before I was born. A reliable compass might have been provided by physical anchors to their memories, such as photographs, letters, or diaries, but they were rarely in evidence. Like many of my friends' families in New York City, mine were recent settlers, emigrants who fled precipitously, leaving much behind. Initially, as an historian, I briefly hoped that documentary traces would help confirm or eliminate the many enigmatic paths to the past they laid down, or at least frame a meaningful context. It was not to be. Nearly all tangible and documentary evidence had probably been destroyed by war and jettisoned in flight. Even with prompting, their recollections never provided much light on what certainly must have been central to who they became.

My family was not alone in putting blinders on trauma, particularly the death of family in concentration camps. But they also dwelled little on their movements from one society and culture to another, on their hopes for stability and a sense of place abandoned and regained several times, and on their personal experiences surviving warfare and religious and political persecution. Lucie and Alexander hinted that both their families were deeply immersed in the artistic, intellectual, and political ferment of Paris in the late 1920s and early '30s, but they said little about how, when they were in their teens and twenties, this environment helped frame their personalities and ambitions. Complicating matters further, any hope that I could establish the accuracy of their stories was continuously thwarted by their playfulness with the truth, their dissembling and inventiveness. To be deprived of a factual foundation, of the grist for the data mill that had been the focus of my professional life, meant that whatever I wrote about Alexander, Lucie and their relatives might well be rife with poorly substantiated inferences, risking being as implausible as the sources themselves. For a die-hard positivist, this was daunting. But this reluctance to write proved less solid than I presumed, and in May of 2019 it melted into air.

Why this sudden change of heart? For a social scientist, retrospective questions about timing, about why changes in beliefs or behaviors among individuals or groups occur at a certain moment, often resist satisfactory explanation and can reside in the realm of niggling enigmas. Less than successful efforts to grapple with the problems of causation and chronology are strewn across the social sciences, such as determining how an individual's resiliency may mediate a response to trauma, or, regarding group behaviors, why there were sudden drops in juvenile delinquency beginning in 1994 and crack cocaine use in 1996. Typically, these questions are difficult to answer convincingly because of the plausibility of multiple competing explanations, but this is more than a matter of complex problems rarely having simple solutions; it is also likely that there are insuperable challenges to collecting data relevant for explaining observable changes in human behavior over time. Context, individual histories and circumstances, deliberately veiled intentions, and so much more obfuscate efforts to identify essential causes and link them to observable effects. Not, however, in my case, when my attitudes toward writing about my extended family were reframed by circumstances that were glaringly evident, relatively recent, clearly circumscribed, and quick to take effect, even to an inveterate procrastinator.

This longstanding curiosity about my family shifted rather quickly into an insistence on memorializing it, beginning with the sudden recognition that life as I had known it might be far more finite than I had assumed. On May 23, 2019, while lying half-naked on my side, a urologist inserted a scope into my urethra, the first of many cystoscopies. I watched on a monitor as the scope inched past a painfully resistant prostate and into my bladder, where I saw intricate networks of capillaries forming red spider webs and beautiful, translucent bubbles, all clinging to each other, undulating gently, moved by an invisible force. In that most undignified of moments, I learned I had cancer, one which turned out to be quite aggressive. Beauty quickly betrayed.

What followed soon after was a dehumanizing process, the dance of medical life-saving that so many cancer patients have experienced. There was the creeping sense that I was powerless before the demands of medical authority. Agreeing to procedures, invasive as they were, was like admitting guilt to an aggressive district attorney to avoid rolling the dice of a risky trial. I was fortunate in many ways, with an early diagnosis, rapid intervention, an excellent and caring surgeon, and the ministrations and affection of family and friends. But it could not prevent, at least for a few weeks, a deep dive into a cancer-omanic vortex, as I scoured the literature for the odds on how long I would keep my bladder, stay in remission, hold onto my hair, avoid metastasis, and live a decent life. By late June 2019 I came up for air and managed to keep statistical obsession at bay, particularly with the help of the late Stephen Jay Gould. His privacy was pierced in 2013 by an announcement in the press that he was afflicted with a particularly aggressive cancer, mesothelioma, which had, according to the research, a median mortality of eight months. Gould confronted this case of statistical determinism with a critique of the abuse of cancer survival prognoses. The median, he argued, was a misleading message. Better to think about the half who would live longer, which he did—much longer. He did this with the advantage of great medical care, humor, a commitment to his work, and much more.[1] His optimism was contagious, and I believe it had a bearing on my case.

Still, there was no avoiding flagging spirits, probably a common reaction to a sickness that is so difficult to detect and definitively eliminate. Morale was difficult to maintain when recovery from surgery was slow and difficult and the treatment so discomfiting. The postoperative, cringe-inducing Foley catheter particularly imperiled equanimity, left in just long enough to wonder if modern medicine viewed infliction of pain as part of the remedy. I began to doubt my resilience in the face of this medical onslaught. A few weeks later came repeated chemotherapy treatments through the urethra with intravesical bacilli Calmette-Guerin, BCG, a tuberculosis vaccine that is pumped into the bladder, retained for a couple of hours, followed by decontamination of the bathroom. First used in 1930 as a treatment for bladder cancer, it remains the only postsurgical intervention for this type of cancer, in effect an immunotherapy. It is fairly effective, with about seven in ten patients going into remission for a time. What determines long-term survival is another niggling enigma, as is the question of why, after ninety years, no other treatment has been adopted. Bladder the ignored, the uninteresting, the last in line for path-breaking research? I asked this question of a distinguished research scientist at Sloan Kettering, who specializes in early stage bladder cancer. Why so little progress

---

1 Stephen Jay Gould, "The Median Isn't the Message," in *Bully for Brontosaurus: Reflections on Natural History* (New York, W. W. Norton & Co, 1991), 473–478.

after ninety years? Were urologic oncologists relatively underfunded? Was the science stymied? The response was that to do nothing was worse, hardly uplifting and confidence inspiring, followed by an observation that research was focused on the more severe stages of this cancer, straining my belief that candor is always the best practice with patients.

Recovering from cancer surgery and weekly trips to Cooperstown, NY to be pumped with live TB bacteria by a jovial nurse hidden in a hazmat suit, I started confronting certain challenges that were sudden and unexpected, and still are unabating. There is the challenge to resist complaining and to live as if this illness never occurred; to do otherwise makes it harder to block out thoughts of imminent mortality and, worse still, threatens to dispirit those I love. And there is the challenge of refusing to live with that most "onerous citizenship," as Susan Sontag described it.[2] Public knowledge of cancer places you in that realm where others presume imminent death and where the illness is suffused with militaristic metaphors—of the war against, the battle with, and successfully killing the destructive invader that attacked with no warning. To meet these challenges, I decided to keep the illness as private as possible and to find a new, life-affirming activity. Writing this memory of memories about people who asserted their humanity after surviving something far worse than a treatable illness certainly came to mind. But I was still not ready to begin writing about my extended family for another year.

---

2 Susan Sontag, *Illness as Metaphor* (New York: Farrar, Straus, and Giroux, 1978), 3.

The pressing need to write came into focus in late 2020, by means of a coincidence. By coincidence, I mean an unexpected chance event. Some might imbue coincidences with a greater meaning, proof of an intentional force guiding the universe, of astral bodies, or of a deity. But my interest in spirituality and organized religion never took root; it was systematically eroded by parents who had firmly concluded that such beliefs were fallacies, countermanded by the absence of proof that they existed, and the clear evidence that no justly guided universe, whatever its form, would have permitted the creation of Nazi ideology or genocide. It was a small step for me, during the 1960s and '70s, to seeing spiritual beliefs as manifestations of false consciousness, as "sacred canopies" to support the maintenance of social order in a world of inequity and unexplained tragedy. A coincidence, then, for me, is just an accident, the by-product of the law of truly large numbers—a statistical adage that with a large enough number of incidents, something very unexpected is likely to happen. Paying attention to a coincidence, noticing it as something really noteworthy, is a choice, either intentional or subliminal, and with the result that the accident can take on meaning. Coincidences, in this sense, can trigger a sudden realization, either of something we had not recognized before or highlighting something we were just ignoring or suppressing. That is exactly what happened to me.

My coincidence took the form of a book by the poet David Lehman.[3] Friends sent it to me, in part because Lehman

---

3 David Lehman, *One Hundred Autobiographies: A Memoir* (Ithaca, NY: Cornell University Press, 2019).

spent part of his life in Ithaca, near where they live, and in part because his memoir is a beautiful rumination on the life-affirming qualities of writing at a moment when thoughts of mortality are irrepressible. The overlaps in Lehman's life and mine are extensive, aside from cancer. We both spent time teaching, less than happily, at Hamilton College, and we are both the children of uprooted Jews who fled the European bloodlands and came, after several interim stops, to live in the US. Both of our families left few traces to help us understand the deep impacts of trauma, and our fathers died before we could have conversations that let us explore what went unspoken. I also understand that, in many respects, little actually binds us. Lehman writes about his intellectual formation from association with some of the twentieth century's leading poets and literary critics and through his immersion in the canons of literature. But the coincidences were striking enough to draw my attention to his approach to understanding his past, which in turn compelled me to write.

Lehman's search for self-understanding blends excursions into what may very well be truthful autobiographical episodes, but he also uses obvious deviations from fact, inventing alternative versions of himself, as did all of my family. Throughout Lehman's one hundred autobiographies, scenes from his past and present while under duress follow no chronology or narrative path. Instead, they are alternately rhapsodic, morose, and playful snapshots of past events, some are brief glimpses of passing encounters, others narratives of memorable interactions, all efforts to find anchors amidst his unmooring by serious illness. None of these recollections and personal histories, real and imagined, are framed as resolutions of complex emotions. All of the qualities of Lehman's autobiographies, the mixture of truth and invention, the alternation of specificity and a broad narrative sweep, the clear import of some and the veiled and nuanced quality of others, characterized much of my family's storytelling. Lehman, my partial doppelganger, helped me design my own memory of memories, even if what Lehman constructs is a poetic reflection on his own efforts to maintain his humanity, and what I hope to accomplish is to reflect fully the humanity of my family of survivors.

CHAPTER 3

Looking Back Through the Haze

As I have said, this extended exploration of my extended family's pathways to resilience was launched in September 1973. Before starting on my way to explore the emigration of Soviet Jewry to Israel and France, I stopped in New York City. Alexander had died nine months earlier, and I was still wandering in a netherworld of mixed emotions that can accompany the loss of a parent, including numbness and a sense of guilt for having left so much unresolved. I thought a conversation with some of my parents' friends, mostly onetime neighbors, would help clarify my confusion about Alexander's life before I was born and his behavior after relocating to New York in 1952. Many came, representing a kaleidoscope of experiences in common with my parents', including European Jews uprooted in the 1920s and '30s, survivors of the '40s, and artists blacklisted in the '50s. They comprised a living history of the American left in the twentieth century, including those committed to finding posthumous justice for the Rosenbergs, Alger Hiss supporters, antinuclear protesters, partisans struggling to revive their dream of socialism in the wake of Stalinism, and civil rights activists who had participated in Freedom Summer. In the privacy of our home in the 1950s and early 1960s, Alexander would, I thought, unfairly refer to them as *salons communistes,* leftists of discourse in the safety of their living rooms, not people of action. Of course, so was he, and like them, he had suffered for his beliefs.

These family friends came, that fall in 1973, to celebrate Alexander, their companionship and shared beliefs, and their sympathy for a member of the next generation, one of their own, a red diaper baby. For the most part, they reminisced about Alexander's artistry and celebrated his skills as a humorous raconteur. True to my family's narrative, nothing was said about past loss, grief, or trauma.

Two among those present took a radically different tack, one that was startling and memorable. Both were psychoanalysts. I had known them all my life, played with their children, and, during some late summers, visited them in Provincetown, when they had closed their offices and relaxed in each other's company in a beachside replica of their city community of artists and analysts. These two elder statesmen of psychoanalysis pulled me aside, both wearing the masks of avuncular concern. I asked them what they could tell me of my father that would help me understand him better. Their response was forcefully analytic, not at all avuncular. Alexander, they said, was someone they deeply admired for his artistic brilliance, whose company they relished, but, they said, pausing dramatically, you know, of course you know, that he was never interested in truthful self-revelation.

He preferred invention over veracity, used deflection rather than sincerity, and chose humor as a defense against agonizing disclosure. His autobiographical stories, they went on, constituted a narrative of ongoing revision. His artistry was not limited to the piano. We have known you all your life, and to avoid the psychological damage that comes from viewing Alexander as an imposter, an emotionally unavailable and ultimately unknowable parent, you will be well served, they advised, to view his personal narrative through the lens of family romance.

While at that moment I had little understanding of this Freudian concept of a fraught relationship between child and parent, these two analysts were clearly determined to alert me to the danger of an emotional cocktail of grief mixed with a confusion, even resentment, borne at least partially of paternal confabulations. They may also have had concerns about the intergenerational transmission of trauma, although they never mentioned it. At that moment they proposed a remedy which I found difficult to ignore. To avert the consequences of the looming emotional turmoil they saw in my future, this internal struggle through unresolved family relationships, they recommended I merge my forthcoming travels with a search into some measure of truth about my father. Create distinctions between fact and parental falsity, they urged, establish some clarity of understanding to dispel some of the haze from parental invention. And what can you say about my mother, I asked? Their quixotic response: she is a rock. With that, the conversation ended.

Both these family friends were students of Anna Freud. In her long career, Freud played a critical role in establishing and refining the lineaments of child psychoanalysis. Among her singular contributions, she deepened understandings of the stages of childhood development and explored the multiple, ego-driven mechanisms of defense that are unconsciously used to protect oneself from disruptive and unpleasant feelings. In retrospect, I was surprised that my conversation with the two psychoanalysts was so immediately and persistently compelling in its recommended path forward. At that time, I had a full measure of youthful certainty, forged in heady undergraduate discourse, that Freudianism was an unverifiable philosophy, unscientific at its core, founded on sexist suppositions, and just plain passé. Granted, both were distinguished, much published analysts, and I had a lifetime of admiration and affection for them compounded by a respect for scholars that came with my freshly minted college degree. Even more, at a difficult time, they had attempted to protect me from Vietnam. When the first Selective Service draft lottery in December 1969 selected the order of admission to the war, and my lottery number put me nearly first in line, these empathetic analysts reached out, offering me the possibility of a psychiatric deferment. "Come spend a week with an analyst," they offered, "with your background, you will not have to serve." I opted to resist the draft, but their effort to find me a way out, their willingness to push the boundaries of professional conduct, created a bond of gratitude and trust. And while the psychological complex of family romance was incomprehensible to me at the time, and still seems overly broad and factually ungrounded, there was an immediate power to their solution. Verifying the past may have been a remedy in search of a problem, but it provided me with a focused beacon for resolving my confusion about my family, for clearing at least some of the haze. And I could not entirely reject what I saw as a kernel of truth in their advice.

Alexander's powerful, Janus-like personality, his urbanity, wittiness, and charm coupled with chronic confabulations and infrequent lapses into what seemed, to them, to be efforts to drown deep sorrow, could, they feared, have adverse consequences for me that I might begin to address by identifying family fictions, allowing me to better understand and appreciate my father. And that my mother was a rock, was another believable note of caution from the Anna Freudians. I had already surmised that she had survived past traumas, about which I knew little, and had endured a marriage to an oft-absent and mercurial spouse with a stolidity and stoicism that limited her capacity to provide emotional supports for her children.

These family friends, in their drive-by psychoanalysis, succeeded, if that was their intent, in convincing me that I would be well served to find credible markers about my family—what I could rely on as truthful touchstones amidst all the rest. This hope was reinforced by an emerging enthusiasm for historical research. Burrowing in the seemingly inexhaustible French archives, in those documentary rabbit holes, reinforced my hopes for some verification. Working long enough, I might uncover enough to create a rich developmental context to my family. Not that my researcher's enthusiasm was without limits. Ambition never displaced doubts that a family history could reveal more than hints about the experiences and influences that could have shaped my father into a dissembler extraordinaire with such contrasting personality traits or why my mother was a rock. Historical archives that might have records of the last three or four generations of my ancestors are largely repositories of institutional artifacts. Archival records are largely formulaic, driven by the bureaucratic demands and constraints, with only rare nuggets that provide revealing insights into the past experiences and motivations of individuals. Still, I hoped that the archival haze would never be too dense, that factual touchstones could be found offering at least partial glimpses into a verifiable past of my forebears, if only to direct me away from false trails. What follows in this chapter and next are the results of my fact finding. After that, I will let the family narratives speak for themselves, without assessing them for their veracity, but instead appreciating them for their own voices, for the effects they had on listeners, for the way trauma and resilience interacted as my family created an air of humanity to be inhaled by all around them.

My great grandparents and their ancestors were invisible members of the family narrative, and no documentary vestige of them, no matter how insignificant, has emerged. Lucie, who revealed truly little about her parents, was relentlessly silent about those who came before them, with only one rather grandiose hint; there was a thirteen-volume family and theological history written by her father identifying Jewish prophets in our lineage. According to Lucie, this retired man of wealth, nameless in this and all her accounts, withdrew into his study throughout the 1920s and '30s, dedicating himself to genealogy and enriching what he thought was the meager state of French Jewish scholarship. Her father's work, she claimed, was seized by the notorious Milice, the French paramilitary organization that supported the Nazi government in Paris.

Lucie's story of my maternal grandfather's multivolume manuscript was a multilayered parable of her father's persistence and intellectualism, of the family's potential grandeur reaching to the origins of modern Judaism, and of the tragic vagaries of war. The fate of the thirteen volumes, the contents of which in Lucie's telling were largely withheld from her, also magnified the indeterminacy of her ancestry, one ultimately buried by the Milice. While the tale of a presumably destroyed magnum opus was fascinating to a child, in retrospect it seems barely credible, perhaps the result of a flawed memory, or a mistaken chronology, or a partial or complete invention, or quite possibly an oblique glimpse into Lucie's understandable and unresolved anger about French collaboration. The Milice, known for their brutality, was not organized until 1943, two years after Lucie and her mother had fled France. Perhaps her father did stay behind in Paris, but both he and his manuscript disappeared without an archival trace during the war, and their ultimate fate was never included in the family narrative.

Alexander's recollections about his Ukrainian grandparents and their ancestors were also obscured by a haze, in this case one of historical tragicomedy. His stories were a Jewish variant of Kipling's *Just So Stories for Little Children,* with themes such as How Did the Family Acquire the Goyish Name Uninsky? (a richly embellished tale of survival, combining nineteenth-century Cossack violence, orphanhood, and the conversion of a savior to preserve the Jewishness of adopted children) and What Is the Source of My Musical Talent? (inherited from his grandfather and great, great grandfather, both cantors in the Great Choral Synagogue of Kyiv, proof, Alexander would say, that musical talent was usually passed onto alternate generations, with my sister as the Great Exception).

Parental tales of earlier generations hinted, often obliquely, at the family's religious roots, involving Jewish prophets, implausible conversions, and family members chanting liturgical music. For a resolutely secular family, these stories stood in high relief to a child entirely unversed in Judaism, or for that matter, all religion. Perhaps the stories were reflections on the extent of their religious upbringing, something Alexander mentioned only fleetingly and Lucie never. These stories about ancestors were evidently idiosyncratic beacons to our Jewish identity, even if it was no longer was rooted in faith.

My slim volume of factual family history then begins with my grandparents, allowing for one exception to organizational chronology, the accounts of my own beginning. I include this here because it highlights the difficulties of clearing the haze created by the accounts of my extended family. Their memories often expressed multiple, occasionally competing, intentions, and my efforts to confirm and interpret were occasionally disquieting. Lucie occasionally reminisced about the day I was born in June 1952. She told this story because, I believe, it was emblematic of the dramatic turns of a life that was often uprooted and constantly deviating from any well-laid plans. During the war, Lucie found passage to New York, and began accompanying Alexander in his nonstop tours in North and South America.

In 1948 they resettled in Paris, where my sister Eliane was born. But in early 1952, upon learning Lucie was pregnant, they decided to return New York City on what they hoped would be a permanent basis. Alexander was scheduled to perform at The Town Hall on the 4th of February and had many concerts lined up in North America during the first half of the year. In part they expected Alexander would be nearby when I was born in New York.

For these two Parisians at heart, with family still in France and McCarthyism beginning to reach its apex, settling in New York still seemed sensible, so their version went, not only to ensure citizenship for me, but to make it easier for Alexander to revive his lucrative New World career, which had ebbed while based in Paris. He hoped to latch onto the emerging American love affair with celebrity classical artists (Bernstein, Kreisler, Elman, Horowitz, Rubinstein, Stern, and so many others). Lucie and Alexander also often remarked how much they idealized New York City, by which they meant Manhattan, as a place where they could thrive as cosmopolitans. In the 1950s their high regard for the city was apparent, as an international capital of refined culture where polyglots roamed free and they could live relatively free of lethal prejudices. Alexander's then current manager (he changed them often), Bernard R. LaBerge, had an extensive tour in place for 1952 in Canada and the US, in Chicago, Philadelphia, Montreal, and other cities, followed by an extensive stay at The Hague to record several performances during May and June 1952.

When Lucie went into labor in June, she was alone in our New York City apartment. A family friend, a wealthy entrepreneur who had supported Alexander's career in Europe before the war, particularly as a representative of Pleyel pianos, was at the ready. He left his office and rushed Lucie to Flower-Fifth Avenue Hospital, urgently driving from the Upper West to the Upper East Side in his new Cadillac. Lucie had already lost one child to a miscarriage, and she was becoming frantic as I started to crown. All she could remember of that moment were appeals from the front seat to hold on. Lucie, always suspecting that everyone acted out of competing sentiments, believed the concern for her safety was also worry about soiled upholstery.

Twenty-one years later, soon after the remembrance of Alexander with family friends, I went to meet my stork and asked him to reminisce about my parents. He confirmed Lucie's version of my birth but had little to add about my parents' past. Instead, he asserted a role as my stand-in father, advising me to accept my responsibilities and return to Texas, where my mother lived, and reject the offer of a research grant that involved extensive travel. My birth was a conjuncture of crisis and joy, he recalled. When Alexander returned to New York a few weeks after I was born, he went to Fire Island to meet his son and rejoin Lucie, who was staying with friends to recover. He soon learned that as a suspected enemy of the state his US passport was being withdrawn, temporarily ending his career. My obligation now, in 1973, this family friend proclaimed, was to stay by my mother, who had suffered enough in her life, and model responsible manhood rather than traveling to do research. To do otherwise would be feckless and self-indulgent, he intoned. Preferring to address self-imposed guilt, and rarely the type externally applied, I ignored him. All I verified, for my efforts, was that I was conceived in France, nearly born in a Cadillac on the Upper East Side without soiling the upholstery, and that while you can go home again, it can be irritating, and, I found, at times, disturbing. As for archival verification, the only records substantiating this brief history were press releases about Alexander's concerts and my birth certificate.

The haze clouding the past in our family narrative was particularly thick when it came to names. Lucie and Alexander created a near anonymity of parentage. Among my grandparents, none had first names, and patronymics went unmentioned. Even the family name Uninsky, if Alexander's tale was in some way factual, represented a break in lineage after the adoption of my orphaned nineteenth-century ancestors by a nonrelative. Whatever the family name was before it became Uninsky, it had a mythogenic quality and would vary with the telling. Most often it was a variant of Kohen or Kaplan, reflecting, Alexander would explain, the family's probable descent from rabbinic lineage. Lucie's mother, my only grandparent to survive the war, was known to us as "Grandmaman Bisco," using an Americanized last name and a relationship tag in place of a first name.

The depersonalization of my grandparents extended beyond namelessness, lifted only rarely with my father's fleeting recollections, perhaps preemptively anodyne and occasionally tinged with reminders of his early sacrifices for his parents and his musical malleability. ("When I studied at the Conservatoire de Paris, I accompanied silent movies to support my parents, who lost everything leaving Kyiv.") Some stories adopted well-trodden tales of the preparations to embark on a precarious flight from danger. ("My mother sewed money and family jewelry into the hems of our coats.") Lucie offered far less, indicating little more than that her family was wealthy, her father devout, and that both parents were a distant presence during her childhood in Paris.

Lucie's narrative about her mother was spare, and I never learned how she survived the war or what kind of parent she may have been. Grandmaman Bisco lived on our periphery during my youth in New York City, taciturn in the extreme, revealing nothing about either her past life or present activities and interests. My sister Eliane and I had a highly structured and disquieting relationship with our grandmother. Lucie arranged for us to see Grandmaman Bisco twice a year, dropping us off at her elegantly furnished apartment in the Upper West Side of Manhattan. To a preteen, it met my expectations of a grandmotherly home in some ways, with lace on the furniture and the smell of mothballs, but unlike our apartment, there was a TV, and it was turned up to a deafening level and tuned to wrestling, something astonishing to children of parents who abhorred depictions of violence. She barely interacted with us, her grandchildren, and kept to a routine when she saw us—roast beef lunches and milk shakes at Starks, a bustling family eatery on West Ninety-Third, one small step above a Chock Full o'Nuts Café or a Horn & Hardart Automat. We sat on either side of her at the counter, curiously never in a booth; here she created a gulf of anxious incomprehension, particularly when she asked the question that still reminds me of Joan Crawford in *Mommie Dearest*—"Who do you like better, your mother or your father?" My sister Eliane and I were always relieved when lunch was over and we went our separate ways, with Grandmaman Bisco presumably returning to watch Dick the Bruiser and Killer Kowalski settle their disputes.

Lucie consistently ostracized her mother, never speaking to her in our presence or inviting her to our apartment. Alexander ignored his mother-in-law with uncharacteristic dispassion. In the early 1960s Lucie suddenly disclosed that her mother would need to be cared for, and a surprising dimension of my sole living grandparent was revealed. Lucie announced that she would move her mother to upstate New York to be cared for by a family, a costly solution made feasible because, materializing gold from thin air, my grandmother had an uncanny eye for picking blue chip stocks. Fable or fact, neither parent mentioned either stock market investments or Grandmaman Bisco again, except for the announcement of her death in a brief telephone call in 1975. She entered that part of the family narrative that was governed by a rarely broken silence. This surprising, alchemical appearance (or disappearance) of gold from thin air was also a recurring household modus operandi. Uninsky money was shorn of origins and amounts, discussion of salary, bank accounts, or investments was anathema, and money had no particular moral domain, other than it was never to be hoarded. When resources were available, they were to be spent on art, the trappings of elegance, and travel. Funds came with no warning and went with no evident planning or remorse.

Lucie and Alexander rarely revealed tangible and unimpeachable links to the family's past before the war. In the apparent absence of letters, diaries, or photographs, the few objects they possessed from their earlier life, such as the boxing gloves of an adored brother or a score with what appeared to be smudged hieroglyphs, lacked identifiable origins. The one exception was the bronze bust of Chopin, Alexander's additional award for performances of Mazurkas when he won the International Chopin Piano Competition in 1932, and I always wondered how he kept hold of it during his flight across Vichy France. Heavy, weighing fourteen pounds, had he carried it on his bicycle over the mountains to Spain and beyond or left it in safekeeping as he roamed Paris after he was demobilized? I never asked Alexander, perhaps because the bust's unique proof of past glory was beyond question. After his death, Lucie would not respond when asked.

With so little evidence documenting the past, the world of my grandparents and the childhood and young adulthood of my parents was a tabula rasa, upon which Lucie and Alexander were free to inscribe whatever they wished. This is not to say that the artifacts of prior lives were entirely absent from our household, but they were hidden, forgotten, or too painful to reveal while my parents were alive. After Lucie died in 2012, I found a minute cache of photographs, mostly unlabeled and undated. Aside from two of her brother, Monio, upon which Lucie had written to her granddaughter, "this is your granduncle Monio, my brother," one other identified the two young brothers, Alexander and Evsey, both dressed in elegant school uniforms. Lucie also kept two prewar pictures with her mother.

Grandmaman Bisco in 1929 and 1932 with her daughter, the future Lucie Uninsky, aged ten and thirteen. Photos courtesy of the author.

Most of the rest were photographs Alexander took on his travels before the war and publicity portraits. But of my grandparents, this discovered cache contained no diaries, no photographs of those I had never met, no records of their birth, death, marriage, education, or anything they owned. I found only two documents with some mention of my grandparents. There was a copy of Lucie's Danish 1919 birth certificate that was generated in 1938. Further, there was an August 1924 postcard from Serge Weksler addressed to "Mme. et M. Uninsky," without first names, probably written soon after their arrival in Paris in 1924. The card was addressed to them in the 19th arrondissement near the Parc des Buttes-Chaumont. In prewar Paris, this was a neighborhood in transition, where many Ashkenazim had recently landed, along with Greek and Armenian refugees.

The postcard is a picture of Weksler with his arm on the shoulder of a young Alexander, a man-child probably aged fourteen in a three-piece suit, with a gaze of unnatural determination. His praise on the postcard for the young pianist was extravagant, "the world will speak about him as the greatest of pianists." And these two documents form the sum total of the documentary evidence about my paternal grandparents left to me by my parents.

A postcard of the young Alexander Uninsky, posing with Serge Weksler, composer, musical editor, and piano teacher, ca. 1924. Photo courtesy of the author.

The Weksler postcard winks at the past, reflecting the family narrative in a fractured mirror. Alexander's version of reaching France from Kyiv with his parents was spare. The few details he provided pointed to a wondrous intervention of Jewish wealth and philanthropy on his behalf. He recalled that his family was destitute and homeless when they first reached Paris, and he was gravely ill. Somehow, word of the family's dire situation reached Robert Philippe Gustave de Rothschild, banker, devoted polo player, philanthropist, and baron, who somehow also knew of the young Ukrainian's musical talent. According to Alexander, the baron promptly arranged for housing and medical care. Perhaps so. The address on Weksler's card, 117, rue de Belleville, was a social housing complex built between 1904 and 1908 by the Rothschild Foundation to provide affordable housing for working-class households. The apartments, still standing, are near a Rothschild hospital which opened in 1905. When the Uninsky family arrived in Paris, a date which varied with the telling but was likely 1924, they may well have heard from fellow émigrés about Rothschild apartments in the large Belleville complex which were being made available to the recently displaced. Members of the Rothschild family were certainly involved in assisting the emigration of Ukrainian Jews during this period. Or perhaps, even before the Uninsky family left Kyiv, the Rothschilds were their benefactors. There are no surviving records to confirm whether Alexander's memory of Baron de Rothschild's astonishing personal intervention and timely munificence occurred as told, or if the tale was a combination of veracity and fantasy, of art being magically saved by wealth and power.

And what do we know about Serge Weksler, who wrote glowingly about Alexander, and what was his connection to the family? He was a piano teacher, composer, and editor of Chopin's entire piano repertoire for students (fingering included). The Bibliothèque Nationale de France lists ninety-six compositions by Weksler from the 1920s and 1930s, including the brief pieces "Défilé des comsomols" (roughly, the "Parade of the [Soviet] Union of Youth"), "Laughing, grotesque pour piano," and the song for a short comic film "L'Ours et le Pacha" (The Bear and the Pasha).[1] An émigré who was born in Kherson (Crimea) and lived for some years in Kyiv, he was naturalized as a French citizen in 1927 and died in Paris in 1950. He had at least one characteristic in common with my family, a proclivity for reinvention. Serge Weksler used several aliases during his seventy-four years, including Semen Wexler, Serge Choulim and Schoulin, Semen Kharitonovich, and S. Esvé. He may have been Alexander's piano teacher ("son Maitre") for a brief period before Alexander enrolled at the Conservatoire de Paris in the Fall of 1924.

As a starting place for locating any other documents about my grandparents that might be stored somewhere in archives, I relied on family stories of location. I took it as a settled matter, given mention of pogroms, warfare, Revolution, and the Kyiv Conservatory of Music, that Alexander was born in Kyiv, where he lived until he was thirteen or fourteen, when the family left for Paris. Lucie claimed confusion

---

1 "Serge Weksler (1878–1950)," Bibliothèque nationale de France (BnF), accessed March 9, 2025, https://data.bnf.fr/fr/14780170/serge_weksler/.

about where her parents had lived before Copenhagen, where she was born in 1919. She suspected they were from somewhere inside the territorial borders of what was to become the Polish People's Republic in 1952, adding, without a grain of certitude, that the family had owned textile factories. Archival searches in countries where my grandparents probably lived provided no insights into the inner sanctums of my grandparents, their beliefs, personal associations, or interests. Even when the mystery of their full names was resolved, including how their names were transliterated as they moved from one dominant language to another, the archives were largely unenlightening, only occasionally offering fleeting glimpses, the result of a perfect storm of archival destruction wrought by the Russian Civil War, the Ukrainian War of Independence, Poland's historical buffeting by powerful neighbors, and the Holocaust. What information can be found about Lucie and Alexander's parents is located principally in Nazi records, Polish vital statistics, industrial archives, and the occasional attic.

Alexander's parents were Esther (née Schrabman) and Miron Uninsky. The first documented glimpse of their existence, prior to that postcard in the family files, came as a result of Serge Klarsfeld's thorough and taxing work in the 1970s compiling Nazi deportation records.[2] It is in these grim compendia that I finally learned their first names. In the winter of 1942–43, both Esther and Miron were among

2 Serge Klarsfeld, *Memorial to the Jews Deported from France, 1942–1944: Documentation of the Deportation of the Victims of the Final Solution in France* (New York: Beate Klarsfeld Foundation, 1978).

over 3,800 Jews incarcerated in the Drancy camp. It is impossible to know exactly when they were arrested and how long they endured detention. On February 10, 1943, Heinz Rothke, chief of the "Jewish section" (Judenreferat) of the Gestapo in France, wrote Adolf Eichmann that the forty-sixth convoy left Drancy the day before, carrying one thousand Jews to Auschwitz who were deemed "deportable" because they were "stateless."[3] Included on that train were Esther and Miron Uninsky. The convoy lists maintained in the archives by the Centre de Documentation at the Mémorial de la Shoah in Paris are systematic but abbreviated records—names of the deported, alphabetized with their dates of birth, nationalities, and last known addresses. Esther and Miron were listed as Russians from Kyiv; their last address was 11, rue Juliette Lamber in the Batignolles neighborhood of Paris's 17th arrondissement, located in the heart of a far larger Jewish community than their earlier residence in the Belleville section of Paris. Esther was fifty-seven years old and Miron sixty when they were placed on the convoy. Both died in the camp's gas chambers, five days after the train left Drancy.

What little else can be known about my paternal grandparents comes as a result of reasonable inferences, some stronger than others. In Kyiv they were not without some means, if that can be deduced from the one photograph of Alexander as a Kyivan child who, along with his older brother Evsey, were dressed in elegant school uniforms.

---

3 Klarsfeld, *Memorial*, 360.

Kyivan students, Evsey Uninsky, age eight (left), and Alexander Uninsky, age six (right), in their school uniforms, ca. 1916. Photo courtesy of the author.

On one occasion Alexander mentioned that his father had taken a secular path, becoming a haberdasher, a departure from a family that he insisted included generations of cantors. A few matters can be ascertained with certainty. Esther and Miron clearly nurtured Alexander's musical development, enrolling him at the young age of nine in the Kyiv Conservatory of Music to study with Sergei Vladimorovich Tarnovsky. And soon after arriving in Paris, they managed to continue young Alexander's musical education, enrolling him at the prestigious Conservatoire de Paris, allegedly without a centime in their pockets. My paternal grandparents' attitudes and aptitudes reside in a state of near perfect invisibility. Nothing is known about what languages they spoke at home, what hardships they endured in Ukraine and in Paris, how they navigated the political tides of the Russian Revolution, who were their friends and associates, and whether there was an extended family still living in Kyiv or elsewhere who could speak about them.

As is the case for many Jews who left Kyiv in the 1920s, it is difficult to know why they departed at a particular moment. Any number of forces could have impelled them, from waves of antisemitic violence to economic fragility. One can only guess, that perhaps they seized the opportunity of a semblance of an interregnum in Ukraine in 1923 and 1924. It was a time of diminished violence and political upheaval when the government made efforts to encourage Jews to become engaged in agriculture, something which may have been anathema to the Uninskys, urban residents whose devotion to their son's development as a classical pianist was a certainty. They could have selected Paris as a destination for any number of reasons. Many Jews were choosing the city in their flight from antisemitic violence in Eastern Europe. Esther and Miron may have been drawn by Paris' renown as a center of artistic vitality in the early 1920s, the reputation of the Conservatoire, or by the presence of a formidable group of Russian innovators in composition, painting, and dance, including Chagall, Prokofiev, Stravinsky, Chaliapin, Diaghilev, and the Ballet Russes. And perhaps there is the remote possibility that their decision was encouraged from France by the Rothschilds.

While neither my father nor his siblings ever divulged what they knew of their parents' murder, Alexander, for the first time in 1971, acknowledged that other relatives had died in Auschwitz. What prompted this revelation was his shock over President Pompidou's pardon of Paul Touvier, who had been convicted of crimes against humanity for collaborating with Klaus Barbie in the deportation of thousands of Jews from southeastern France. Barely breaking with his long-established silence and deflection about the Shoah, Alexander offered little information, naming no particular relative and revealing only that some of the deported had been cousins, engineers, and, that to the best of his knowledge, none had survived.

In 2008, these relatives emerged from anonymity by happenstance. Jean-Jacques Kantorow, violinist and Lyonnaise conductor, while helping his mother sort through the papers of his recently deceased father, Pierre, found an envelope upon which his father had written: "Personal Affairs of Joseph Uninski, handed over to me for my safekeeping, late summer 1942."[4] Jean-Jacques Kantorow, a friend of Catherine Uninsky Binoche, my first cousin and the daughter of Alexander's younger brother Anatole, brought Joseph Uninski's envelope to her soon after it was found, hoping it contained information about long lost relatives. Kantorow recalled that his father had spoken of a childhood friendship with the young Alexander Uninsky that was rekindled in France. The elder Kantorow told his son that as boys in Kyiv, he and Alexander

4 Affaires personnelles de Joseph Uninski, confiées à ma garde, fin de l'été 1942.

sang together in a synagogue choir. This is one among many recollections that gave me pause about the veracity of memory, given that Alexander's singing voice as an adult resembled gravel poured into a cement mixer.

The 1942 package left with Kantorow, like so much of the family's few documentary records, provided only a suggestive glimpse of the past, less than needed to verify the connection between the Uninskis and Uninskys. It contained a small, sparsely filled address book and several unlabeled photographs. The only entries under the letters T and U were for Alexander's two brothers, Evsey and Anatole. Neither Joseph's own family nor Alexander appeared. Perhaps these exclusions were, in part, a grim strategy of survival in the late summer of 1942. Two of Joseph's family members, Isaac and Louise, had been arrested earlier that year, and Alexander, whose career had blossomed in the 1930s, was a well-known Ukrainian-born Jewish pianist, one of the many whom Nazis deemed deportable. His last performance in France was in late 1940, in Autun in the Saône-et-Loire, to benefit the National Relief and the French Red Cross. This was near where the Uninski family lived, and it may be that Joseph heard of the concert and perhaps even contacted Alexander, who was already planning his escape south. As he prepared the package for Kantorow, Joseph Uninski may have been in the process of adopting a new identity, that of Joseph Uterberry, born in Constantine, Algeria and working in that same city of Autun. I have found nothing to verify this identity change, although after the war the ex-wife of Joseph's brother Marcus told her granddaughter of her granduncle's failed efforts to evade deportation, if he was indeed Joseph Uterberry.

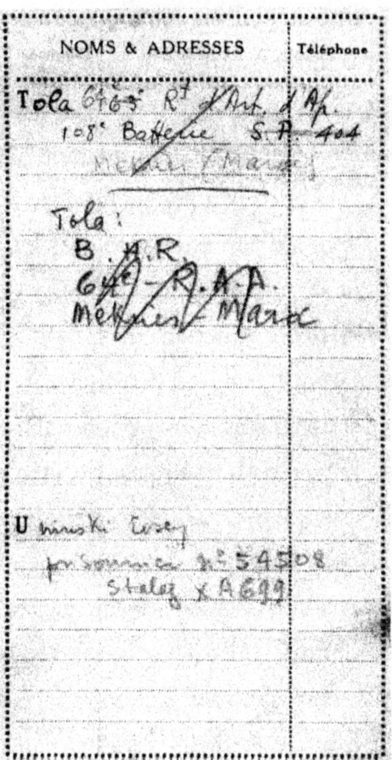
NOMS & ADRESSES | Téléphone

A page from Joseph Uninski's 1942 address book including a lined out military location for Tola (Anatole) Uninsky in Morocco, and Evsey Uninsky's prisoner of war number and stalag. Photo courtesy of the author.

Joseph Uninski's address book, like his ultimate fate, raises questions that are likely to remain unresolved. If Joseph intentionally excluded mention of those who were vulnerable as "unassimilated" Jews, why then include Anatole and Evsey? The address book located Anatole in Morocco with his name and address lined through. Evsey was listed as a French prisoner of war in a stalag. Perhaps Joseph thought their deportation was impossible, one whose address had been in Morocco but was now unknown and the other imprisoned in Germany as a French prisoner of war. Joseph may have suspected that Evsey Uninsky, as one inmate among many, could survive by disguising his religious identity, but he must have known the dangers the address book of a Jew might pose if it fell into the wrong hands. He chose nonetheless to preserve the contacts, even at the risk of storing the address book with a friend who himself was at risk of being deported.

Alexander apparently believed that these Strasbourg-based Uninskis were relatives. It is, however, impossible to substantiate close ties between the families, or whether they were related. There are no records of contacts between Esther and Miron Uninsky and Sarah and Nison Uninski, parents of Joseph and his siblings. Alexander may have encountered Joseph's brother, Marcus, also a pianist who had performed in Paris. Uninsky is also an unusual family name, certainly among Jews, and rarely found outside the very Russian and Orthodox Uninsky District, located in Kirov Oblast, over 1,100 kilometers east of Moscow. But aside from Joseph's address book, there is little to connect the two families and some reason to question whether they were related.

According to the Nazi convoy records, unlike the Uninskys, all the Uninski family members were born in what was to become Poland—Nison in Lowicz, Sarah in Warsaw, and their three sons, Joseph, Marcus, and Isaac, and their daughter or daughter-in-law, Louise, in Sokolow-Podlaski, all at least 750 kilometers from Kyiv, nearly a world away. And little is to be found about these Uninskis: Louise's life was tragically cut short; Joseph and Isaac both studied engineering in Lyon and worked during the 1920s and '30s in the southwestern industrial city of Tarbes, far from Paris. There is even less to be found about Marcus, except that he played at least two concerts in Paris's Salle Chopin. His ambitious recital program on May 25, 1934 was quite similar to those performed by Alexander throughout his career, including two Scarlatti sonatas, two Schubert impromptus, a romance and arabesque by Schumann, a Mendelssohn scherzo, three Chopin Mazurkas, Liszt's "La campanella" on a theme by Paganini, and a Liszt rhapsody. And on June 26, 1937, Marcus appeared again in the Salle Chopin as an accompanist.

The deportation of the Uninskis was recorded by Nazi clerks in Drancy, as it was for Esther and Miron Uninsky. On July 17, 1942, Louise, twenty-two years old, and Isaac, thirty-four, were forced onto the sixth convoy bound for Auschwitz from France.[5] Two months later, on September 23, 1942, Marcus, thirty-one, was deported on convoy thirty-six.[6] On November 6, 1942, their parents, Sarah, fifty-eight, and Nison, sixty-five, suffered the same fate on convoy forty-two.[7] If Joseph Uninski had indeed become Joseph Uterberry, he was deported late in the war, on March 7, 1944, on the sixty-ninth of the eighty convoys sent from the internment camp at Drancy;[8] no evidence of a Joseph Uninski surviving the war exists. No one is alive who knew the Uninskis of southeastern France. Two world wars, the chaotic events of interwar Poland, migration, and the energetic efforts of Vichy collaborators and Nazi occupiers to rid France of "stateless" Jews have denied us

---

5 Klarsfeld, *Memorial*, 55.
6 Klarsfeld, *Memorial*, 310.
7 Klarsfeld, *Memorial*, 342.
8 Klarsfeld, *Memorial*, 525.

nearly all knowledge of the Uninskis before deportation, even after access to the French archives of that era was belatedly granted in 2015.

With the news of Paul Touvier's pardon in late 1971, Alexander openly grieved for the Uninskis but was unwilling or unable to rescue them from relative anonymity in his last year of life. Memories of Sarah, Nison, and their successors are, like so many others lost to past violence, engulfed in a haze. Knowledge of them is largely precluded by traumatic events, the pain of remembering, and the disorder caused by war. Searching for them, trying to acknowledge their lives by reviving an even partial sense of who they were, I am left, like so many others who try to pierce the veil of trauma, with an unfocused sorrow and grief about lives savagely ended and with questions that are unanswerable.

My maternal grandparents, in most regards, were an enigma deliberately created by Grandmaman Bisco, Lucie, and Alexander. My grandmother, during our rather quiet semiannual lunches occasionally punctuated by disquieting conversation, was essentially unknowable, with her Americanized name and a past vigilantly preserved by the living as a blank record. Her husband, in our family narrative, was nameless, shorn of nearly all characteristics, with the details of his disappearance, whenever it occurred, left unmentioned. Lucie successfully concealed her parents' full names until her death in 2012, when I discovered that rather battered 1938 copy of her Danish birth certificate, which contained the transliterated names of her parents ("Kallman Byschkovitsch" and "Chana Kaplan Byschkovitsch"). Curiously, given my family's loose attachment to a factually verifiable family narrative, a portion of the very little they said of my maternal grandparents could be confirmed. Unfortunately, the memories shared were small shards that could never be connected into a coherent whole.

During her ninety-four years, Lucie's version of her family history began with her parents' move, before her birth, from somewhere unspecified in Eastern Europe to Copenhagen, where she was born on January 19, 1919. Before leaving for Denmark, her father reportedly sold his ownership share in textile factories to his brother and used his considerable fortune to settle into a life of Jewish hermeneutics and family genealogy after moving to Paris, somewhere in the 16th arrondissement in late 1919. Lucie would say, of her parents, that she was raised by the cook who, she would bemoan, taught her nothing about cooking. Partially informed guesswork, a short-cut through linguistic and historical complexity, led to more verifiable information about my maternal grandparents.

It seemed reasonable to begin searching for signs of Grandmother Bisco-Byschkovitsch and her spouse in the city of Łódź in the late nineteenth and early twentieth centuries. A center of textile industrialization, there were over 525 factories in Łódź at the turn of the century, at least one-third owned by Jews. Sorting through the online archives of the Łódź Central Museum of Textiles, using different transliterations of the family name, revealed the presence of the brothers Kleoman and Izaac Biszkowicz in the city before World War II. Corporate annuaries stored in the Museum noted the establishment of a "Bracia Biszkowicz" (Biszkowicz Brothers) company in 1894. In 1906 an industry address book listed the brothers as owning a woolens and semi-woolens factory on ulica (street) Piotrkowska, with between 160 and 200 workers and selling

250,000 rubles of product annually (approximately $3.65 million in 2020 dollars).[9] The enterprising brothers were listed as proprietors of another textile mill on Lakowa Street in 1908 that produced woolen, cotton, and other fabrics. Factory surveys indicate that the Bracia Biszkowicz firm was still in business in 1933.[10] Kleoman was most probably my grandfather. According to marriage records listed in Jewish Records Index for Poland, he married Chana Rubinsztein-Kaplan in 1910; the names are clearly aligned with those on the 1938 copy of Lucie's birth certificate. Nothing in the archives indicates when Kleoman sold all or some of his shares in Bracia Biszkowicz, if he did so at all. Chana appeared as part of my childhood, a sphinx with no past or first name. Kleoman disappeared at some indeterminate moment, leaving no trace aside from the impressionistic sketch created by Lucie of a deeply religious, remote man with an abandoned career as a textile industrialist; nothing more is known of him.

After the traumatic events of World War II, my parents were reunited in New York City in 1942. They then embarked on six years of nearly continuous travel as Alexander performed throughout North, Central, and South America, Europe, and the Middle East. There was extensive coverage of his performances in the press, including the occasional interview.

---

9 Kalendarz Informator: na Województwo Łódzkie na rok 1923. [Cz. 2] (Calendar Information: for the Łódź Voivodeship for 1923. [Part 2]), Wojewódzka Biblioteka Publiczna im. Marszałka Józefa Piłsudskiego w Łodzi (Marshal Józef Piłsudski Provincial Public Library in Łódź), accessed March 9, 2025. https://bc.wbp.lodz.pl/dlibra/publication/48706/edition/46543/content.

10 Jacek Kusinski, *Ksiega Frabryk Łódźi* (Łódź: Muzeum Historii Miasta Łódźi, 2009), 130 and 166.

Even eighty years later, Alexander's performative instincts are evident, clearly steering conversations with journalists away from violence, loss, and hardship and toward reminiscences about his friendships with the great composers of prewar Paris and paeans to the poetry of Chopin's Mazurkas. When he did speak about periods during which he was undoubtedly under intense stress or in grave danger, he managed to do so peremptorily and with a deft lightness, as if at a keyboard playing a tone poem. Escape and performance were paramount in his wartime interviews. As he was sought by Nazis in occupied Paris, he astonishingly claimed that he continued to rehearse for months until his flight was unavoidable. Little deterred him from concertizing after his escape from France to South America. His abbreviated descriptions implied an almost effortless and uneventful departure from wartime Europe, devoid of setbacks and struggles, save one, a brief imprisonment in Madrid. His claim to have bicycled from Paris to Spain, a part of family lore, first appeared in the 1940s interviews. When the press asked about his family, Alexander was routinely evasive and vague, occasionally unresponsive, and inconsistent in the glimpses he provided. He never mentioned his brothers and sister to reporters, saying only that his parents were still living and were in Paris, occasionally in the south of France, or elsewhere in some indeterminate location. As for my maternal grandparents or Lucie's siblings, the press record is blank. By the time I was born, a haze had already enveloped the lives of Esther, Miron, Chana, and Kleoman, one that was never lifted in the family narrative.

CHAPTER 4

An Extended Family Known and Imagined

The grandparents I never met were an evanescent presence, their traces erased by the corrosive whirlwinds of hatred, decades of violence, sudden flights for survival, and by the silence of the living. The family tree was stunted and exfoliated in Alexander and Lucie's narrative, and my efforts to revive it, to verify the hints and enlarge upon the traces, extended my acquaintance with blind alleys. It is by no means a unique experience to have so much of one's past shrouded in darkness, with the lives of ancestors only a ghostly, unknowable presence. It occurs among countless families, forced into precipitous flights from genocide and total war. Many of my cohort in postwar New York shared foreshortened personal histories. They also were born to immigrant parents who survived the great turmoil of the 1930s and '40s, and they too heard family narratives centered on a recent past, skirting or blurring the period before the great transition to life in New York.

This time-shortened focus of the family narrative created a sense of vibrant immediacy in our lives when we lived in New York, a heightened appreciation of the here and now that my family shared with many other recent arrivals to the city. This was, in part, a postwar commitment to renewal by any number of paths among the uprooted and dislocated, including a focus on economic restoration, reinvigorating a sense of purpose, and immersion in a new community. But it seemed that Alexander and Lucie's sense of immediacy, more so than with other adults in our community, was buffeted by strong currents that detached them from fixed moorings in their newfound land. Involvement in New York society coexisted with a countervailing feeling of deracination that was often close to the surface. They enthusiastically participated in the life of the city but also floated in a mindset of being persistently apart. Although they were US citizens, they often acted as if they belonged to no nation, still stateless refugees traveling with the Nansen passports they claimed to have obtained before the war.

Until they died, Alexander in 1972 and Lucie in 2012, both seemed alienated from, even antagonistic to, the multiple cultures that co-existed around them, even more after we moved to Dallas in the early 1960s. Their sense of not belonging always seemed profound and sincere, hardly an affectation, instead a wholly intrinsic part of their characters. Although they never openly reflected on its sources, their apartness was likely borne of the traumatic experiences that had stripped them of family, place, and security, coupled with a highly refined intellectual and esthetic elitism.

This essential state of uprootedness took many forms, from a distaste for any overt expressions of chauvinism to an aversion of anything redolent of fixedness, particularly home ownership. Although the *New York Times* was at our door every morning, they did their best to impede the flow of mainstream US culture into our lives, with no television or radio until I was a teen. We would see movies, but only classics and new European films showing at MOMA and at the nearby Thalia Theater, named for the muse of idyllic poetry and comedy, something Alexander undoubtedly found irresistible. I still vividly recall going to the Thalia one afternoon in 1961 to see *Madame Sans-Gêne* (literally, "Madame without Embarrassment"), my cinematic introduction to comic, norm-breaking lust and to the young Sophia Loren. Aside from jazz, which my parents had come to love in prewar Paris, American mainstream and popular culture never rose to even a guilty pleasure for Lucie and Alexander, who favored only what they saw as the higher forms of artistic achievement. While in New York, they were immersed in the arts, reveled in them, kept abreast of emerging trends and innovations, but never ranged far from the leading museums, art galleries, and classical music venues.

Although they occasionally called the city a "World in One," they never acknowledged a sense of attachment to urban New York beyond their own community of artists and psychoanalysts, many of whom were also among the recently arrived, fully enmeshed in their careers, prosperous, and still far from assimilated, linguistically or culturally. It was clear that Lucie and Alexander sought and found a group of friends who shared their deep-seated sense of being both relieved to be in the US and feeling unmoored. Their move to Dallas in the early 1960s was an exile on Main Street for both, stripped of their peers and lacking a Metropolitan Museum of Art and a Carnegie Hall. This was a sharp descent from sacred to profane, although Lucie suffered a somewhat more intense cultural and psychological shock than Alexander, who continued to concertize abroad, rarely playing in the US after his run-in with the Red Scare. The sense of displacement was instant. Lucie and Alexander had planned to live near the University, in an unincorporated section of Dallas, University Park. We soon learned it was a community with property restrictions forbidding the sale of houses to Jews and anyone who might be considered nonwhite. We settled instead in a semirural community outside the "City of Hate," for the full Texas experience, with a stable down the street, country and western music playing on truck radios, cowboy hats, and teachers who demanded "sir" or "ma'am" at the end of each sentence. Lucie and Alexander felt deeply uprooted, deprived of the art world they had relished in Paris, lost in the war, and then regained in New York City. And they were also without access to their polyglot community with similar histories. Texas was a very foreign land, where my parents were constantly reminded they were aliens.

This persistent uprootedness from place and from much of the culture of their recently adopted land was in keeping with the life Alexander and Lucie shared once they arrived in the New World during the war. They were incessant itinerants when they united in 1942, traveling together continuously, as Alexander performed throughout North and South America, and then, after VE Day, in Europe and the Middle East. In late 1948 they established their first fixed address since the war, settling in Paris where my sister Eliane was born. Lucie remained there for nearly four years while Alexander continued touring. In 1952, they resettled in New York City.

Whenever the subject was raised in the 1950s and early '60s, Alexander and Lucie forcefully rejected the idea of returning to France. France was still home, they would explain, but there was greater economic opportunity in the US, and warfare, even world wars, would likely stay an ocean away. There was more to their decision to remain in New York besides income and safety, terms they rarely used, the former too vulgar and the latter unattainable. Alexander insisted that moving to the US was a matter of personal principle. Former Nazis and collaborators may have been defeated, but they were never vanquished, and to be an artist required sufficient distance. This was a statement about never forgetting, persistent danger, and perhaps his acknowledgment that he had not sacrificed during the war like his brothers and needed no ongoing reminders. Given that Alexander concertized throughout Europe during the 1950s and '60s, his stated preference for living in the US was perhaps a useful fiction. Similar was his explanation that postwar he recorded exclusively in The Hague because the Dutch had heroically resisted Nazi occupation and protected its Jewish population, a claim he possibly knew was apocryphal. Alexander was, in reality, under contract with Philips Records, which was based in Amsterdam and had recording studios in The Hague.

There were additional explanations for not returning to France. Both parents saw the effervescent cultural life of New York City as offering a refreshing spark of artistic life reminiscent of the prewar cultural capitals of Europe, perhaps less revolutionary but diverse, creative, and energetic. For Alexander and Lucie, the city probably offered a psychological and physical buffer against the past and access to the artistic nourishment they so relentlessly sought. But if they harbored any hope of permanency by choosing to settle in New York, it was not to be.

A 1953 publicity picture of the Uninsky family at home, a year before their flight to Toronto. Photo courtesy of the author.

In 1954 the family precipitously left for Toronto, when, at the tail end of McCarthyism, Alexander's US passport was withdrawn, ending the possibility of a planned international tour. We returned to New York in 1956, and departed for Texas in 1962, a place Alexander would say should have required passports for entry. He may have been thinking of the Nansen variety, which provided the stateless the right of international mobility.

A family narrative colored by immediacy and deracination had certain unmistakable features. Most apparently, Lucie and Alexander placed only slight importance on the passage of time, rarely providing a chronicle where the past served as prologue and events unfolded in logical succession. As with many families in our New York community, there were apparent omissions and glaring discontinuities. Traumatic events received glancing treatment, if mentioned at all. The fates of missing family members were treated invariably either with silence or an evident absence of reflection. My parents' earlier experiences of involuntary displacement, coupled with their abiding sense of unbelonging, no doubt undermined any temptation to dwell with much nostalgia or affection on those communities where they had earlier lived, resettled, or even vacationed.

This altered past extended to the mundane, revealing only hints of emerging family life before the war. My parents never described past residences and, aside from Alexander's involvement with a wide community of Parisian artists in the 1930s, they made only the vaguest allusions to prewar friendships. There were no tales of coming of age, few memories of education, or of an extended golden age during childhood. This incomplete narrative was told discontinuously, removed from the context of a specific moment, with anecdotes, reminiscences, and comic tales routinely moving back and forth in time. By frequently removing topics and personalities from a precise historical context, they heightened a dominant sense of immediacy in the family narrative, compressing their past into an enlarged present. Their memories were liberated from linear time, and personal histories had no inescapable consequences.

Even though the family narrative was neither bound by a logic of successive events nor enriched by accounts of what one might have expected, it was easily embraced, in large part because of an exuberant, vivid storytelling often populated by the great and near great. It also had the strength of a certain consistency that led to familiarity. Lucie and Alexander often returned to their favorite themes, cleverness, humor, and hard work as sources of resilience in a dangerous world, the importance of defying inequality and discrimination and denouncing the poisons of violence and hatred, and the centrality of creating and appreciating great art, an essential part of a life well lived.

Although their parents were barely present in their recollections, Alexander and Lucie created central roles for their siblings in the family tragicomedy. Their brothers and sisters were linked to a recurrent set of themes and vivid characteristics that heightened the theatricality of the narrative, and each of them was stamped with certain well-defined and gendered characteristics. Alexander consistently embodied heroic resilience in the service of art. He was able to use his repertoire of extra-musical skills, among them intellectual, linguistic, and comic, to extricate himself from mortal threats; these permitted him to serve the singular and lofty purpose of perfecting and performing his vision of pianistic art, one that suffused both the Romantic canon and modern compositions with a range of qualities there were poetic, cerebral, and, at times, surprisingly muscular.

Alexander's sister, Elisabeth, who my father referred to derisively as the fluttering *papillon* (butterfly), was his antithesis, living without guile, without interest in art, cleverness, or ambition. She served as an example, no doubt a cruel, sexist, and condescending one, that Great Trauma could be survived by some, not by means of courage and talent, but as a matter of good fortune and obliviousness.

Lucie consistently appeared as emblematic of strength and selflessness, persevering with a pronounced stability of character and self-sacrifice, surviving war and betrayal, creating a protective cocoon for her spouse to continue a much-interrupted career, carrying on as parent in chief in the absence of her spouse, and maintaining her principles in an alien environment.

Evsey, Alexander's older brother, was the polymorphic epitome of sweet and caring goodness and a person of self-effacing bravery who, after demonstrating the inherent virtue of living the artistic life, managed to prevail by adapting to dire circumstances with modesty. He began adulthood as an aspiring artist in prewar Paris, then endured five years as a prisoner of war, and emerged, postwar, as a father of many who accepted the role of a village *tavernier*. He served wine for years on end, sold fishing tackle, and, Alexander would invariably add wistfully, no longer searched for the personal satisfaction of a long-elusive artistic identity.

Alexander's younger brother, Anatole, like Evsey, was portrayed as having shifted personalities to accommodate exigencies, but more extravagantly and forcefully than Evsey, making the transition from a penurious and free-spirited playwright manqué before the war, to a hero of the Resistance for a free France, then turning the page postwar, participating in summary executions of retribution known as *épurations sauvages*, brutal purges of collaborators. By the early 1950s, his role in the family narrative shifted fundamentally; it was now described as a louche and anarchic life, with debts from chronic gambling covered by confidence games and embezzlement schemes that undermined successful business ventures. He even abused the kindness of family and friends whom he never sought to repay. In the family narrative, Anatole was emblematic of tragic heroism, whose higher-order dreams of artistic accomplishment were thoroughly redirected by the Shoah and the violence he witnessed and wreaked, serving both as a soldier in the Just War and as an agent of revenge afterward. Anatole's path from artist to con man highlighted the need for forgiveness in the family narrative, routinely offered by Alexander and Lucie to honor personal sacrifice and because, they would insist, his charm was irresistible, even though they themselves were often the marks my uncle bilked.

My uncle Monio, Lucie's older brother and my father's best friend, was adored by my parents, and his brief life was recounted in skeletal, hagiographic form as an intellectual polymath of great promise and political righteousness whose life featured only pinnacles and no valleys. When he was mentioned, relatively rarely in the family narrative, it was accompanied by lists of achievements, but nothing emerged of his personality. He was the archetypical mensch who went to law school, fought for prisoners' rights, supported the Popular Front, and pursued a doctorate in philosophy. His death, undated but probably occurring in 1940 or 1941, was shrouded in mystery, conjuring the image of great promise denied.

Lucie's sister, Lola, appeared rarely in the family theater, but her role, an embodiment of malevolence, was a striking counterpoint to the prevailing themes. Never associated with the arts or intellectual endeavors, the lifeblood of the Uninsky and Biszkowicz men, Lola was an agent of betrayal.

Her escape from perils of wartime France began with flight to Porto and culminated with a conversion to Catholicism and marriage to a Portuguese police psychiatrist. While religious belief for Lucie and Alexander was tangential to their vision of an ethical life well lived, an archaism stripped of relevance by senseless vitriol and violence, Lola's adoption of the life of a converso was an unforgivable affront to all Jews. Her choice, after having escaped to a place of relative safety was, for my parents, the height of amorality, an unforgivably cynical and self-serving choice in a Europe convulsed by antisemitism. Her perfidious nature was confirmed by marriage to a servant of the Portuguese forces of repression, and if that were not enough, the narrative also included hints of a fabulously skilled trans-Atlantic attack on the financial welfare of her sister and mother. After the Nazi surrender, Lola, by then an Argentinian, allegedly plotted and successfully executed an appropriation of the family fortune stored in the legendarily impenetrable Swiss banks. Anatole's depredations, at times at the family's expense, could be forgiven of a hero who struggled against fascism, while Lola's financial duplicity, also harmful to family, clearly could not, given that it was compounded by an ignoble lack of courage and a betrayal of her people.

Gender typification coursed strongly through these roles, although not without certain eccentricities and inconsistencies. Far more than the women in their families, Alexander, Anatole, Evsey, and Monio, as young men in prewar France, had high aspirations, and they chose paths at the functional periphery of their society, at odds with ready assimilation to mainstream society. Alexander, who studied at the Conservatoire de Paris, and Monio, at a school of law, were portrayed as intellectually restless. Unlike many of their talented peers, who were slotted into well-defined career paths rather early in their educations, they reportedly wandered hungrily from their principal academic institutions to emerging fields of interest at the Sorbonne during the late 1920s and '30s. Evsey, the painter, and Alexander, the pianist, moved seamlessly between their classical training and norm-breaking artistic expression. Anatole, so the narrative went, seemed drawn from the cast of characters in Puccini's *La Bohème,* writing avant-garde plays while gambling incessantly and drinking heavily. These nonconformist roles, which spanned a wide range from principled intellectual opposition and artistic innovation to a louche insouciance, were the exclusive domain of my father and uncles.

Perhaps this gender-specific narrative stressing intellectual and artistic restlessness reflected my father's abiding, romanticized image of male members of the Russian intelligentsia, who he believed provided models for challenging the worst of established order. Little of this seemed to have its origins in the social and political ferment Alexander witnessed in his youth, although he often expressed admiration for certain key figures, particularly the anarchist Peter Kropotkin, and, curiously, Alexander Kerensky, briefly the Russian Provisional Government's Socialist Revolutionary prime minister in 1917, and perhaps more importantly for my father, an occasional bridge partner in the early 1950s. Most often, family discussions of the intelligentsia focused on the role of heroic nonconformism as portrayed in the literature that Alexander read as a youth in Kyiv (particularly Dostoevsky, Bely, and Leskov) and later discussed, he recalled, with fellow émigrés in France.

Both parents spoke rhapsodically of a prewar Paris that, in the first three decades of the twentieth century, welcomed a coterie of brilliant and dynamic Russian émigrés who inspired them. There was always an unmistakable maleness infusing my parents' idealization of path-breaking intelligentsia. The creative brilliance of Alexandra Exter, Natalia Goncharova and other innovative Parisiennes, all also émigrés from Eastern Europe, never appeared. Only men, Sergei Diaghilev, Marc Chagall, Wassily Kandinsky, Sergei Prokofiev, and others, whose artistry marked paths that diverged markedly from the dominant elite aesthetic, played a prominent role in the creative world within which Alexander, Anatole, Evsey, and Monio thrived.

With the coming of war, male bravery, previously limited in the family narrative to intellectual, artistic, behavioral, and political expression, was recast in terms of the physical struggle against fascism. The wartime fearlessness of the young Uninsky men was layered, organized with a hierarchy of valor. Anatole, the younger bohemian brother, was accorded the highest mark of courage, making the conversion from feckless bohemian to purposeful Resistance warrior, through VE Day and beyond. Organizing operations in Brittany, he was said to have recruited colleagues from a colorfully diverse group of artisans, criminals, and political activists, stolen arms and munitions, engaged in hit-and-run actions against the occupiers, escaped capture on several occasions, and lived to never tell a tale, scorning any recognition of heroism.

Soon after France declared war on Nazi Germany in September 1939, Evsey and Alexander both enlisted in the French army, but their bravery in the family narrative manifested itself by their intention to engage and the fact of their survival, which was apparently lightly marked by combat, if at all. Putting aside their distaste and disappointment with the deepening and darker antisemitism in France, they chose to defend the country they hoped had accepted them as accomplished and assimilated Frenchmen. Alexander was clearly committed to remaining in France and spoke of applying for naturalized citizenship with the Central Office of Russian Refugees just before enlisting.[1] Soon after deployment, Evsey was captured, and this small and fragile man endured years in a POW camp, successfully hiding his religion. Alexander, demobilized after his unit on the Maginot Line was overrun, returned to Paris in June 1940, where his presumed assimilation melted away, and he became a Soviet Jew, marked for arrest as a danger to the state. For a time, he lived a furtive existence, apartment surfing in Paris. This was, I suspected, Alexander's insertion of magical thinking into moments of great duress, infused with a comic touch, for wherever he landed there were reputedly pianos upon which he could rehearse. A commitment to music was his form of resistance, his love of art a secular saving grace, but physical resistance was dropped from the narrative. When he thought arrest was imminent in 1941, Alexander fled to Latin America and renewed his career.

Evsey's foreshortened and Alexander's relatively limited, even nonviolent, roles as soldiers created the image, never directly but by inference, that fate had interfered to preserve

---

1 The Office Central des Réfugiés Russes (OCRR) was created in May 1925, after the French government recognized the Soviet Union. It was established in large part to continue the protection of refugees that had, until that point, been provided by Russian imperial consular authorities.

their art. Being spared the worst, they were given the opportunity to pursue an essential part of their own humanity. I sometimes thought about this part of the family narrative, recalling the two brothers' struggle to survive, on a bicycle across France and Spain or as a prisoner of war, as something of a morality tale about courageous persistence serving a greater purpose—art and artistry had to be preserved to help forestall society's dehumanization. Not that either brother ever elaborated upon the military phase of their outright resistance to fascism; neither ever provided details about their army training or battlefield experiences. These were buried in the past, with Evsey answering direct questions about this part of his life with the Gallic shrug of "ask me no more," and Alexander always deflecting, typically smiling wryly that his time in the army led him to detest nature, once he had seen it from behind the barrel of a gun. Alexander's friend, Lucie's brother Monio, was never remembered as a combatant in those rare moments when my parents mentioned him in family reminiscences.

Only Lucie, not Elisabeth or Lola, appeared in the family narrative of prewar Paris. Unlike the men in the family, she neither aspired to be an artist nor an intellectual, nor was she inclined, of her own accord, to struggle against social and political norms. Lucie would recall that in prewar Paris she was never convinced of her intellectual acumen, a consequence she implied of being regarded as academically untalented by her emotionally distant father, who doubted the value of educating his daughters. She was also, by her own account, a *jeune fille rangée*, literally a "well-behaved girl," but often translated, as in the case of Simone de Beauvoir's memoir, as a "dutiful daughter." In using this phrase, Lucie was not referencing Beauvoir's critical commentaries on class, religion, and sexuality, but rather noting that her upbringing trained her to be an assimilated, uncontroversial Frenchwoman, and certainly not a nonconformist. When she recalled moments of youthful activism, they were not initiated of her own accord, so she would say, but only with the encouragement of her brother Monio, who urged her to join some of his causes, including rallying support for Léon Blum's National Front and raising funds to aid the Spanish Republicans in their struggle against Francoist forces.

Elisabeth's wartime experiences were distilled by Alexander to the mere mention of her having survived, and, in our several meetings from the mid-1970s on, my aunt left it at that with a dismissive wave of her hand and an abrupt change of topic, a clear warning to leave the past alone. The flight of Lucie and her sister Lola to Portugal in the spring of 1940, soon after German forces entered France, was an event never recalled in heroic terms by either parent, and certainly not in detail. It must have required no small amount of courage and prescience, along with good fortune, but little was said about obstacles encountered and overcome during the long road trip that included crossing the closed border with fascist Spain. It was a part of the past never recalled through the lens of wartime bravery or portrayed as traumatic. Most strikingly, this fragmentary story was overlaid with an image of ease and given the circumstances, of solicitude on Lucie's part, riding from Paris in a family car to help her sister. In this telling, Lucie, who only learned to drive in 1962, held Lola's newborn on her lap while Lola drove to the city of Porto, seemingly without incidents of any note, nothing requiring sang froid or tricksterism, and quite tellingly, all done without any mention of male assistance.

Neither Lucie nor Alexander ever divulged how the Biszkowicz family managed its Portuguese exile. Monio and his parents, Chana and Kleoman, disappeared from the narrative. At this point, gender stereotypes of women surviving at war diverged. Lola's story was a character study of profound betrayal, ruthless self-interest, and subservience to a man. She appeared in the family narrative only twice after arriving in Portugal, leaving in 1941 for Buenos Aires and returning to Europe after the war to raid the family funds.

In stark contrast to her sister, Lucie's time in Porto was a relatively blank page, characterized by her independence of action and flavored by comic deflection. She would only say that having lived in Porto for over a year, she was prompted to emigrate because she could not stand another mouthful of dried *bacalao* (cod). Providing no details on how she managed it, in early 1942, Lucie extricated herself from wartime Europe and moved directly to New York City. This daughter of wealth arrived there penniless but soon obtained her first paid employment. To support her newfound independence, she labored in a watch assembly center in Manhattan, putting "hands on blank faces." That same year, her brother's best friend, Alexander, arrived and played his Carnegie debut. This was, in the family accounts, a happy coincidence that led to marriage two years later after a concert in Maryland.

Once united in the New World, Lucie adopted the role of Alexander's steadfast and resourceful partner, the young grande dame of a successful artist. This was, as they both recalled, a partnership, albeit an unequal one. She became his musical adviser, expertly critiquing his performances at a time when Alexander suspected that few in the public who heard him outside of New York City could fully appreciate his pianism. When my parents spoke of this time, they recalled the profound satisfaction that success had brought, but there was never any discussion of mutual affection. Lucie was engaged in the hard work of sustaining Alexander's career momentum. In support of that effort, she remade herself, developing a public image as the glamorous companion to the dashing young artist, beautifully clothed as she had never been before, and clearly capable of supporting her husband's career.

Alexander and Lucie Uninsky on tour, arriving at an undisclosed location, ca. 1943. Photo courtesy of the author.

When my sister Eliane was born in 1948, Lucie's role was transformed again, shifting from an active partner in her husband's career, an art-focused life that involved nearly continuous travel, to a sedentary life of ease, supported by an absent husband. Now a Parisian mother, Lucie moved into postwar bourgeois domesticity, probably what Alexander expected of her, but which she clearly adopted with relish. She recalled managing a household for the first time, even learning to cook with the assistance of staff, and becoming caregiver to her exhausted spouse upon his return. Alexander on tour apparently ate little and drank to excess; even if the opportunity arose, he was hopeless in the kitchen, more likely to "watch the egg and boil his watch." Every time he returned home, she would prepare meals from his childhood in Kyiv that ostensibly comforted him with pleasant memories of a childhood that neither parent ever revealed. For several subsequent days, Alexander indulged in this private mother-comfort restoration, with meals that might include *schav* (a green soup of sorrel or spinach), borscht, holishkes (stuffed cabbage), *syrniki* (sweetened cottage cheesecakes sauteed in butter) to build his strength, and, on occasion, calf brains for intellectual vigor. Lucie, at least at this point in her life, remade herself with a remarkable malleability. Once an essential partner in building a career, she was now transformed into a household manager and maternal figure caring for a child and spouse.

CHAPTER 5

Pushing Aside the Haze

Although it became obvious that little could be credibly ascertained about my grandparents, I had long hoped that a more complete and accurate family narrative about my parent's generation would emerge from the haze created by Lucie and Alexander. There was never any doubt that my parent's version of the past was brewed in the context of unimaginably intense contrasts. In reality, serial episodes of traumatic exposure to danger, persecution, loss of family, immiseration, and displacement had been interspersed with artistic success, a life of ease, and the fellowship of outsized, creative personalities. In the hands of others, the narrative that unfolded over years might easily have become a tragedy of disappointment and regret, a tale of gain leading inexorably to loss, a lesson in life's primordial unfairness. But my family's accounts of the past had a protective and didactic air, dwelling not on horror but on essential characteristics for survival. They used wit, imagination, and misdirection to create uplifting stories and anecdotes that moved attention away from traumatic events that they either minimized or omitted.

Lucie and Alexander, in particular, presented themselves as evidence that in the difficult world they must have experienced, life could be achieved without an ending marked by grief, anger, disappointment, and resentment. Lessons were certainly being taught, particularly about their sources of resilience, but there were also times when seemingly magical interventions or exceptionally fortunate circumstances intervened, pulling them from impending disasters. Here and there these incidents explained the seemingly inexplicable. On those occasions, the pillars of their credibility shook, but given their skills as storytellers, they never crumbled. It is tempting, in retrospect, to know why this was so. Especially with their young children, these unexpected interventions heightened interest with an air of mystery and were told with such conviction they seemed within the realm of the plausible. Later, when teenage skepticism had settled in, these exceptional moments of good fortune were portrayed as linked to Alexander's talent, when his artistry, it seemed, naturally invited support from elite benefactors. However, it became evident over time that fortuitous interventions occurred for other family members not widely known for their creative gift, and it may be that the simplest explanation of these seemingly fantastic events is the most telling, that the less family members said about troubled times the better.

During the first of many trips to Europe, in 1973, I sought to fill in the silences of Lucie and Alexander, to better understand the confabulated and expand the confirmable, and, most importantly, to somehow reveal the sources and methods of this family's extraordinary resilience. I met repeatedly with Alexander's three siblings during the last twenty years of their lives. Anatole, the youngest brother, was always a challenge to locate, occasionally hiding from creditors or engaged in activities that were certainly frowned upon by authorities. Evsey, in his bistro in Saint-Rémy-sur-Avre, and Elisabeth, in her modest apartment near the Bois de Vincennes on the edge of Paris, were always easily found. Lucie's sister in Buenos Aires never responded to my efforts to contact her. But clearing away my parents' and their siblings' narrative haze was no mean task. One and all, Elisabeth, Anatole, and Evsey shared Lucie and Alexander's penchant for invention, deflection, and omission that, at times, had the unmistakable signs of a collective and remarkably sustained effort to immunize or isolate the next generation from their past. To a certain extent, this was confirmed in what became a singularly unenlightening exercise in futility—exploring the past with my French cousins. The eight children of Elisabeth, Evsey, and Anatole, all living in France, had only a pixel or two of information to add to the family history. Anatole had never had a role in raising his daughter; Elisabeth's son knew only of the family's postwar lives; and Evsey successfully created the alternate reality of a fully assimilated, rural family for his six children.

And there were more blind alleys. Archival sources regarding my parents' generation were only a bit less rare than they were for my grandparents, and diaries and correspondence nonexistent. Alexander and Lucie never identified friends from prewar Paris, other than artists, and only one of them was still alive when I began traveling in Europe after 1973. Jean Hélion, the distinguished painter who had served in the

French army, escaped capture, and waited out the war in New York, dismissed my questions about his prewar friendship with Alexander. Instead, he quoted in his sing-song Franco-English accent, the well-worn opinion of L. P. Hartley in *The Go-Between* that the "past is a foreign country; they do things differently there."

Confirming my family's story, taking up the challenge of the two psychoanalysts who helped launch me on this path soon after my father's death, could never be about revealing what was undeniably and irrefutably true. The claim of absolute confirmability in personal narrative is often a canard, particularly when it is clear that reticence and inventiveness are also both at play. Only a few sources, principally archival, provided nearly unimpeachable glimpses into the Biszkowicz-Uninsky past, and a rough, believable outline took shape amidst the otherwise largely unverifiable narrative. The result of my efforts, however, only confirmed what was often unsurprising, dealing with the very bare bones of the family story. An undated picture discovered of Alexander in a French uniform, for example, indicates that he probably served in the war (although the lawyer in me knows it has no probative value), but information that sheds light on his brief mentions of service near the Maginot Line driving supply trucks, or how he survived upon returning to Paris, are not to be found.

Alexander Uninsky, probably before his military assignment, ca. 1939. Photo courtesy of the author.

A class photograph in front of the Conservatoire de Paris in 1926 confirms, absent school enrollment records and living peers, that Alexander, at the age of sixteen, was studying with the pianist and composer Lazare-Lévy, even if nothing is available to verify the few stories of his experience there.

Lazare-Lévy and his piano students in 1926 at the Conservatoire National de Musique in Paris. Lazare-Lévy is in the center, Alexandre Uninsky in the upper right. Among the others in the photograph who can be identified are Monique Haas (top left), Pierre Maillard-Verger (top center), Louise Clavius-Marius (second from the left, middle row), Gabrielle Giraud-Latarse (to the right of Lazare-Lévy), and Colette Cras-Tansman (bottom right), all of whom had distinguished musical careers. Photo courtesy of the author.

Anatole is briefly mentioned in Resistance archives, but he appears nowhere in any histories of the period, and nothing I could find testifies to his exploits that formed a central part of the family narrative. When it comes to my family's recollections, fact-finding often entailed a fall into a rabbit hole to mundanity.

After some years of searching for clear lines to the past, my search for stringent standards of confirmability gave way to accepting plausibility, particularly about important facets of the Uninsky-Biszkowicz tragicomedy that cried out for explanation. This was particularly the case for Lucie's brother Monio.

Monio Biszkowicz, age twelve, in 1925. Photo courtesy of the author.

Portrayed in adulatory terms and mourned furtively by my parents, he disappeared from the family accounts about the time Lucie and Lola arrived in Portugal in 1940. Absent documentary confirmation, I relied on versions of events provided over time and independently by Evsey and Anatole. Given Anatole's frequent recourse to flimflammery and Evsey's seemingly ingrained reticence to divulge much of the past, deriving a credible account from this type of consonance may be a dubious step taken. Still, after the war, the two Uninsky brothers lived different lives apart from one another, and rarely communicated; I have at least a better than shaky conviction that their occasional overlapping versions of the past were not the product of collusion. This standard of confirmation, called triangulation by my colleagues in program evaluation, is a lower one than some, but at least it provides a semblance of some believability where none other exists.

What did happen to Monio, the politically progressive polymath? According to Evsey and Anatole, Monio was the bright and adventuresome activist of my parents' narrative, interested in criminal justice reform and deeply involved in a struggle against resurgent xenophobia and antisemitism in prewar Paris. He became close to the Uninsky family in the mid-1930s, when, after finishing law school, he branched out to another field, studying for a doctorate at the Sorbonne with the celebrity philosopher Henri Bergson, winner of the 1927 Nobel Prize in literature. It was in these classes, my uncles recalled, that he befriended Alexander, who also attended the Bergson lectures. It is impossible to know with any certainty what attracted both the activist and the artist to Bergson's lectures. Alexander, for his part, vaguely recalled his interest in the philosopher's ideas about creativity, freedom, and novelty. In addition, at this time, Alexander's musical career, after winning the Chopin prize in 1932, was becoming incandescent, and he may have been motivated to further root himself in French society by becoming part of the academic elite he idealized, forging a path of intellectual assimilation. Or so his brothers believed. During this time, the Biszkowicz and Uninsky families became closer. Through his friendship with Monio, Alexander also came to know Lucie, a teenager who, my uncles fondly remembered, idolized both her brother and the young pianist.

When war was declared, Evsey and Anatole soon lost track of Monio, and they only learned of his fate from Lucie after she was married and, in 1948, had resettled in Paris. During those early postwar years Lucie would occasionally visit Evsey with her newborn daughter, and even though his life was far from settled, Anatole took every opportunity to visit with his brother and sister-in-law. It was on those occasions, my uncles eventually revealed, that Lucie spoke of Monio's disappearance.

My uncles were at first reluctant to speak at all about Monio, wordlessly implying something tragic had occurred with telltale downward glances and long sighs. Their hints of wartime misfortune revealed more than any family member typically offered about such dark moments. My interest in Monio intensified, but for several years, the family maintained its silence. Perhaps they were guarding Lucie's privacy, or they thought me too inexperienced and unworldly to manage what they were hiding. Eventually they relented, each in his own way. In the late 1970s, Anatole responded to my questions about Monio during what the French call an evening *bien arrosée* (well watered). It was a rare moment of lubricated candor about the war. Evsey later revealed something similar during an atypical display of undisguised sorrow about a lifetime of disappointments, which was clearly triggered when we together visited the painter Jean Hélion. Both Evesy and Hélion had been captured at the outset of the war, but unlike my uncle, Hélion escaped the prisoner-of-war camp early on and wrote a bestseller about his experience, *They Shall Not Have Me.*[1] Hélion had become a leading modernist and was painting in his chateau near Evsey's village. In their own ways they told

---

1 Jean Hélion, *They Shall Not Have Me: The Capture, Forced Labor, and Escape of a French Prisoner in World War II* (New York: E. P. Dutton, 1943).

me, Anatole morosely and Evsey somberly, without embellishment or explanation, about the tragic death of Monio.

As the Nazi army approached Paris in the Spring of 1940, Monio decided to follow his mother and sisters to Portugal. In the presence of Lola and Chana he took his own life. On this dark slate of suicide, much was inscribed.

Monio Biszkowicz in 1939, shortly before he left France for Portugal. One of several family photographs Lucie Uninsky never revealed to her children during her lifetime. Photo courtesy of the author.

Monio's action, Lucie told her brothers-in-law, was born of intensifying anguish, the cumulative effects of the conduct of the French toward the Jewish community before and during the war, and his guilt over the decision to leave while others fought. But, according to Anatole and Evsey, Lucie also understood Monio's action as an unmistakable expression of profound outrage, an elemental disgust over Lola's conversion of convenience, one that Monio saw as actively supported by their mother. Lucie recalled her own subsequent sense of suffocating isolation in Porto. She felt completely alone in her grief, with Alexander in Latin America, her father inexplicably absent, and alienated from her sister and mother, who were beyond acceptance. None of this, of course, is confirmable, but for Evsey and Anatole, Lucie's account rang true. For the two brothers, who may have become somewhat inured to matters of death and expressions of grief after their wartime experiences, Lucie's despair was striking. In part, it was out of character for their sister-in-law to express a grief so intense, so close to the surface, particularly seven years after Monio's death. That the suicide was other-directed, serving as a final condemnation of Monio's mother and sister, also still bordered on the unimaginable to my uncles in the 1970s, nearly thirty years after Lucie's account.

A verifiable version of events? Certainly not, but a believable one because of its singularity. During the twenty years I visited on and off with Evsey and Anatole, this was the only time they spoke of suicide or of any traumatic event, or even of Lucie's emotional well-being. Lucie's account of Monio's death, in their memories, stood in stark contrast to their other contributions to the family narrative, which rarely inclined toward illuminating family dynamics. This was also most certainly an atypical moment in their past, to see the usually stolid Lucie so bereft. Evsey and Anatole evidently believed Lucie's account of Monio's death, and their accounts of the tragedy were all the more compelling because they were, for them, unusually and strikingly similar. And I was inclined to believe their versions because it helped clarify facets of the family narrative that had long confused me—why Lucie and Alexander grieved so privately for Monio and so completely ostracized Chana, Lucie's mother and my only surviving grandparent, and why Lucie so adamantly resisted my efforts to elicit memories of her brother. Or perhaps convenience conveys credibility in the murky domain of trauma and memory.

While Lucie and Alexander infrequently spoke to me about Monio, and never about his death, I learned from family friends and Alexander's students that in our later years in Dallas, my father began including accounts about Monio. Placing Lucie's brother in an invented pantheon of the brave, Alexander reportedly began to speak of his talented friend's efforts to galvanize resistance to the activities of the far right in France in 1939 and 1940, particularly against Action Française and the Croix-de-Fer. This was new information and clearly an account of heroic futility; it was a natural but likely invented extension of Lucie's recollections of her brother's earlier support for Blum's Front Populaire and raising funds for Republican forces during the Spanish Civil War. Monio's demise, in this account, was presumed without specificity. Perhaps not coincidentally, these revelations came at a time, in the late 1960s, when Lucie was having difficulty adjusting to life in the Southwest. She was, after several years in Dallas, often dismayed, and occasionally distraught by her surroundings. Accounts of Monio's renewed anti-fascist activities may have been Alexander's curious approach to short-circuiting Lucie's disquiet, providing an alternative, invented narrative, a way for Lucie to feel some elevated sense of pride. During these years, it became clearer that parental confabulations, at least those I recognized, served a deeper purpose of displacement, pushing aside grief and negativity and, at times, protecting their privacy. But it also seems unlikely that Lucie would ever have accepted any effort to revisit Monio's death, invented or otherwise. Replacing Monio's self-destruction with a story of persistent struggle against fascism may also have been intended to deflect Alexander's own feelings about his role in the war. This was a time in Alexander's life when arthritis, the frustrations with being an artist in residence in a school of music remote from the great cultural centers, and a decline in his recording career were wearing away at his equanimity. He may not only have been offering comfort to Lucie, but also himself taking comfort in telling a story of heroism about his closest friend who did not survive the war.

Alexander's moodiness in the months before he died was far from a secret. Many suspected his death at the early age of sixty-two was a suicide, something which briefly graduated from rumor to a Wikipedia factoid, but there was no evidence of a self-inflected death in the postmortem. In his final years, he drank more Pope's telephone number (his less than private joke about the whiskey VAT 69) and was more acerbic with his university colleagues, but this was by no means a steep decline to despondency; he never edged toward signs of suicidality, and his dissatisfactions and physical pain did not overwhelm his love of music and his engagement with performance. His tours in 1970 and 1971, if anything, were longer than during the late 1960s. In his last year, 1972, he was thinking of his future, excitedly planning a tour to celebrate his fifty-year career. This calculus suggested he had first performed professionally in 1923 at age thirteen, although he actually began touring in 1927. The earlier year suited him better, he told me, a confection for publicity purposes. Fifty, a jubilee year, would resonate more with the public than forty-six.

Whenever I saw Alexander perform in the late 1960s and early '70s, it was clear that on stage he was another person altogether, completely immersed in an often explosive and always wide-ranging display of musical emotions. He often said his goal was to immerse audiences, opening listeners who were new to the music to a deep appreciation, and for those who were familiar with the pieces, engaging them in a reinterpretation, to have them listening anew. He wanted his public to move beyond the superficial enjoyment that came from technical showmanship, a type of appreciation which he derided, to a deeper understanding of great compositions. He hoped to achieve what always seemed impossible to me, to evoke colors with his pianism, to musically draw impressionistic visions of nature, and to project the specific emotions he believed were expressed in the scores, whether baroque, romantic, or contemporary. On stage, at the piano, Alexander was alive, in love with musical poetry, and consumed by his version of artistry. It was inconceivable to think in those moments that he was capable of feeling helplessness. He was clearly comforted by and fully committed to performance.

It was in these times, which turned out to be the last years of his life, that I began to see Alexander as a circus performer. I imagined him walking on a lifelong tightrope strung between a traumatic past and a fulfilling, creative present. He was, I concluded, inventing memories to keep his balance whenever it might be undone by lingering horrors that could never be entirely sublimated. But imputing specific motives for an invented narrative is clearly a risky business in the context of trauma, an effort that is itself an unsteady walk between fact and fiction, especially when those memories are recalled by gifted storytellers.

Lucie may also have precariously inched forward on a tightrope between nightmare and sunlight; a raconteur, like her husband, she was more interested in recounting Alexander's past than her own. And she also embellished her recollections, but when it involved the Biszkowicz family, she may have maintained her precarious balance by insisting on a narrative dotted with conspicuous omissions rather than inventions, with silence perhaps offering her some measure of security, or at least some emotional distance. Even when I was a child, these exclusions clearly begged for elaborations that were never offered. Names omitted were a particular source of curiosity. When asked, Lucie would only feign confusion about the origins of her family name, "was it Estonian or Latvian?" and then skip quickly to the anglicized Bisco and never mention her mother's first name nor explain why Grandmaman Bisco was so extraneous to our lives. Lucie's father was never given any name, first, patronymic, or last. In Lucie's telling he was sparsely sketched, a wealthy, two-dimensional philosopher king, closeted in his study, and then suddenly, like his son, an invisible man, gone without a trace. Her omissions and misdirections were rarely supplemented by other family members, and little tangible has survived to provide insights into Lucie's life before she settled in New York City in 1952. There is nothing to document her years as a daughter of privilege in Paris in the 1920s and '30s or as a refugee in Portugal in the 1940s.

After her death, I found precious little documentation from her earlier life in Europe: a series of 1949 photographs with her newborn daughter in France; press clippings about Alexander from 1942 to 1945; and a French residency visa issued in 1949 listing her Paris address in a formidable Haussman apartment building that still stands in the 16th arrondissement, on Rue de Civry, steps from the Bois de Boulogne. From the time she first arrived in the US early in the war until 1948, as she shuttled nearly incessantly with Alexander throughout North and South America and to and from France, Lucie was photographed often, descending from planes, waving from ocean liners, part of a glamorous couple; sometimes she posed with him at the piano, with her gloved hand usually posed lightly on his shoulder, while she gazed admiringly at his fingers on the keyboard.

Lucie Uninsky observes Alexander Uninsky playing for his first teacher at the Kyiv Conservatory, Sergei Tarnovsky, in Chicago, Illinois, November 1944. Copyright permission courtesy of The Tully Potter Foundation.

Despite Lucie's depiction of parents who were disinterested in her education and her own equivocal estimation of her scholastic aptitude, she claimed to have graduated from the highly regarded and very selective Lycée Fénelon in June 1938, the first high school in Paris to enroll women. There, she may well have been a classmate of young women of talent and ambition. A few years before Lucie attended the school, its students included perhaps the three most famous French women of their generation: Simone Weil, a philosopher and distinguished politician; Louise Bourgeois, a sculptor; and Simone de Beauvoir, feminist, social theorist, and philosopher. Although she only revealed her attendance at Lycée Fénelon in 1975, Lucie never provided any proof of having been educated there, and none is available from the school as it is now constituted. Nonetheless, her claim of a baccalauréat, along with her considerable linguistic skills, were sufficient to obtain employment as an English as a second language instructor in the Dallas Independent School District, where she taught for over twenty years after Alexander's death. She was beloved by her largely Latin American and Vietnamese students, and when I spoke with them, I heard, or wanted to hear, that they were learning to speak English with traces of Lucie's French accent.

Conversations with family friends, many of whom continued to live in our close-knit Upper West Side building, added credible glimpses of Lucie in her new incarnation in the early 1950s, a mother of two, the matriarch of a musical family, and a woman, like many Jewish refugees, with little inclination to discuss the past. Her community of painters, actors, directors, musicians, and psychoanalysts spoke of Lucie's strength of will, her well-controlled temper couched in humor and tamed with a smile, and her remarkable capacity for forgiveness. On several occasions during the 1950s, they recalled, when Alexander returned from tours, his luggage was placed outside the apartment door the day after he arrived, a short-term banishment and public shaming for infidelity. Somehow, each time, a private reconciliation ensued.

Among my father's colleagues at the Aspen music festival in the 1950s and several neighbors in Manhattan, it was common knowledge, often a metonymy for gossip, that Alexander went into a short-lived, self-destructive tailspin that included narcotics. First provided him by a lover when on tour, or so they claimed, heroin may have assuaged Alexander's arthritic pains and helped the lifelong insomniac sleep, but addiction could also have been a product of family mythmaking. According to this account, Lucie, alone and in seclusion, supervised a cold turkey withdrawal, swaddling Alexander in blankets, helping manage the agonizing struggle until he reappeared, recovered, emaciated, and depleted. The few photographs from this period show an exhausted man with sunken cheeks and an uncharacteristically grim expression. Soon after, in late 1954, in flight from McCarthyism, the family departed for Toronto, where Alexander was an artist in residence at the Royal Conservatory of Music. It was a brief tenure, less than two years and never discussed by my parents, other than Lucie's dismissive and unelaborated remark, told many times, about the unendurable parochialism of the city that found my father's behavior "scandalous," a sign perhaps that he had fully recovered. Alexander's Toronto sojourn left barely a trace in the conservatory archives, other than that he taught a master class with the Chilean pianist, Claudio Arrau. My sister, a child of eight when we returned to New York in 1956, later claimed to recall little of our time in Canada, and I, four years younger, now remember only a longing to return to the city.

This story of cataclysmic decline and painful recovery was told by colleagues, friends and neighbors, partly, I suspect, because they thought it believable of a man who must have endured great psychic and physical pain, but also, I think, because it fit with the image they all had of Lucie, a grande dame of music, supportive of the artist and his art, a persevering woman, a rock. Among those contemporaries confirming what may have transpired, knowledge of past traumas and lasting impressions of well-defined personality traits may have influenced what they deemed credible.

If Lucie's rather nonspecific and episodic narrative of her own life through the early 1950s largely defies confirmation, it is even more the case for her immediate family. Her accounts of her parents and siblings, like her autobiography, were sparse and discontinuous, and whatever documents might have added to this bare family history seem to have been largely swept away by sudden migrations and war. The two immediate family members who survived the war added nothing to the narrative, with Grandmaman Bisco, ostracized and unpleasantly laconic, and Lucie's Argentinian sister Lola, no doubt aware of her sister's profound hostility, unrelentingly unresponsive.

Alexander's three siblings, by contrast, all survived the war and were communicative, although in a strictly circumscribed manner, providing no documents of the past, and maintaining, like Alexander and Lucie, a determined sense of immediacy, insisting more on their lives as lived, skirting questions about their youth, parents, and wartime experiences.

My paternal aunt, Elisabeth, was nearly invisible in the family narrative, accorded no artistic talents or youthful restless spirit like her siblings. It was clear, aside from rare visits from Alexander when he played in Paris, that she lived entirely apart from her brothers. Archival searches to find traces of her past activities have been fruitless, aside from a notice of her burial in Creteil, not far from her last residence. Elisabeth responded to my questions about her childhood and life before and during the war with accounts of how much she enjoyed her present life, a contented widow with an adoring son, who shed no light on her past and knew next to nothing of his mother's brothers. The *papillon* of the family narrative fluttered, not perhaps in the suggested oblivion, but above any apparent sadness and regrets, quietly satisfied with small pleasures. Whatever traumas she had undoubtedly endured during the war, the deportation of her parents and a likely solitary path through the occupation without her brothers nearby, were nowhere near the surface.

Evsey did indeed study with André Lhote, painter, sculpture, and influential critic of modern art, whose eponymous academy during its thirty years had over 1,200 students in the visual arts, including Hans Hartung, a forerunner of lyrical abstraction, the sculptor Louise Bourgeois, the singer Serge Gainsbourg, Dora Maar (painter, poet, and Picasso's muse), and the photographer Henri Cartier-Bresson. Evsey never achieved anything close to such renown. It does not appear that he managed to enter the vibrant gallery scene in prewar

Paris, although Lhote did select him to be one of seventeen students shown in the academy's first exhibit at the Galerie Pittoresque in Paris in 1937. On a poster announcing the exhibit, Lhote introduced the works of his students with florid praise, describing them as paintings of "audacity [with] violent color of plastic deformations," expressions of his belief that artistic "disorder inspires." He hoped the artists shown in the exhibition would continue to challenge the art world and "linger in the land of poetic experiences."[2]

The few of Evsey's prewar paintings that survive are Fauvist, clearly in Lhote's early style, playful, colorful, and far from naturalistic. What little Evsey said of his prewar artistic career, of what he said about the past at all, was tinged with regret, that he failed to emerge from the master's influence to develop a style of his own. Anatole had a different regret, that his older brother had not heeded his urgings to use his technical skills to make a fortune in fakes. The artful dodger had hoped for an artful forger.

Evsey's dreams of establishing his mark among Parisian painters were put on hold in 1939, when he enlisted in the French army. The only evidence of Evsey's wartime experience came to light in that recently discovered address book of Joseph Uninski, who in 1942 left it in the care of Pierre Kantorow. Alongside Evsey's name was written "prisonnier N° 54508, Stalag X-A 699," a POW camp in Schleswig, 133 kilometers north of Hamburg near the Danish border, and over a thousand from Paris. Evsey most likely was placed in

---

2 "Gallerie Pittoresque: Exposition d'Artistes de Monpartnasse," Andre Lhote, 1885–1962, accessed March 9, 2025. https://andre-lhote.org/media/academie/AL_Galerie_Pittoresque.pdf.

confinement with thousands of other French soldiers in 1940, and there he remained, according to his brothers, until 1945. No one in his family could ever recall Evsey discussing his experience in Stalag X-A.

Correspondence of fellow POWs spoke of hard labor and an intense companionship of peers.[3] In his *Journal de Captivité: Stalag XA, 1940–1945*, Louis Althusser, the enormously influential postwar philosopher, wrote of his five years in the same camp as an arduous and radicalizing experience, leading him, he remarked, to become a Marxist.[4] It also, Althusser believed, precipitated lifelong bouts of severe depression. His postwar life was that of a legendary professor, a prominent theoretician of the French Communist Party, and a celebrity intellectual in Paris at the École Normale Supérieure. Evsey's life after liberation certainly stood in stark contrast. Running a rural bistro in Saint-Rémy-sur-Avre, a rural village of less than 1,700 inhabitants in the 1950s, he led an apolitical life of stability and introspection. His commitment to art became sub rosa. In off-hours Evsey painted alone in a locked room off the kitchen, mostly for his own pleasure. His public persona was of a calm, hard-working, and uncomplicated man, father of many, contentedly married, who, unlike Althusser, never strangled his wife.

Anatole, the youngest Uninsky sibling, was remembered as the family's beguiling boy, doted upon by his parents and

---

3 Robert Dael, *Au Stalag XA: Textes et correspondance du représentant des Français prisonniers, protecteur et ami d'Althusser (1939–1945)* (Paris: Editions L'Harmattan, 2019).

4 Louis Althusser, *Journal de Captivité: Stalag XA, 1940–1945* (Paris: Stock/IMEC, 1992).

older brothers. When my parents spoke of him, they always used what I assumed was an affectionate diminutive, Tola. Alexander believed Tola had great potential, a precocious reader who was inspired as a teenager in the 1930s by the theatrical works of an international avant-garde being performed in Paris, including Apollinaire, Anouilh, and Pirandello. By 1935, at the age of sixteen, he was said to have started drafting his own plays, hoping, so Alexander may have believed, to become the family's third artist. Alexander also spoke of a raffish teenage Anatole, a side of his younger brother that he believed he had abetted with *argent de poche* (pocket money) once Alexander's success was ensured in the early 1930s.

Anatole reportedly would tell his older brothers he was seeking authorial inspiration, hoping to rub elbows with established authors at watering holes where writers and actors were known to be found at all hours. He was also drawn to risk in the last years of prewar Paris, particularly by betting on horses whenever he had a few francs to spare. Much was omitted from this description of an intelligent, carefree young man, so gifted at casual ingratiation, Lucie would say, that he never lacked for a free drink. In these recollections of Anatole, who was twenty when the war began, no mention was made of his education, his reactions to the intensifying antisemitism of interwar France or any political sensitivities or commitments, whether he ever put pen to paper long enough to complete a draft, or what his parents thought of his early gravitation to a bohemian lifestyle.

By late 1939, the Uninsky siblings were dispersed, Evsey and Alexander training in different military camps, Elisabeth perhaps remaining in Paris, and Anatole, somewhere unknown. Evsey, after his release from the stalag, demonstrably adopted a new persona and was rarely in contact with his siblings, preferring to focus his attention on his growing family and managing his rural bistro. Elisabeth, once the war began, lost touch with Anatole, and the two, by all accounts, never spoke again. The narrative of Anatole's life during the war and through the 1960s was maintained by Alexander and Lucie. They saw Anatole frequently once they returned to Paris in 1948. As they reported, Anatole made a sudden, seamless transformation by means of warfare, from insouciance and hopes of a literary career into a Resistance combatant. At war's end, enraged by the government's efforts to dampen discussion of collaboration and to continue its colonial agenda, Anatole allegedly refused to stand down; instead, he decided to wage wars of revenge, not only against *collabos*, but also against the Fourth Republic itself, working occasionally to support the Algerian resistance to French rule in the mid-1950s. By the late 1950s, a different persona emerged, still a charmer extraordinaire and inveterate gambler, but now a businessman who, while successful in terms of profits, resisted operating within society's norms. Anatole, my father would say with barely concealed admiration, made a fortune as the first to import coin-operated pinball machines to France, a curious and unconfirmable story, and then lost all his investment capital at the casino tables.

Alexander often made light of his brother's penchant for putting his hands in the *poches* of others and taking their *argent*, never mentioning the impact on the targets. He playfully dignified what was clearly embezzlement, theft, and fraud, framing them as acts of an economic anarchist, one whose recent past led him to reject government authority and the principle of private property. Anatole was a hero, after all, and much could be forgiven, or at least recast in a gentler light. There was, also, a bit of moral balancing, insisting that Anatole was a sloppy anarchist who invariably stumbled into the forces of order, who themselves found room to be forgiving. Only here did heroism clearly bring its earthly rewards in the family narrative, as judge after judge allegedly commuted Anatole's jail terms, even pardoning him, supposedly out of respect for his prior deeds on behalf of the *patrie.*

Anatole's life before, during, and after the war is essentially undocumented. There are no records of him as a young man, nothing to reveal school enrollment or graduation, publications, or any tangible evidence of social engagement, delinquency, or political activism. He may well have been as depicted by his older brothers and Lucie—a playful, uninhibited youth fully engaged in café culture, artistic ferment, and the Longchamp racetrack. And my parents' tales of Anatole's postwar life, before I first met him in 1974, focused far less on his campaign of violent retribution and support for Algerian rebels than on his gambling debts, serial peculation, and arrests. Having failed to discover any warrants, court appearances, or convictions involving Alexander's younger brother, I am forced to conclude that stories of judicial indulgences may have been pure inventions. Nonetheless, when I finally located my itinerant uncle, then fifty-five, certain traits conjured in the family narrative were easy to see. Anatole was then fully engaged in a small-time criminal enterprise in Switzerland. Traveling with him for a few days in the summer of 1974, his transgressive character amazed me, a mixture of guile, charisma, and wit, directed toward obtaining down payments from retailers for counterfeit goods that he never intended to ship. The ongoing spectacle of systematic fleecing was done casually with elegant variations and became a roaming set piece about human gullibility in the face of effortless charm. The role would only be dropped briefly when he was alone with me, raising a glass to celebrate his day, but his twinkling, flimflamming identity never permitted any further entry into his past actions and present motivations.

Forgiving Anatole, or at least accepting his behavior without condemnation, came easily because of the family narrative. Accounts of my uncle's exploits, stealing weapons from occupying forces, escaping capture, fighting behind enemy lines, disrupting army transports, and preparing the way for Allied forces were all mythogenic fodder for childhood dreams. On my first encounter with Anatole, these memories of his singular heroism were as vivid as ever, riding a wave of credibility that partly stemmed from his striking physical resemblance to Alexander. I was unprepared for the surprise that he was nearly my father's double, and those first days together in 1974 brought accounts of his past feats to full force in the present, as well as the sense that forgiveness, or at least a wide latitude, was owed. Alexander's running narrative about his brother acquired, for a brief time, a more solid foundation, particularly explanations of why my father's concert tours in the early 1960s yielded paltry revenues, something he accepted with what seemed like near indifference. Anatole, so it went, was amassing gambling debts in casinos across France, posing as his well-known brother, signing "A. Uninsky" on his IOUs. Alexander talked of paying these debts out of love and concern for his brother, a hero's ransom, a burden that was in "protracted diminuendo," he would later jest, steadily shrinking as Anatole was banned from one French casino after another. Of course, all of this could have been one of many distractions from another diminuendo, evident even to a preteen, a decline in Alexander's career, with fewer concerts and recordings in the early 1960s, necessitating the move to Dallas in 1963 to take up a position as an artist in residence at Southern Methodist University.

The impact of the striking fraternal resemblance between Anatole and my father faded over time, as did my hopes for confirmation of my uncle's wartime experiences. He was anything but forthcoming about the 1940s, providing a slim opening only near the end of his life, when he began mentioning his intention to live near his wartime comrades. In late 1991, I learned that Tola's health was declining, leading him to abandon his anarcho-criminality and settle in a retirement home near the central Breton village of Plouguernevel. He chose the location, so he said, to be near a few surviving Resistance combatants, but when I visited Anatole during his last months, he demurred when asked to identify his comrades. Nor would he confirm Alexander's off-hand explanation, that his brother had been plucked from obscurity into the Resistance, recruited to fight for France in Brittany by Geneviève de Gaulle, the General's niece. Anatole seemed surprised by my retelling of this anecdote, saying only he despised de Gaulle as a poor general and failed leader, which is why he refused honors from him when offered, something else I could never confirm.

Until recently, all that could be verified about Anatole's activities during the war was that he was included in the governmental registry of Resistance fighters, number 581,059 on an alphabetical list of 604,593 *résistantes et resistants.*[5] Anatole's guardedness about his wartime activities must have preoccupied him from early on. Unlike most others in the registry, he was listed as unaffiliated with any of the main Resistance movements or networks. Whatever role he in fact played during the war, it does not appear in historical works on the Resistance, and he left barely a trace in the French army archives, only a note identifying his nom de guerre, Yvan Marcel Robert.[6] The significance of this alias eludes explanation, either as a personal, literary, or military reference. Robert became part of Anatole's postwar identity, by adding it as his middle name and, in his last days even insisting that he was known in Plouguernevel not as Anatole but as "Colonel Robert."

What seemed particularly inexplicable about his place in the family narrative was the insistence that he made a nearly instantaneous transition from a feckless young man with no military experience to a resilient and effective Resistance combatant. This appeared to be another component of my family's occasional use of magical thinking to avoid more prosaic explanations. Then Joseph Uninski's address book from 1942 provided some insight. Joseph had only one address for Anatole, and it was crossed out—the "64ème Régiment d'Artillerie d'Afrique,

---

5 "Service historique de la Defénse," Ministère des Armées, accessed March 9, 2025, https://www.servicehistorique.sga.defense.gouv.fr/en/node/42089.

6 "Anatole Robert UNINSKY," La ministère des Armées, accessed March 9, 2025. https://www.memoiredeshommes.sga.defense.gouv.fr/fr/ark:/40699/m005a290f697d7c1.

Meknès, Maroc." It is unclear whether Anatole, twenty years old when France declared war on Nazi Germany, enlisted in the French army with his brothers, but somehow in 1940 he managed to leave continental France for North Africa. Meknès was a substantial military fortress in northern Morocco, used decades before World War II as a principal base for France's ruthless establishment of colonial control. By 1939, it served as a critical site for reorganization of the French Armée d'Afrique. Although an address book presents a slim foundation for definitive conclusions, it is possible that Anatole trained alongside Moroccan volunteers, other refugees from the mainland, and French colonials.

The Sixty-Fourth Artillery Regiment and other French forces based in Meknès, including several infantry regiments and reorganized Legionnaires, saw nearly constant action throughout the war. It may well be that Anatole was an active combatant and learned many of the skills that he would need in the Resistance. So much, however, remains a complete mystery—when he departed for Morocco, how long he may have served in North Africa, when he returned to fight in the Breton Resistance, and why this time in Morocco was never a part of the family narrative of Anatole's wartime exploits. It could be that Joseph lined out his Moroccan address when Anatole reappeared, which would put him in France sometime between 1941 and 1942. I would like to believe my uncle took heart when, on New Year's Eve, 1943, the Sixty-Fourth African Artillery regiment of the French army landed in Naples along with nearly twenty thousand Moroccan and French infantry soldiers and made their way through Italy to southern France by August 1944. So much conjecture, so little confirmed about a charming man whose life made an astonishing trajectory from a hazy past of possible artistic bohemianism to a probable but unacknowledged period of heroism and ending, most clearly, as a small-time confidence trickster.

As one would expect, compared to his siblings and Lucie, Alexander's life was a relatively open book of many easily confirmed moments. There are hundreds of reviews of his performances, the first of which was in 1925 when he was fifteen. By 1928, he was already a pianist of stature performing often in Europe and Latin America, then nearly constantly after 1932, when he won the Chopin prize, until the war, which only briefly interrupted his public performances. Aside from a Red Scare hiatus in 1954 to 1956, he continued concertizing until his death in 1972, while also producing over fifty recordings, primarily with Philips.

An arrangement of several of Alexander Uninsky's record jackets with a 1945 publicity poster. Copyright permission courtesy of Adrian Morningstar.

Amidst all encomia lavished on him by journalists during his career, Alexander, the public figure, steadfastly maintained his insistence on privacy in interviews, providing only glancing and less than candid insights into traumatic experiences and carefully diverting press interest away from his family. What little he divulged about his personal life in press interviews occurred during a short time span, when he was touring North and South America between 1942 and 1945. Journalists then were understandably curious about his experiences in France during the war and his escape from fascism. Alexander's accounts were not only guarded but revealed a countervailing impulse to embroider the past with snippets of incompatible details. His journey of escape from France, from Paris to Madrid and then onto Latin America, was an object of constant improvisation and revision, focusing mostly on his 1940 arrest in Spain, the result either of having entered with no papers, bad luck, or because he was identified as an undesirable by Falangists who turned him over to the police. His freedom from prison in Madrid was attained variously by a daring escape, bribery with a diamond ring, or because José María Nemesio Otaño, the recently appointed Director of Madrid's Superior Conservatory of Music, admired his playing and convinced the authorities to release him.

It was clear, in all his interviews, that Alexander often infused answers to personal questions with comic invention, at times tinged with ribaldry, instead of providing candid or verifiable responses. How did he meet Lucie, after having last seen her as a twenty-year-old in 1939 Paris or Porto in 1940? By accident, on Fifty-Seventh Street in front of Carnegie Hall, or on Forty-Second Street (at the time a notorious red-light district), or by chance in Omaha, a version my father loved to repeat at parties through the '60s, both mocking what he thought was American naïveté and punctuating the joke with an exaggerated Russified pronunciation of "Om-a-kha." Or, without a noticeable segue or prompt, he would shift the subject away from wartime trauma and personal inquiries, launching into an "anecdote," a favorite being a post-recital appearance of an aging, unidentified, Polish nobleman who came backstage to praise his performance of Chopin's second sonata and to request he play the third movement, the "Funeral March," at his internment. Alexander's response—"Certainly, and where and when will that be?"—was emblematic of his public persona, redirecting attention away from the tragic or traumatic while acknowledging his artistry with humor and without excessive hubris.

Although in private Alexander spoke of his friendship with many musicians, in public he rarely mentioned other classical performers, recalling instead his close association with four composers who he said inspired and encouraged him through the 1930s: Maurice Ravel, Sergei Prokofiev, Igor Stravinsky, and Darius Milhaud. When it came to his siblings, there was no need for obfuscation or humoristic redirection in his conversations with the press. Anatole and Evsey joined Elisabeth cloaked in privacy, along with Lucie's family and most of the formative influences in his early development as a pianist. His brief musicological musings about the piano canon and contemporary composers figured far more prominently than any other topic, drawing attention to his wide-ranging repertoire and his readiness to explore composers' musical sources and intentions. After the war, Alexander's public persona, in press, on the radio, and in occasional television appearances, existed in this highly circumscribed musical environment. More than before, it was shorn of historical context, his own musical education, family members, and the traumatic experiences that marked his life.

While Alexander's narrative told at home was more detailed than his public versions, his private recollections about his path through troubled times were, as in public, characterized by a caginess often shaped by levity. There was a persistent avoidance of discussions related to family and friends murdered in the camps, warfare, and how, despite so much loss and trauma, he had managed to prevail. In his domestic version of the family narrative, Alexander's childhood in Kyiv from 1910 to 1923 was sparing in detail, highly selective, and, at times, spectacular. There were rare and brief stories of the civil war from 1917 to 1921, but nothing about the pogroms of 1919 or what may have instigated or facilitated the family's voyage of emigration to Paris in 1924. Recollections of warfare following the 1917 Revolution and the subsequent civil war and Ukrainian War of Independence were tempered in the telling, witnessed by young Alexander in an implicit cocoon of safety. The tales had a cinematic quality, soldiers divided by the Dnieper River, lobbing shells and firing madly at each other, but absent graphic details. And the stories invariably turned seamlessly to Alexander's early musical commitment, recalling, for instance, how the episodic rattling of automatic weapons created a disruptive metronome, interfering with his piano practice.

Alexander recounted only one performance in the Russian Empire, a signal musical episode infrequently told, and then only when I was quite young. His talent already widely known when he was six, he was called to perform for Tsar Nicholas II, one year before the October Revolution. Never one to tell traditional fairy tales involving danger and fright, such as Baba Yaga who occasionally cannibalized visitors to her hut that walked on chicken legs, this was his version of storytelling for children. It was an awe-inspiring tale of genius and artistic triumph, and, in retrospect, wholly improbable. It stood in stark contrast to his own disdain for the pianism of prodigies, no matter how talented. Artistry, in the family narrative, came with intrinsic skills shaped on the anvil of time, hard work, and constant self-examination. And the 1916 invitation to perform for Russian royalty in St. Petersburg would have been beyond the pale for a young Jewish pianist from the Pale. It would have occurred soon after the conclusion of the Beilis trial, a moment of heightened antisemitism in Kyiv involving the sensational accusation of a Jewish clerk's ritual murder of a Christian child. In retrospect, this autobiographical tale of precocity, so unusual in the family repertoire, was likely a part of the self-reflexive ironic and tragicomic repertoire so central to Alexander's narrative. For me, it was a glittering and entrancing tale of my father's special talent, and for Alexander, even if fictive, it may have been part of an internal conversation about the power of art to triumph over hatred and irrationality.

Early recognition of Alexander's talent did indeed occur, provided by Sergei Vladimirovich Tarnovsky, the leading professor of piano at the newly formed Kyiv Conservatory. He recalled, years later, while teaching in the US at DePaul University, that Alexander's rare gift led to an early admission in 1917, his youngest student at age seven, one of two children among a group of young adults. Tarnovsky clearly was a keen judge of talent, having earlier, in 1914, admitted another child to his class, the eleven-year-old Vladimir Horowitz. Beyond these fragments, details about Alexander's musical education in Kyiv have never surfaced. Tarnovsky revealed nothing of his relationship with young Alexander, and no amount of urging encouraged my father to speak about his parents' interest in music, how they may have nurtured his talent, or his relationship with Horowitz, a companion in Kyiv Conservatory classes for over three years. Only cartoonish images of the adult Horowitz weaved their way through Alexander's narrative, combining mockery with elements of sadness, envy, and admiration. Horowitz emerged as a brilliant peculiarity in our family conversations, a consummate showman with an idiosyncratic technique whose phenomenal success, we were reminded, was frequently interrupted by illness and self-doubt. There was a persistently backhanded regard tinged with jealousy for a classmate and colleague who Alexander labelled as that most fortunate of artists, one whose family settled in New York years before the outbreak of World War II and who married into the Toscanini family.

Alexander would occasionally imitate his former classmate's singular technique as part of a summertime family quiz, "Name That Pianist," acknowledging, clearly begrudgingly, that such a distinct pianistic style was worthy of admiration. Only after Alexander's death, did a faint signal of the relationship between the two pianists emerge. Horowitz contacted Lucie from time to time, and in 1976, learning I was in Ann Arbor, his secretary called to offer tickets for his forthcoming recital at the University's Hill Auditorium. My housemate answered the phone, and thinking it a prank, replied, "Horowitz? And I'm the Queen of England," and abruptly ended the call. The after-concert conversation was limited to my brief apology and a curt dismissal. I never had the chance to speak with him again. A second time was one too many improbable calls for my indomitable housemate. On a subsequent occasion, he claimed to be Marie Antoinette when Isaac Stern called to offer tickets for his upcoming concert with the Detroit Symphony, where he would perform the Rochberg violin concerto recently composed for him. This time, there was no post-performance chill, instead warmth and graciousness, and we had a wide-ranging conversation, much of which was directed at my partner Kira about her field of study, Russian history, focusing particularly on the work of his friend, Isaiah Berlin. There was no opening to discuss Alexander other than Stern's statement of affection for Lucie and Alexander. Not that the son of a musician should have expected more from a post-concert conversation; unfortunately, that is all I ever managed to extract from the great violinist about my family. It was disappointing that, for whatever reason, I never had the opportunity to discuss Lucie's memory of the moral and financial support Stern provided the family in the wake of blacklisting.

The Red Scare was featured as one of many moments when the family narrative was punctuated by the timely, if not magical, interventions of the wealthy and famous. When the Uninskys arrived in Paris in 1924, penniless migrants and Alexander gravely ill, Baron Robert Philippe Gustave de Rothschild apparently arranged for housing and medical care. Once Alexander recovered, Esther and Miron applied for

Alexander's entry to the Conservatoire de Paris. At age thirteen, he entered the advanced class of Isidor Philipp, pianist, composer, and music critic, who was best known for his five major works on piano exercises. Philipp emphasized the fundamentals of technique, perhaps, for a young teen, excessively. In a matter of months, Alexander asked to be transferred to Lazare-Lévy, pianist, composer, and legendary pedagogue. Eagerness to work with Lazare-Lévy may have had other sources beyond a wish to escape from Philipp's strict discipline. Alexander may have been more comfortable learning from a Jewish teacher, and the shift was also likely influenced by financial constraints. Here again was another fortuitous intervention by a wealthy and famous benefactor; Lazare-Lévy allegedly offered his lessons without charge.

Alexander would describe this acceptance and nurturing by a great musician and teacher with whom he readily identified as a turning point in his development as an artist. Unlike other faculty, Alexander recalled that Lazare-Lévy insisted on expanding the horizons of instruction in the Conservatoire, encouraging discussions of the relationship between music and the other arts and introducing contemporary philosophy and politics in his classes. Whether this approach appealed to Alexander's existing inclinations and even planted the seeds of future enthusiasms, including his interest in Henri Bergson, it is impossible to know, but the bond between the two endured until the maître's death in 1964. Alexander left no doubt that the Lazare-Lévy's expanded view of musicianship, coupled with the Conservatoire's rigorous training in music theory, accelerated his development as a pianist, fortifying his gift. In June 1927, at the age of seventeen, we know that he graduated with honors and a performance prize from the Conservatoire's annual competition. Five months later, he made his recital debut at the Salle Chopin, reviewed in the arts journal *Comœdia,* which proclaimed the pianist "a young virtuoso, [who] when his talent is fully mature, will become master of the keyboard."[7] He seems to have matured meteorically after graduating, and during ten months of 1928, performed over one hundred concerts in France, Argentina, Colombia, Venezuela, Spain, and Portugal. In 1932, registered as a stateless person, he won the second quinquennial International Chopin Piano Competition, and his performance schedule continued to expand. Flight from France in mid-1940 resulted in only a brief interruption of his nearly incessant concertizing, briefly slowed again by flight to Canada to escape political persecution. Whatever caused his declining prominence in the early 1960s, physical ailment, temperament, or a declining ability to master torment, the drive to make music was persistent, and in his last years, his performance schedule began to accelerate.

As an artist, Alexander reached a high level of impressive consistency, as is clear in any survey of his reviews during the last thirty years of his career. They all glitter with acclaim, a pianist "unequivocally placed with the keyboard giants of the day," "unsurpassed," "spell-binding," and so on, but this reveals little of his personality, the meanings of his memories, and how he dealt with trauma. For this, I am limited to his

---

7 «Les Récitals de la Semaine», *Comœdia,* November 21, 1927, 3, accessed March 9, 2025, https://gallica.bnf.fr/ark:/12148/bpt6k7651943d/f3.image.r=Uninsky?rk=42918.

own narrative, which while the fullest of the family, can hardly to be taken at its word. His version was highly selective and inconsistent and, with little tangible evidence or convincing peer testimonies, largely unverifiable. Much the same can be said of Lucie and all my aunts and uncles, that their narratives, when they chose to provide them, elude confirmation.

Beyond rich evidence of Alexander's career, what lives on about the Uninsky and Biszkowicz families of my parent's generation are my memories of their narratives. They were part of a generation of immigrant Eastern Europeans who endured a series of violent traumas and wildly fluctuating circumstances that may have been unprecedented in their ferocity and frequency. With a past such as this, one which could have easily been corrosive, crushing, and destabilizing, it is nearly unimaginable that they nonetheless maintained a sense that the past could be reimagined as prologue to a positive, rewarding, and creative future. For Lola, the trauma led to a sparingly outlined tale of betrayal, Monio's fate was excluded from the narrative, clearly too painful to recount, and Elisabeth survived, seemingly without effort, engagement, or relationship to the past. But for the remainder of the family, while trauma was obliquely acknowledged but never detailed, the emphasis of the narrative was unmistakably on resilience, persistence, creative intelligence, and courage to resist or honorably escape persecution. What was revealed in storytelling about the past and in the behaviors I witnessed was a levity of being and a prevailing sense of immediacy that rarely was overtly shadowed by trauma. Particularly Lucie and Alexander, and to a lesser extent Tola and Evsey, their storytelling and comportment was infused with humor, guile, and magical solutions to what seemed like insuperable obstacles. Each of them, in their own way, created a rough survival guide toward lives that permitted them to persist, reimagined, after unthinkable traumas. Their invented lives from troubled times are what remains, a gift of talented raconteurs, that deserves to be remembered in their voices and through their behaviors as a record of resilience. That is what follows, in all its idiosyncrasies, inconsistencies, and anachronisms.

CHAPTER 6

What Is This?

Even now, after fifty years of intermittent mulling over this family's inventive and often mesmerizing stories, persistent obscurantism, and disparate personalities, from the quietly domestic, heroic, to outlandish norm-bending, it has come to this, a story without an identifiable structure. I began with what seemed a straightforward plan, to conduct a combined archival and oral history, deepening my understanding of a family's voyage through cycles of calamity and success. By so doing, it seemed reasonable to assume, I would achieve greater clarity about the varied strands of my received family narrative. With patience and persistence, it perhaps would be possible to fill in the many omissions and sweep away the historical haze created by confabulation, lapses in chronology, hyperbole, episodes of striking good fortune, and comic interpolations.

Pushing for greater clarity about the details of my family history was probably a means to several ends. It always seemed credible to me that cleansing a subjective version of the past with the bright light of objectivity might tell me more about the degree to which I had been raised in the shadow of severe trauma. I never hoped to find determinative links between their earlier experiences and the people they became, but I could reasonably hope to resolve my own concerns about what might have moved them to offer their particular family narrative and behaviors. It had long perturbed me, certainly since that meeting with psychoanalysts who knew Alexander and Lucie well, that I had little understanding of what had shaped my upbringing and how that may have affected me. Was my parents' fluidity with the truth driven by a protective impulse, to avoid transferring their well-disguised anger or guilt about the past? Was their narrative a form of partial or selective forgetting to permit them to carry on and to allow their children to live without the burdens of this family's past? Would a more factual account of their background alter my understanding, appreciation, and affection for them and what they had tried to inculcate in me?

As should be clear now, that plan, this quest for clarity, could not possibly have reached a satisfactory conclusion. Too much of how this extended family chose to conduct their lives and manage their turbulent past was obscured by their omissions, inventiveness, and reticence, and nearly all documentary evidence that might have revealed much of their thoughts and behaviors, past and present, was lost. Instead, I propose following another path, to identify and explore the dominant themes apparent in the layers of memories and years of observations and interviews. The aim is not to define or illustrate general rules about long-term social and psychological impacts of serial exposure to trauma. Rather, I hope to pry open patterns of my extended family's thoughts and behaviors from these recurrent themes and to make plausible inferences about how they managed to persist despite it all. Exploring these themes, such as religiosity, strategies of safety, and the uses of humor, helps reveal their mechanisms of resilience and their pedagogic approaches intended to safeguard their children from what they believed to be enduring dangers.

This approach to understanding an extended family's persistence does not readily conform to a recognizable professional or literary framework. The result here is most certainly not a personal memoir. It is about me only to the extent that interpreting my memories of their memories and contemporaneous interactions with such singular and often quixotic people must, it seems clear, take into account my own evolving perspectives about them. Rather, this is about puzzling through what made my parents and their siblings who they were and what they may have intended by their narratives and actions at different times. As a result, the focus is an admittedly subjective endeavor to identify themes of consequence illustrating components of their resilience. The family narrative was far from an instructional manual for survival and the management of trauma. Quite the contrary, contemplating their memories and comportment often is akin to listening to a cacophonous composition, one lacking linearity, asynchronous, and failing to provide a recognizable conclusion.

This is also not a family history. So little is known about their exact experiences, pedestrian and traumatic, that may have shaped the Biszkowicz-Uninsky clan; they too artfully cloaked what they thought of both the signal and ordinary events that shaped their lives. In the case of this extended family, an historical analysis would have to operate in a near vacuum, hardly a harbinger of an accurate, objective interpretation of the past.

What follows, for lack of a better term, is a hybrid historical and personal work. It is akin to a mosaic composed of evolving recollections and credible snippets of information. This approach resides firmly in the world of reasonable conjectures, where creative accounts are not discarded merely because they are improbable and fanciful. This approach often has felt like a walk in a new location, trying to reach somewhere without a language to communicate with passersby but amassing just enough data to bring this community of survivors to life in ways that extend their chronicle, hopefully making it more comprehensible if not necessarily believable.

There can be little doubt that the impacts of exposure to serial trauma were mediated by innumerable forces. When sifting through what could be known about my parents and extended family, and what they wanted to be remembered through their narratives, the urge to pigeonhole those forces, to put them into well-established analytic categories, arose often. It is tempting to use established explanatory frameworks to structure what otherwise seems to be a cloud of information; it helps establish some order on what seems chaotic. My inclination was initially to search for existing frameworks, particularly sociological and psychological, to establish causal inferences linking trauma experienced to specific structures of memory and particular behaviors. This approach was difficult to resist after more than a decade as a social historian, followed by career as an attorney and director of nonprofits whose work focused on violence prevention and evidence-based therapeutic services. But early on it was clear that this was not a suitable approach. The family's considerable inventive skills, their playfulness with ideas, historical events, and language often obfuscated cause and effect. There is little doubt that there was an intentional effort to minimize information about surviving trauma and to create highly personalized and often evolving understanding of their postwar lives.

My hybrid family history, based largely on my memories of family reminiscences conveyed over many years, observations of their behaviors, and limited documentation admittedly has few guardrails to establish veracity. Nonetheless, collecting memories of survivors—to understand patterns of what they are conveying to those who choose to listen and closely observing their behaviors over an extended period, in the near absence of other information—is a critically necessary approach to deciphering some of components of persistence and resilience they have elaborated. This is particularly the case for those many families who have fled traumatic circumstances and resettled far from their native lands, like my nuclear and extended family. Many retain extraordinarily little, if anything, tangible to factually anchor their memories. These survivors of trauma who fled to find safety were essentially free of constraints when formulating their family histories, even to the point of reinventing histories to solidify their resilience. It is my hope that this hybrid history allows us to have a firmer grasp of what shapes their efforts to maintain their humanity and to thrive.

CHAPTER 7

Names Given, Names Taken

Although this was rarely dwelled upon in their recollections, several members of my family adopted new first names in the 1920s and '30s. This was far from unusual among the immigrant community of prewar Paris. The same, it seems, occurred among many of the newly arrived who decades earlier entered the US through Ellis Island, where quite often both first and family names changed. The latter was not the case for Alexander, his two brothers, and Lucie, who retained their last names during the interwar years, which in their French forms adhered closely to the East European originals. Their newly adopted first names, however, were quite distinct from their given names, not at all misadventures in transliteration, and, unlike the originals, not of Jewish origin. Intentionally or reflexively, they were engaged in an act of disguise, replacing part of their identities. Lucie and Evsey never offered explanations for their name changes. In family stories, my father changed his for a better stage name, and Anatole only discussed the necessity of adopting a nom de guerre. Other plausible motivations, such as the hopes of finding greater acceptance among their French peers and any personal dislike of a chosen name, never arose. Perhaps, once immersed in a fluid Parisian world of rapidly changing politics and arts, they felt liberated by the constant flux, more able to take greater command of their identities.

With their last names intact, they were clearly not disguising their national origins, which some otherwise might have viewed as a pathway toward assimilation into French society. Alexander and his brothers may not have felt the need to insulate themselves from institutionalized antisemitism, given that the family name was not readily identifiably as Jewish, but probably not Lucie Biszkowicz, whose last name was clearly Ashkenazi. Whatever the causes for their renaming, it was yet another sign of a recurring theme of elasticity of identity evident in their narratives and comportment, including Alexander's ability to playfully mimic the styles of other pianists and the malleability of Lucie, Evsey, and Anatole from the 1930s through the 1950s, as their personalities and interests shifted profoundly. Lucie evolved from a young woman ensconced in a life of comfort and conformity to a *grand dame de musique* and then onto domesticity and stolidity. Evsey made a seemingly effortless transition from a solitary painter in search of a modern identity to a barkeeper patriarch of a large brood. And Anatole, the bohemian playwright, seamlessly leapt into the role of warrior and angel of vengeance and ended as an anarchic practitioner of financial flimflam.

Like so much else in the family narrative, authenticating the given names of my parents, aunts, and uncles was challenging, another journey littered with documentary dead-ends that were the result of destructive, troubled times. The archival evidence of birth names is particularly sparse—the 1938 copy of Lucie's 1919 Danish birth certificate and a few residency status filings with the Central Office of Russian Refugees in the mid-1920s. In both types of documents, the names may well have been modified by the recorders' misunderstandings of names spoken by recent immigrants or by the filers' deliberate alterations of the names. In the Copenhagen copy of her birth certificate, my mother's name was recorded as "Alice Byschkovitsch." The daughter of Orthodox Jews, this was likely a transliteration of a Hebrew name, Alisha or Ilisha, meaning "noble." Her new name, Lucie, was adopted without formalities sometime before she left for Portugal. My mother never indicated that the name she went by was anything other than her given name, which, in France is usually understood to represent "brightness" or "radiance."

Lucie's younger brother was called Monio on those infrequent occasions he was mentioned. In 1924 Lucie's parents, Chana and Kleoman Biszkowicz, went to the general consulate of Russia in Paris to register their twelve-year-old son's presence in Paris. The document dashes any expectation of careful transliteration, with "Samuel Bichkovitch," born in Poland, listed as the son of "Kelman Bychkovitch" and "Hana Rubinstein."[1] Given no other brother was ever mentioned by Lucie, Monio was most probably Samuel. His first name may have been an intentional or accidental French transformation of a Hebrew birth name given in Łódź, Shmuel ("god has

1 L'Office français de protection des réfugiés et apatrides (Ofpra), Fonds Russes, Document 181, accessed March 9, 2025. https://archives.ofpra.gouv.fr/archive/resultats/russes/n:134?type=russes (archive accessible only after creating an account).

heard") or Emmanuel ("god is with us"), either of which has a diminutive of Monio.

According to documents submitted by her parents with the general consulate of Russia in Paris, Lola, as Lucie's sister was known in family stories, was named Charlotte.[2] In retrospect, it was in keeping with my parents' dislike of my aunt and their senses of humor that they may have selected a new identity for her. At times they used the Spanish nickname for Lola, Lolita, possibly a private reference to Nabokov's controversial novel about the sexual preference for prepubescent females. Like the fictional Lolita, Lola could have been, for Alexander and Lucie, both the consummate seductress and a victim of circumstances beyond her control, although the latter never led to my parents' sympathy. The Argentinian converso and raider of the family's Swiss bank account was beyond any redemption. Or they may have been using the diminutive for the Hebrew and Spanish name Dolores, which they certainly knew meant pain or sorrow in both languages. In the end, knowing whether the diminutive Lola was even used by Charlotte remains suspended between confabulation and credibility, floating in the layers upon layers of invented family narrative with only glimmers of a factual basis.

Unlike my aunt Elisabeth, who maintained she was given that Hebrew name ("God's promise") at birth, her Uninsky brothers were rather tight-lipped about their given names. After Alexander died, Lucie decided to reveal that my father

---

2 Office français de protection des réfugiés et apatrides (Ofpra), Fonds Russes, Document 182, accessed March 9, 2025, https://archives.ofpra.gouv.fr/archive/resultats/russes/n:134?type=russes.

was born with the biblical name Aaron, which perhaps explains why she used the diminutive "Nona" at home, rather than "Sasha," the nickname for Alexander that his friends and colleagues often used. In documents recently discovered in the Central Registry of Russian Refugees, my grandparents in 1925 claimed his name was "Arnold," often adopted by Ashkenazi immigrants because of its resemblance to Aaron or simply the result of a recorder's misunderstanding.[3] According to Lucie, it was Lazare-Lévy who convinced the young Aaron/Arnold to pick a non-Jewish and internationally recognizable stage name to further his career in a world of intensifying antisemitism. When his name first appeared in the French press in 1925, while still a student at the conservatoire, he was already, at age fifteen, "Alexandre."

Neither Anatole nor my father ever used the name Evsey when they spoke of their older brother, but his wife, Monique, insisted it was his given name, one that he used when he launched his career as a painter before the war. Often transliterated Yevsey, it is a rather unusual Jewish name whose etymology is difficult to ascertain. By 1937, in the catalog for an art exhibition of André Lhote's students, his name had already become "Choura," pronounced *Shura*. Perhaps Evsey selected Choura, a nickname for Alexander, in homage to his brother, to ease his path to artistic recognition with a name without Hebraic roots, or because it was well known in the creative world of prewar Paris, the sobriquet of Alexandra Danilova,

---

3 Office français de protection des réfugiés et apatrides (Ofpra), Fonds Russes, Document 2631, accessed March 9, 2025, https://archives.ofpra.gouv.fr/archive/resultats/russes/n:134?type=russes.

ballerina in Diaghilev's Ballets Russes. Before and after the war, Evsey signed his prewar paintings "Ch. Uninsky." When asked why he used that signature, this wry and usually laconic man responded that using only his last name would provide Alexander praise he did not need and signing with "Ch." alone might deprive him of his own long-awaited attention.

Long after I met Anatole it occurred to me that he was the only Uninsky sibling without a biblical name. He was usually referred to as Tola in family reminiscences, used as a term of affection in the childhood stories about him, and, it seemed, the Russian diminutive of Anatole, along with Toto and Tolichka. Eventually, after many requests for his given name, my uncle acknowledged it was Tola. This is, in retrospect, rather ironic, for Tola was one of the judges of Israel, about whom very little is known, a fitting name for an uncle who left so few traces. In the late 1980s, when I asked Tola about the reasons for selecting Anatole as his name, he responded with a characteristic deflection. Perhaps the Tola of prewar Paris preferred a first name that was both goyish and linked to his artistic ambitions, such as that of the French Nobel Prize winner in literature in 1921, Anatole France, which was the pen name of Francois-Anatole Thibault. When he retired in Brittany, where he fought in the Resistance, Tola preferred to use Robert, his nom de guerre.

The ease with which names could be changed to meet exigencies was not forgotten when Lucie and Alexander took up residence in New York City. Malleability of identity was a life lesson they apparently wanted me to learn early on. When I was born in June 1952, Alexander was still in The Hague, where he was recording. By telegram, Lucie announced the birth of a boy, and, according to the family account, they initially decided on the Slavic name Boris, in honor of a close Parisian friend who, I later learned, died soon after the war. Then they reconsidered and decided to add an additional name, worried that a Russian first name would only bring me misery in an America where the Red Scare was in full swing. When I asked why they chose Philip, they invariably claimed that a prince's name would provide me unimpeachable credentials as a nonsocialist. Not that there was any evidence of their conviction that first names could have a talismanic quality, which in this case was to ward off the risk of being labelled as a red diaper baby at the height of McCarthyism. They may have only wished that I had, like them, an identity without a religious and political identification, for Boris was a popular name among Soviet Jews in the 1950s. Whatever their motivation, this was a naming tale in the family tradition, always linked with some irony, an abiding wariness, a sense of the value of malleability, and possibly true. I was always grateful they left Boris as my middle name, providing me more than sufficient psychic distance from the duke of Edinburgh.

CHAPTER 8

What's Not in a Name?

In October 1973, as mentioned earlier, I began my research trip and voyage of discovery through Brezhnev's Russia and Ukraine to study the accelerating emigration of Soviet Jews to Israel, Europe, and the United States. The plan was to terminate my work in the USSR in Kyiv, where I also imagined it would be possible to contact long lost relatives. Entering Russia through Vyborg, a tip of the hat to heroic idealism, I followed Lenin's route before the revolution, on his way to St. Petersburg's Finland Station. After several weeks in Leningrad, I continued south through Novgorod and Moscow, coaxing my aging Volkswagen bus over the more than 1,700 kilometers to Kyiv, my father's birthplace. My research goals were to understand what motivated the emigration of Soviet Jews now that the door was cracked open and to track the routes, detours, and byways taken out of the country. I planned to interview those who had obtained their exit visas, as well as refuseniks whose dreams of emigration were blocked. Not that this agenda rolled out as planned. I had expected that most of my actions would be seen as provocations by authorities and arranged for meetings as clandestinely as possible.

The semi-official response began with a minor form of harassment by the state travel agency Intourist, which kept changing hotel reservations at the last minute, placing me further and further from my intended destinations. This was a simple and effective method of limiting planned activities, and official interference did not escalate significantly. Perhaps I was too young and preposterously uninformed for Soviet authorities to deal with me more harshly. I was, after all, driving a thirteen-year-old, rusting camper that was irreparable in the USSR, and they may have reasonably assumed that sooner or later I would break down and be shipped out.

The Jewish communities along the route in Russia surprisingly did not see an American in a German car as unwelcome, a meandering threat to their well-being. Those with visas to depart often stated that their risks had already been confronted and partially resolved, while many refuseniks agreed to meet with me, hoping for contacts in the American Jewish community that might lead to exit ramps from an intolerable situation. Refuseniks and visa holders alike may have also viewed détente, the recent cooling of tensions between the US and the USSR, as an opportunity for more open discourse with visitors from the "West," even, sometimes, as a corrective to what was seen as newspaper disinformation. Everyone knew, several acquaintances joked, that in *Pravda* (Truth) there was no news (*izvestya*), and in the newspaper *Izvestya,* there was no truth. Some of my new acquaintances pointedly reminded me that access to information was a bread of life, and they were hungry. But there was always a grimness at play in these interactions, a sense that any conversations might have unpredictable consequences. Precautions were taken, evasiveness drawn from pulp novels, as if we all knew how to be sufficiently discrete and were right in believing that the benefits outweighed the risks. Much of this understanding resided in the realm of winks and nods and in retrospect was particularly foolhardy on my part, possibly creating additional adversity in threatened lives.

This sense, that a perceived cooling of a repressive environment extended beyond the Jewish community, even provided opportunities to conduct the occasional interview with notable dissidents. Among them was the great poet and memoirist, Nadezhda Mandelstam, a true "guerrilla of the imagination" as Seamus Heaney memorably described her. Ill, barely able to lift herself from her couch, she spoke of the need to persist despite obstacles of war and government repression, as did the modern painters whose works covered her walls, all of whom were banned from exhibiting but continued to paint. Pursuit of unfettered artistic expression and preservation of the right to be creative were paramount, which is why she fought to keep her husband's poetry part of the present. I wondered, as I left her apartment, how much it seemed as if she were speaking of members of my family, especially Alexander.

After three and one-half months in Russia, I headed to Ukraine. I hoped a different republic might change what had recently become the increasingly disagreeable issue of lodgings further and further from the communities I hoped to meet. In January, with bald tires skittering on icy roads, I approached Kyiv. My first goal was to find the Great Gate of Kyiv, whose grandeur I only knew musically from Alexander's exuberant recording of Modest Mussorgsky's *Pictures at an Exhibition.* The thousand-year-old structure was easily found and, as imagined, was both imposing and magnificent. Nothing else from that moment on occurred as anticipated, particularly my efforts to interview members of the Kyivan Jewish community and to locate relatives still living in and around the city. And my efforts to finally understand how the family came to have a decidedly non-Jewish name were stymied.

Early on in my Kyivan layover it was clear that an American in jeans with a cloud of curls driving an old German car with rust holes in the side and a muffler barely muffling posed a greater risk to anyone seeking to avoid the attention of Soviet authorities there than in Russia proper. The contrast with Leningrad and Moscow was plainly evident. There, it seemed détente under Brezhnev left open the possibility of casual conversations with passersby who were interested in US culture and counterculture, one that that ranged from the tangible, such as Levis as a form of currency, to a thirst for information and discourse with an American who knew enough Russian to banter. The impact of détente was not at all evident in Kyiv. After a few days of averted glances and cold shoulders, along with expressions of dislike, including the invective "bourgeois hippy," it was evident I was provoking less a sense curiosity and interest than one of unnecessary risk. There was a particularly clear reticence in the Jewish community to speak about their circumstances or aspirations, cemented by a warning whispered one evening near Kyiv's Great Choral Synagogue, "you are a fool [дурак; *durak*] to endanger people."

Perhaps because I was young, and certainly motivated by a sense of entitled purpose, I felt that my well-being hinged in some measure on clearing away some of the haze enveloping the family narrative. So I began to cast about for information about my Kyivan relatives. My long-term quest was an act of singlemindedness absent discretion. Rebuffed time and again by passersby and officials discouraging a *durak*'s behavior, I moved to deliberate efforts to shock; I even asked for directions to the ravine of Babyn Yar, site of the mass murder of Jews and non-Jews, knowing full well that the location was not yet officially recognized. Yevtushenko's 1961 poem "Babi Yar," I felt, somehow gave me license to ask: "No monument stands over Babi Yar. A steep cliff only, like the rudest headstone."[1]

Aside from this interpersonal iron curtain, it was clear that there was an additional barrier, my own transliteration blues. No one from my parents' generation ever disclosed how Uninsky was written in Kyiv, whether in Russian or Ukrainian Cyrillic. Reverse transliterations starting from Latin alphabet versions was far from obvious because my family's pronunciation of "Uninsky" varied widely, depending on the language spoken. Anyone in Kyiv might have been a relative if their name in Russian was Юнинский or Yнинский, or if the Ukrainian spelling was Юнінський or Унінський.

In 1974, searching through Ukrainian telephone books, business directories, and other official listings, no Uninskys were found under any spelling, even approximate ones. Perhaps claims of family narrative were true, that Uninsky was an unusual name and that by the mid-1930s the Kyivan family diaspora was largely complete. It could have been that the few who remained did not survive the Holodomor (the Great Famine of 1932-1933) and the German World War II invasion.

---

1 Yevgeni Yevtushenko, "Babi Yar," trans. Ben Okopnik, Remember.org, accessed March 9, 2025, https://remember.org/witness/babiyar yar.

In recent years, internet resources, including searches through census records and digitized Ukrainian telephone books dating from 1935 on, have also yielded no one with my last name living in and around Kyiv.

When I finally learned that my paternal grandmother's maiden name was Esther Schrabman, as transliterated in the deportation lists, no one alive in the extended family who knew her—Lucie, Evsey, Tola, and Elizabeth—would break the silence about both Esther and her husband Miron. Without further information, a plethora of transliterations into Ukrainian and Russian seemed possible. For all of them, the silence of the sources was as complete for the Schrabmans as it was for the Uninskys.

And so, it seems, the past of my Kyivan progenitors remains hidden, aside from Alexander and Lucie's cursory recollections. There were possibly cantors in past generations, and Esther and Miron may have owned a haberdashery, as Alexander occasionally mentioned, but confirmation of any details of their lives and those of their ancestors seems unobtainable. This includes the origin story of the allegedly non-Jewish Uninsky family name, a tragic, cliché-ridden childhood tale told only by Alexander. Our name, he insisted, was an accident of history, and in each telling, imprecision lent an air of invention. Originally, our surname was Kohen, perhaps Kogan, possibly Kaplan or Kagan, my father could not be sure. At some point in the 1800s, either during an unspecified act of violence by Cossacks, who appeared stereotypically in family stories as pointlessly brutal in the past but entertaining performers in the present, or during one of many pogroms, which were presented, somewhat inaccurately, as an ever-present danger in nineteenth-century Kyiv, the children of our ancestral family were orphaned. As in other traumatic moments of the family history, a person of wealth and privilege intervened, as, for example Baron Rothschild rescuing the homeless and poverty-stricken family arriving in Paris or Isaac Stern supporting the blacklisted Uninsky family in New York. In this instance, it was a childless Count Uninsky, who adopted the children as his own and subsequently converted to Judaism.

Broadening the search to the whole of the Russian Empire for some evidence of this benevolent Count yields little of relevance.[2] There is certainly no connection to the priest named Uninsky, ostensibly martyred in early 1920 in the remote Siberian town of Blagoveshchensk, on the Chinese border. The fantastical family origin story of pogroms and adoption, like so much of the family narrative, stands on its own, its accuracy impossible to verify. It may have been an elaborate, if unconvincing, corrective, a way of sweeping aside any later confusion, that although we were not religious and had a goyish name, we were nonetheless Jews. Perhaps this story told for children, an improbable, magical restoration of family by one who withstood antisemitism to the point of adopting orphans and converting to their religion, was a way of insisting that verisimilitude had its limits, that there were moments when attachment to reality had to be suspended. Pogroms were too awful to contemplate, like so much else that was omitted from the family narrative.

---

2 The name Uninsky does not appear in the list of noble families of the Russian Empire maintained from 1797–1917: Общий Гербовник дворянских родов Всероссийской Империи (Obshchii Gerbovnik drovianskikh rodov Vserossiiskoi Imperii).

CHAPTER 9

Discarded Past and Reinvented Present

In April 1945, my uncle Choura Uninsky, born Evsey, was released from his long stay in Stalag X-A 699 and began his one-thousand-kilometer trek back to France. Although Choura never spoke with me about his confinement or his journey home, he may have told Alexander. But even if Choura discussed his five years of hard labor in a prisoner-of-war camp with my father, it went no further, never appearing in the family narrative. Alexander himself offered only a spare account of his brother's return to Paris, delivered in the most general terms and summoning the image of a solitary man trudging through war zones for weeks, only occasionally assisted by short rides from Allied army trucks. It was a secular tale with biblical overtones, Choura bearing his burden patiently and stoically. Trauma was muffled in the telling, with suffering of any sort left to the listener's imagination. There were no intimations that Choura felt self-pity, was overcome by his travail, or even felt distraught. Succumbing to life's agonies, no matter how extreme, was explicitly addressed only once by my uncles, and only after much urging, when they eventually revealed the suicide of Monio, Lucie's brother and Alexander's friend.

According to Alexander, Choura had managed to survive during his wartime imprisonment because he was able to hold tightly to the goals of reclaiming a painterly life when he returned to the creative community that had sustained him before the war. As with so much else in the family story, chronological discontinuity and mystery then intruded upon the narrative, burying any obvious or even plausible links between what came before and after. The two years of Choura's life, from his release in 1945 through 1946, were a blank, a discarded time from which a new Choura emerged, an ex-Parisian, no longer a bachelor, a person whose creative past bore no resemblance to his more prosaic present.

This notable gap in the family narrative, the two years that ended when Choura decided to abandon both Paris and his painter's palette, occurred in each family member's account. One might assume that when Choura returned to Paris in 1945, instead of beginning where he left off after years of lost autonomy, he certainly must have found his prior life demolished. His parents and two brothers were unaccounted for, all his possessions probably had been sold or appropriated, and the community of artists around André Lhote had dispersed. He soon must have learned about the full breadth of the Shoah's monstrosities. He undoubtedly faced an unendurable constellation of grief, disorientation, anxiety, and helplessness, incentive enough to discard this part of the past.

Choura, it appears, never discussed what happened to him from 1940 until he reappeared in rural France in 1946. No one in his family, not his siblings, Lucie, spouse, or children could recall my uncle ever exhuming any memories from those dark times. They all knew that Choura had been a POW during World War II, like so many others, and little more. I have long suspected that my uncle's selective wall of silence may have may been intricately linked to deep sentiments of alienation or rejection. It is probable that Choura's return to Paris after liberation was the culmination of a profound breach with his surviving family. For five years, he probably heard nothing from them while in Stalag X-A, with Tola underground and Alexander abroad, steadily on the move. It was unclear whether Elisabeth, who carefully placed shutters across her wartime past, was ever in contact with Choura during the war, or, for that matter, afterward. Choura never responded to questions about Elisabeth, creating a zone of mutual exclusion for brother and sister.

There is little doubt that Choura had been close with his brothers before the war, but his confinement was followed by a postwar diaspora of sorts that cut them off from one another. Efforts to contact Alexander and Tola, if he had tried, could very well have failed, or conversely, Choura may have been out of touch purposefully. Tola, the younger brother was not far from Paris, active in Brittany through 1947, according to Alexander, living a clandestine life dotted with acts of retribution. On constant tour in North and South America from 1945 through 1947, Alexander worried about his siblings, he insisted, but was unable locate them. Choura's isolation from family, which began in 1940, ended in 1948. Reunion was sparked when Alexander returned with Lucie to Paris and began performing in Europe again.

In 1949, at some undisclosed location, the three Uninsky brothers, Lucie, and a friend spent time together. From left to right, Tola, Mme. Monet, Alexander, Lucie, and Choura. Photo courtesy of the author.

By that time, Choura's postwar transition was complete, with his path from one persona to another unexplained and open to conjecture. According to Lucie, Alexander, and Tola, the Choura they remembered from before the war was no more in 1948. His transformation was all-encompassing. Choura's past life, as a bachelor consumed by creative aspirations, was entirely swept away, seemingly replaced by its antithesis, one enmeshed in domesticity, a small bistro, and rural affairs.

Choura's reincarnation was radical, much like Tola's, where the past bore little relationship to the reinvented present. When trying to explain his postwar identity in rural Saint-Rémy-sur-Avre, both Alexander and Tola recalled how they were at first stunned by a choice so out of character. They initially assumed their older brother, now thirty-eight, was seeking a rural retreat that would serve as inspiration for his art and provide a well-deserved peace of mind. But Choura, they found, had other ideas, and had acted upon them with alacrity. A quiet, shy, solitary man before the war who preferred the comfort of his canvases to an active social life, or so his brothers remembered, he was now married and proclaiming his interest in raising a large family. His intent became reality, as Monique, his wife, gave birth to six children in less than ten years.

Alexander and Tola gently mocked their brother's full-throated choice of what seemed to be classical small-town French domesticity, barely hiding their longstanding condescension toward what seemed to them to be a downward slide into working-class life. Most out of character, however, was Choura's decision to become proprietor of a village bistro, pouring early morning glasses of breakfast wine for farmers, selling pale blue packs of Gauloises and the yellow-papered Gitanes Maïs that stuck to lower lips, making simple lunches of omelets and croques monsieurs, and closing every evening in time for his own family dinners. Painting, his brothers and Lucie understood, had become an afterthought.

Avoiding any discussion of Choura's long confinement or the deep shock he must have experienced upon learning of his parents' fate in Auschwitz, Tola and my parents intimated that the stunning transformation of the once promising painter was the result of the physical and mental stress he had endured. This was implicit in the way they referred to him, as if he had two names, "*pauvre* Choura." The implication was not just that he was poor, but also by the tone they used, worthy of pity, a lost soul, who, they would invariably add, had been a fragile child, weakened by whooping cough. When speaking of Choura, Alexander, Lucie, and Tola usually focused on the present, particularly on Choura's growing family, joking that the older brother was hurriedly making up for lost time. Choura himself was never inclined to explain his transformed identity to his brothers and sister-in-law. To them, he limited explanations of his emergence as a village shopkeeper to a story of economic necessity resolved by good fortune that, in retrospect, seems a fable.

Upon his return from Stalag X-A, the French government, as it did for many other released prisoners of war, likely provided him twelve thousand francs based on his five years of service, the equivalent of one hundred dollars in 1945, enough to keep him going for only a few months. When the opportunity arose, he seized upon a state agency's offer to provide *anciens combattants* with licenses for bistros that had fallen into desuetude due to wartime fatalities. As fate would have it, Choura explained, his license was in Saint-Rémy-sur-Avre, which would certainly not have been his first choice. But governmental ingenuity and largesse offered an irresistible opportunity, and financial necessity was not only the mother of reinvention, it united him with the mother of his brood.

A bistro license as manna explained Choura's unexpected choice of relocation and profession, but it was no doubt a confabulation of convenience, a fortuitous intervention, this time not by persons of power and wealth, but by an anonymous bureaucracy, the Ministère des Prisonniers, Déportés et

Réfugiés, Direction du Rapatriement (Ministry of Prisoners, Deportees and Refugees, Repatriation Directorate), and its successor, the Ministère des Anciens Combattants et Victimes de Guerre (Ministry of Veterans and War Victims). Nothing in the historical literature indicates that any agency actually offered bistros to willing takers, least of all these two ministries, hastily formed at the end of the war, underfunded, and overwhelmed by the complexities of repatriating and resettling 1.8 million POWs.

Initially believable on its face, Choura's explanation was probably, in part, playful. The Uninsky brothers all had a winking relationship with the word "bistro," delighting in explaining that the word originated during the 1814 Battle of Paris, when Russian soldiers, hurriedly demanding drinks before they were ordered to move on, would yell at servers to be "quick," *bystro* in Russian (*быстро*). As a child I heard this origin story from Alexander and believed it; when Choura told it to me years later, he said it to demonstrate his historical knowledge and to tease his nephew. It was apocryphal, he would laugh, because the first taverns called bistros did not appear until much later in the nineteenth century. He thought the word might have come from *bistouille,* a mixture of coffee and alcohol favored in Picardy and Normandy, but he suspected the etymology of bistro was still unknowable.

As much as the origin of the word bistro is a mystery, so too is the true source of Choura's tavern in Saint-Rémy-sur-Avre. From the moment I met him in 1974, however, it was clear that he had adopted the role of an ordinary rural tavern keeper. He bantered with men at the bar, serving wine, talking of the weather and farm machinery. But he also stood apart, with an accent close to my father's, blending French, Russian, and Yiddish in a way that revealed he was from nowhere, and in a sense, from everywhere. Yet his branch of the Uninsky family was undoubtedly an integral part of this poor rural community. Monique and Choura went to village gatherings, attended local sporting events, and made sure that the bistro served the village, trying to satisfy local demand in as many ways as possible, from fishing rods to the essentials for children attending school. And there were hens in the backyard to ensure that all omelets had the freshest local eggs. But references to Choura's past were nowhere in evidence. He never adopted the mantle of one who sacrificed for France and never discussed the Shoah. There was no modern art in this Uninsky household, no classical music, and nothing that hinted of Choura's childhood as an Orthodox Jew.

Perhaps, after living under the control of others for five years, and, one can surmise, disguising his identity as a Jew from his German captors, Choura had developed an ability to surgically partition his identity. It may be, out of necessity, that he had developed a skill of compartmentalization, one which permitted him to erect a protective shell around his prior identity. This shell may have hardened after the war, experiencing immiseration, detachment from his siblings, and learning about the fate of his parents. All of this may have solidified his determination that the past would not serve as prologue. But his adopted rural personality was, it turned out, incomplete; traumatic experiences had not utterly transformed him. Another part of Choura was hiding, out of sight; after several meetings over a period of five or six years, when I had apparently gained his confidence, I summoned the will to ask about his reinvented self. His response was not about his decision to become a *tavernier*, what kept him attached to this rural community, or whether he retained any part of his Jewish identity. What he revealed was that his adopted identity seemingly offered him the privacy he sought and required, providing him a place of safety to reaffirm his commitment to painting. He was aware of current trends in the Parisian art world but no longer in touch with his former colleagues, and he never discussed art publicly or with his family. He had started to paint again in the late 1960s, behind a locked door, away from prying eyes.

When asked why he was so secretive about his paintings, and even for several years more, unwilling to show them to me, Choura would only say it would remain that way until he was certain of his originality and artistic weight. Perhaps the ability to imagine his art, even in the absence of canvases and oils, had enabled him to survive past ordeals. That, however, we will never know. It was a subject that Choura refused to speak about, part of what seemed to be a discarded past. But what was never shared verbally was certainly not forgotten. One afternoon after he had acknowledged he was painting again, Choura pulled a dusty canvas from behind many others. At first glance, it appeared to be a depiction of a concentration camp, a stark work in black and white of a chained, gagged, and emaciated figure behind barbed wire wearing only what appears to be a military cap. This was, Choura explained, his only effort to visualize his ordeal as a prisoner.

Painting by Choura Uninsky encapsulating his experiences as a prisoner of war; untitled and undated. Photo courtesy of the author.

But nothing more was said, not a word about the stalag or the Shoah. And then, without explanation, he offered me a photograph of the work, a personal history never verbalized and needing no explanation. The painting was quickly replaced in a dark corner and has not been seen since.

To a certain extent, Choura's capacity to shift identity and interests was a crucial example of the family survival instinct amidst changing circumstances. But there were essential differences among the forms of their resilience and malleability. Lucie managed a seamless postwar evolution, from musical impresario to motherly comforter, as the times seemed to require, in the interest of others. Lucie's wartime and postwar experiences were undoubtedly life-changing, and her resilience took the shape of selfless adaptation. However, these changes were never open to exploration or in any way seen in the context of her prewar life. By the early 1950s, she had adopted a clearly defined stolidity, living in what often seemed an unshakeable presentness.

By contrast, Tola's prewar ambition of becoming an author may have been undermined by gambling and drink, but that persona was transformed as he passed through the crucibles of a just war of resistance and into one of violent revenge. He emerged unable to abide by society's rules, a fact interpreted by his family as a natural extension of personal sacrifice. His prewar habits of gambling and heavy drinking remained and were perhaps accentuated. But war had created an inveterate and competent rule breaker, and from there it was a small step to his becoming a grifter gleefully looting any and all, practicing a form of economic anarchism.

Lola, never clearly depicted before the war, was reimagined as a kind of malevolence created by war. She apparently survived by what others in the family saw as determined amorality, first by converting and then by looting her family's fortune. Elisabeth, my enigmatic and evasive aunt, may have changed in some ways over the course of the war, but if so, it was apparent to no one. She was portrayed as the exception to this rule of malleability; she survived by floating above the din.

Alexander's identity, as an artist committed to performance, was fully formed before the war; that driving force remained a constant in depictions of his daily life during the war and after. Even when sought after as an undesirable, he managed to practice continually. Escape to the New World in the midst of war seemed driven by the need to preserve his gift. The drive for artistic achievement, it appeared, could not be derailed by tragedy. Other readily identifiable traits from before the war, particularly Alexander's intense commitment to issues of social justice and intellectual restlessness, continued, but in a subdued form, largely confined to family conversations.

CHAPTER 10

Grifting in Plain Sight

In early June 1974, Tola/Anatole/Robert Uninsky, my youngest uncle, was nowhere to be found. Family members only knew his last address, an apartment on 6, rue Malher in Paris's 4th arrondissement, and that had been vacated a few months before. Neighboring residents were unforthcoming about Tola's whereabouts, as were strangers in neighboring bistros, until one night, chance intervened in a *bar* à *vin* near the apartment. A man who described himself as a *pote* (pal) of my uncle produced an address, and soon after I was driving to Lausanne.

Tola's account of his journey to Switzerland resembled the unconfirmable, magically infused form of recollection that populated the family narrative, but in a morally inverted universe. It was a story of peculations and charming deceptions, rather than a selfless pursuit of artistic truth, and it involved a timely intervention that rested on the fortuitous of death of a detested figure, not the support of a benevolent and wealthy patron. In March of 1974 Tola began his prison term in Paris for a financial *indiscrétion,* as he delicately put it, the nature of which he was reticent to reveal. Matters of culpability were deflected breezily with a wave of his hand trailing wisps of smoke from his cigarette; if being jailed was traumatic or a source of ignominy, it was indiscernible. Involuntary confinement, it seemed, was transitory and easily dismissed. On April 2, 1974, President George Pompidou died, and his temporary successor, Alain Poher, in keeping with what Tola believed to be a longstanding custom for economic crimes upon the death of a president, commuted his sentence, and he was released.

Tola's liberation was a tale of karmic retribution. His conviction and prison sentence had occurred during the administration of President Georges Pompidou, a politician he held in utter contempt, particularly because of the government's urban renewal program that Tola despised as a modernist despoliation of Paris. Pompidou had reshaped the skyline with the Montparnasse Tower. He then destroyed a treasured neighborhood, Tola's own, by beginning construction of what would be an eponymous temple of modern culture, the Centre Pompidou, the plans for which, my uncle grumbled, revealed a capitalist homage to an oil refinery more than a modern art museum. Pompidou's most egregious act was the 1971 demolition of Les Halles, the glass-and-iron wholesale food market beloved by denizens of the night, like Tola, to be replaced by a train station and shopping center. It was still only a muddy crater in 1973, when Tola claimed he watched the anarchist director, Marco Ferreri, film a reenactment of Custer's last stand for *Don't Touch the White Woman!*, a satirical indictment of genocidal violence that for Tola also served as a fitting retort to a failed French administration.

In later years, all paths that might have led to the verification of Tola's tale of abbreviated imprisonment reached dead ends.

There were no traces of his criminal convictions in 1973 or 1974, and the assertion that presidential deaths in France triggered, customarily or statutorily, reduced sentences for economic crimes was pure invention. Tola's tale, perhaps a secular form of divine justice for Pompidou's wreckage of Paris, also made no reference to Alexander's explanation, to a just resolution honoring a war hero; there was no fortuitous judicial intervention acknowledging Tola's role in the Resistance. Tola insisted his liberation was by a welcome happenstance, one that was entirely fictive, the timely death of a president for whom he certainly did not grieve.

Eventually, as we came to know each other, one a curious young American in shocked awe of his uncle and the other a grifter extraordinaire, Tola clarified what had prompted his sudden flight from France, ostensibly after being released from prison. He held onto his tale of a commuted sentence, but right after the cell doors opened, he fled from his victims who were apparently in hot pursuit, among them fleeced creditors and embezzled business owners. Whether or not any of that story was true, what was plainly evident, as I got to know my uncle, was his gift for survival on the run. Soon after crossing the border to Geneva, he was, astonishingly, in possession of a legitimate Swiss business license, a credential not only difficult to obtain during the 1974 oil crisis, but normally impossible for someone with a criminal record.

Obtaining permission to exploit the Swiss marketplace seemed a plausible situation for Tola, the gifted charmer, but nothing prepared me for his improbable residence in Lausanne. He was living in the guest apartment of Marianne Piccard, widow of Auguste, a Swiss national hero of science.

Auguste was known for pursuing record-breaking extremes, ascending to unprecedented levels of the stratosphere in a high-altitude balloon of his design in the 1930s and descending by bathyscaphe to the ocean's lower depths in 1948. Perhaps Tola was attracted to the legend of the daring and inventive scientist, both being men of extremes. In my uncle's case, from bohemian wandering as a youth, he was elevated to warrior heights, and then fell to criminal depths.

Tola's tale of his voyage from prison to Lausanne was wholly incredible yet somehow believable, told with charm and apparent sincerity. When he left Paris in early May 1974, just ahead of his creditors, he first made his way to Italy and contacted one of the Piccard daughters, an aspiring pianist of some wealth who had briefly studied with Alexander. She was so delighted to meet the artist's brother that she invited him to stay on her estate. Perhaps she was influenced, Tola mused, by his strong resemblance to Alexander. For a month or two, he enjoyed adopting the pretense of being to the manor born, even learning to press olive oil, a time-honored pastime of the leisure class.

When he left for Switzerland, Tola asked the young Piccard for a letter of reference to her mother in Lausanne. Mme. Piccard welcomed Tola to the apartment above her residence, with the provisos that he pursue his love of writing and maintain a near monastic existence with no visitors. In addition, a devout Calvinist, still in mourning clothes twelve years after the death of the great Auguste, she expected my uncle to respect her need for quiet and to hew to a highly regulated life without alcohol and cigarettes. Tola, a chain-smoking, heavy-drinking gambler, who had long since abandoned his youthful dreams of being a scribbler, was hiding in plain sight.

During my weeks in Lausanne, Tola took me touring, performing his other identity of a salesman with a trunk full of merchandise. In one town after another he stopped in haberdasheries, taverns, tobacconists, and village shops. His adopted manner was a roving theater of plausibility, a charming, hardworking wholesaler taking payments for orders of an idiosyncratic and underpriced repertoire of what he privately called *hazarai* (junk), including silk shirts, Turkish candies, burnt wine aperitifs, and meerschaum pipes. To seal each order, he generously offered customers samples, a way of marking his generosity and good intentions. At the end of one week in early July, my last day in Switzerland, we stopped in a bar in the village of Laupen to watch the FIFA World Cup final between the Netherlands and West Germany. Most of those present volubly cheered in Swiss German against the Dutch team, and for the first time I saw Tola's pleasant demeanor slip away, if only fleetingly. As we left, he chortled about fleecing buyers of their down payments. The Swiss deserved nothing less, he muttered, after serving as bankers for the Third Reich and providing a safe haven for collaborators such as Paul Touvier. Before shifting to another topic, he made sure I shared his nightmare image of Swiss vaults full of gold bullion melted from teeth pulled from the mouths of the murdered. When we returned to Lausanne that evening, Tola invited me to his apartment in Mme. Piccard's house, which was empty for a brief time while she was viewing a film at his recommendation. There he opened the window to smoke, and we drank farewell glasses of wine.

The next morning, when I checked out of the room Tola had reserved, I learned that he had not paid my bill as promised.

His farewell presents, a meerschaum pipe and a silk shirt made in Hong Kong, were inauthentic, cleverly made instruments of deceit. His grift was effortless, but hardly motivated solely by historical vengeance against politicians, collaborators, and Swiss bankers. His charm and carefully studied demeanor of innocence and harmlessness were well-worn clothes that made the man, in France, Italy, and Switzerland. Even I was a mark, an easy one, a young naïf searching to understand and admire a childhood hero who had helped vanquish the Nazis. Tola's justification for his criminality in Switzerland was that retribution was generally deserved because the nation had benefited from the Shoah, but it was also clear that no one was immune from his depredations. He was engaged in equal opportunity chicanery, even including his brother, Alexander, whom Tola impersonated and indebted at casinos across Europe. Nothing about my uncle spoke of a coherent plan of life, certainly not one based on accumulation of wealth or a path toward leisurely retirement. The first time I met him, in 1974, Tola was particularly convincing as a wholesaler, possessing the imprimatur of the Swiss government, and his fraud was relatively effortless, if rather small-scale, but it was never designed as a modus operandi that would keep arrest at bay for long. His flimflammery was always short-lived, and anarchic, shifting in form and victim.

Years later, when we spoke, my uncle explained that he had benefited from good fortune during that summer of 1974. The Swiss police were closing in and, he claimed, his arrest was probably imminent. On my last day in Lausanne, when he planned to celebrate with me in his apartment, he had taken steps to ensure the house was empty so we could celebrate in ways that his landlady would certainly disapprove. Tola had encouraged Mme. Piccard to attend a classic American comedy *Arsenic and Old Lace,* assuring her that she would enjoy the performance of Cary Grant. She returned home outraged over the comic depiction of serial murders by elderly women and immediately evicted Tola, who left for Paris the next day, as it happened, just ahead of the police. Tola may have legitimized his grifting in Switzerland as a form of karmic vengeance, but there is little doubt that his was a life of equal opportunity depredation, including from his own family. Here was the risk-taking, hit-and-run life of just resistance converted to an economic anarchism of unceasing escapes.

CHAPTER 11

The Inextinguishable Gift

It was a given in my parents' version of the family narrative that the brothers Uninsky were innately talented. Each was born with a "gift," as they called it, an ability to create the exceptional from the mundane. From a young age, all three were identified as artists in becoming. This talent distinguished them from others and created avenues of survival in dangerous times. Inherited ability, a secular blessing of sorts, would not necessarily develop into artistic virtuosity. Talent had to be nurtured by the masterful instruction of a great pedagogue. A certain personal character was also required, one capable of a steadfast devotion to the hard work of refining the necessary techniques, of mastering the craft. And even if the gift blossomed through instruction and with dedication into mature artistry, it only had value if it reached an audience bringing poetic light to a darkening world, and this was, given the tumult in which the brothers lived, often a matter of chance, both fortuitous and inopportune. Only Alexander somehow managed to elevate his talent to performative virtuosity, reaching across four continents early in his career. Still, the complete expression of innate talent need not have been expressed exclusively in the world of art. In the face of the seemingly insuperable challenges the family faced, the gift extended to an inextinguishable creative talent, capable of taking on new, not necessarily artistic forms.

For Lucie and Alexander, a developed artistic gift was an essential bulwark against the waves of mediocrity constantly threatening to drown civilization in pap. Identifying this form of exceptional creative vision required a closed circle. Only those who were themselves gifted or who were intimately connected to their community could recognize it without difficulty. This might include critics, but only rarely so. For the rest, they were helplessly condemned to dwell in unawareness, an inability, Alexander joked condescendingly, to distinguish Władziu Valentino Liberace from Arturo Benedetti Michelangeli (a pianist Alexander greatly admired). In their anecdotes and reminiscences, my parents associated only with the artistically gifted, who were, overwhelmingly, musicians. Admission to their pantheon of the gifted meant that these artists had demonstrated originality, a mastery of technique, the capacity to spellbind, and more. These qualities were all ineffable, beyond ordinary mortals to understand, although my parents knew it when they encountered it (just as Supreme Court Justice White recognized pornography). Recognizing the gift in others even, on occasion, required prescience. According to Alexander, his good friend, the modernist composer Darius Milhaud, often told the perhaps apocryphal story of a student whose compositions he found lacked the spark of genius. He urged the young Dave Brubeck to abandon neoclassical music and follow his muse in jazz.

When Lucie and Alexander populated their past with the gifted, their motivations were transparent. They were in part creating an uplifting account of accomplishment, where Alexander's gift was recognized by a group of equally exceptional peers. There was also the motive of instilling a sense of pride by locating their children in a social order higher than the one we experienced in our daily lives. In our teens, Eliane and I occasionally saw this as name dropping for its own sake; nonetheless, the stories had a flair and humor that was usually compelling and, which by their very nature, humanized celebrities.

The community of famous soloists and composers appearing in the Uninsky family narrative was a gendered one, populated nearly entirely by men. Women endowed with the gift and able to become great artists were truly the exception. First and foremost among them was the cellist Raya Garbousova. A close friend of Alexander's since they met as students in Paris, both recent émigrés from the Soviet Union, they embarked on international careers as teenagers and never lost touch with one another. It was the case that from the 1930s through the 1950s, the period when most of the family anecdotes about gifted musicians took place, women were generally underrepresented as featured performers on the concert circuit, and to a somewhat lesser extent, they still are. The exception, of course, was opera, which Alexander and Lucie often attended, but great voices, male and female, never appeared in the Uninsky pantheon. It seemed, inexplicably, that the operatic community irritated them both and were often targets of their silliest musical humor, particularly their oft-repeated apocryphal aphorism of the link between deeper voices and feebler minds.

Until my sister Eliane was born, only men were described as inheriting "the gift" in the Uninsky family. A violin prodigy, she was encouraged from a young age, with excellent instruments and instruction that was carefully selected to nurture her talent. Despite their efforts, Eliane chose medicine and parked her bow and rosin. Although Lucie and Alexander were less bound than most by discriminatory beliefs, when they explained Eliane's decision, it was, at least in part, highly gendered. Men, they offered as a partial explanation, were more able than women to withstand the physical and emotional strains of constant touring. Although the signs were evident, neither parent couched Eliane's decision to abandon performance in terms of her emotional problems, and instead also offered a second explanation, that women, no matter how gifted, clearly faced greater intrinsic obstacles as musicians, on the face of it, a truism at that time.

If inherited talent was not a guarantee of an artistic destiny, it was undoubtedly an elemental creative ability. It improved the possibility of surviving the most profound obstacles; with the gift came improvisational skills and inventiveness, an ability to adapt to unforeseen, drastic circumstances. The gift might blossom into artistic greatness if nurtured by others who had the rare ability to instruct without suffocating creativity and if the artist possessed a single-minded commitment to seeking perfection. Otherwise, it turned out, the gift, while itself inextinguishable, would lead elsewhere, facilitating improvisations along indeterminate paths, like the jazz Alexander loved. This facet of the family story, however, had one other important element. The history of each Uninsky brother's gift was enlivened by the extraordinary, including my father's inexorable rise to international artistic fame, Tola's nearly superhuman resistance to fascism and charmed, raffish life of criminality, and Choura's nearly inconceivable capacity to shed one identity and find contentment in an entirely refashioned self.

Lucie and Alexander's accounts of the gift were part of a broader tale that extended far beyond classical music, one that described for my generation the many skills for surviving what might be life-shattering setbacks—adaptability, cleverness, perseverance, and a readiness to recognize and seize the initiative. Three brothers born with the gift ultimately arrived at three entirely different outcomes, each of which was comprehensible in terms of the family narrative, and even, given the circumstances, somehow admirable, flaws and all. This story of the inextinguishable gift as a pathway to some form of success was always enthralling and merits retelling as it was told. What follows largely adheres to my memory of their memories and avoids efforts to test what may have been confabulations against the strictures of historical and logical confirmation. Their story was better, a gift in and of itself.

Tola was an infant when the Uninsky family arrived in France, and by 1936, at age seventeen, he had already set his sights on becoming part of the transgressive, often surreal, avant-garde movement in Parisian theater. Although his linguistic skills and creative talent were up to the task, Tola's dedication waned without mentorship, and he slowly found more interest in playfulness than playwriting. But with the onset of war, Tola's belief in carpe diem coupled with extraordinary good fortune offered him the opportunity to redirect his gift from waywardness, bars, and racetracks to a creative, purposeful life of guerilla warfare. By chance, whiling away an afternoon late in 1939, he met Geneviève de Gaulle-Anthonioz, niece of Charles de

Gaulle, who was taken with his charm and wit; she asked him to help organize the French Resistance in Brittany. Tola's gift morphed to creative violence, seemingly without mentorship, a path colorfully embellished by Alexander with exploding railway lines, daring escapades and narrow escapes, and associates with memorable names; my favorite was Louis à Quatre Doigts (Four-Fingered Louis), an alias perhaps drawn from a popular, early twentieth-century farce about a village criminal missing one digit.[1] In the telling, Tola's quickly crystallized talent for Resistance combat emerged from the mother of all necessities, an obligation to fight the just war. By implication, the chrysalis of Resistance violence, including when he briefly became a *liquidateur* of collaborators, reinforced, even nurtured, existing qualities of Tola's character and talent—inventiveness, an anarchic tendency, and a profound amorality. Tola emerged from warfare into a life of full-blown criminality that often seemed a parody of postwar capitalism. This was the last phase of my parents' accounts of Tola's curious talent. During the 1950s and '60s, in between arrests, the former warrior, now charming huckster, moved effortlessly in and out of profitable ventures, pinball machine entrepreneur, an importer of luxury cigarette lighters, and a marketing manager for an industrial sanitation enterprise, among others. This idiosyncratic list of economic successes all ended with Tola absconding with most or all of the profits. Tola's extraordinary gift was propelled by some of the same circumstances and innate characteristics that drove Alexander, although in felonious form: striving for perfection;

---

1 René Morax, *Les Quatre Doigts et le Pouce (ou la Main Criminelle): Farce villageoise en un acte* (Lausanne: Librairie Th. Sack, 1905).

choosing a creative path in his field; and continuing with an undaunted persistence.

The Choura described by Alexander and Lucie was in many ways quite the obverse of his brother Tola, abstemious, averse to gambling, far from outgoing, and, despite Tola's urgings before and after the war, able to resist the allure of potential income as a forger. A teenager when the family arrived in Paris, Lucie and Alexander conjured the image of Choura as a fledgling painter already focused on his gift and determined to have it flourish. During the late 1920s he resolutely sought the tutelage of more experienced artists, settling in the mid-1930s on André Lhote and his academy on the rue d'Odessa in the heart of the Parisian artist community in the Montparnasse district.

Choura Uninsky with one of his Fauvist paintings, ca. 1938. Photo courtesy of the author.

Although he was steps from La Coupole, one of several brasseries where painters often congregated, Choura reportedly spent little time there, focusing instead on his art. Lhote soon recognized Choura's technical abilities, particularly his stylistic adaptability. That skill led to work as one of the great master's studio painters, and Choura's primary source of income before the war involved completing some of Lhote's canvases. This was the wrong mentorship for someone who had not yet gained virtuosity. It suffocated the young painter's gift, taking Choura on a detour into a terrain of painterly mimicry, one, Lucie and Alexander concluded, from which he never emerged. Choura never revealed to me much from those years, but he confirmed a central theme of the family narrative, that his efforts before the war to find a style all his own, free from the mandarin's influence, were futile.

In the years before the war, Choura may not have received much encouragement from his brothers. While Tola hoped his brother might "find" an unsold Picasso, Alexander could only recall Choura's singular lack of originality, his inability to discover an original painterly vision. My father always had a great appreciation for the painters active in prewar France, particularly Chagall, Picasso, Matisse, Léger, Miró, and Kandinsky. Choura's paintings, he often repeated, projected none of the excitement and innovation of these masters and were clearly under the influence of Lhote, a painter who Alexander, probably unfairly, dismissed. There was a combination of sadness and disappointment in Alexander's descriptions of Choura's paintings, which were primarily in one of the master's principal styles, Fauvism. One work summed up my father's invidious perspective, Choura's portrait of his brothers, which he remembered as a particularly derivative and poorly executed Fauvist painting. In the late 1970s, Choura offered me the portrait, which had somehow survived the war. Completed in 1937, one can understand why my father disliked it. Alexander and Tola inhabit a two-dimensional Fauvist world typical of Lhote's very early work, an approach that the painter had discarded during the first World War. The two well-dressed men are barely recognizable, sitting across from each other with a tilted and distorted chessboard between them. They are clearly disinterested in the game, staring without affect toward the viewer. They are seemingly bored and aimless, the counter-opposites of Alexander and Tola's personalities as portrayed in the family narrative.

Choura Uninsky's 1937 portrait of his brothers, Tola on the left, Alexander on the right. Photo courtesy of the author.

Of course, one painting is slim evidence of Choura's indebtedness to Lhote or his talent, but there was no doubt what the successful pianist thought about his brother's fledgling career as a painter.

If Choura's artistic virtuosity never emerged, a lesson about the dangers of the wrong sort of mentoring, Lucie and Alexander admired him nonetheless for his gift of survival. This frail man was an exceptional example of wiliness, persistence, and courage. How else, Alexander would ask, could a French Jew with a Russian name emerge from Nazi imprisonment? The absence of evidence, of illustrative tales, never served as an obstacle to Alexander's interpretation. Even in the context of deprivation, of a nearly total loss of autonomy, Choura rose to the occasion, proving his adaptability, and managed to insulate himself from the worst consequences, no doubt with the aid of fellow inmates. As with Tola, war was an incubator for new forms of the gift. After his liberation, Choura successfully and seamlessly became someone else in the eyes of my parents, an entirely foreign Uninsky, simple, content, uninterested in the arts, a rural small businessman, and remarkable for what he had survived, not what he achieved.

Alexander's journey from child prodigy to mature artist was placed at great risk numerous times, but it was never derailed and only briefly curtailed by religious and political persecution, illness, revolution, and genocidal war. His emergence as a musician occurred rapidly in a family narrative that downplayed the obstacles; instead, it built on a foundation of innate talent that would never have matured to virtuosity but for his devotion to mastering technique and music theory, his access to guidance from masterful instructors, his parents' unerring ability to navigate around antisemitic obstacles, and the timely intervention of good fortune. Early on and often, the goddess Fortuna repeatedly provided a wind at his back, revealing his gift in a timely manner, or so Alexander concluded. The tales of how his rare gift was advanced by artists and timely benefactors were many, including that improbable recital before Tsar Nicholas II, an exceptional early entry to the Kyiv Conservatory at age seven, his rescue by Baron Rothschild in Paris, and then his instruction, free of charge, by the legendary pedagogue, Lazare-Lévy.

Even with Fortuna's winds at his back, Alexander was careful to acknowledge that his innate talent benefited from rigorous instruction in music theory and technique that also offered him room to experiment with his creative instincts. Although he never spoke about what led to artistic success, it was more than evident in his behavior when he was home. The gift required dogged persistence, stamina, relentless perfectionism, and raw ambition, particularly a quenchless thirst to find new audiences. When Alexander was on tour, Lucie would summon the image of a lifelong whirlwind of performance. After graduating from the Paris Conservatory in 1927, at age seventeen, Alexander quickly left the nest and immediately embarked on a hectic performance schedule, appearing more than twice weekly for over three years, shuttling between Latin America and Europe. In 1931, according to Lucie, Alexander first performed Prokofiev's Third Concerto with the composer unexpectedly in attendance, another moment when the gift was aided by serendipity. According to my father, Prokofiev, who had never heard of him, was so enthusiastic about the interpretation of the concerto that he overcame his legendary irascibility and antisocial personality and immediately befriended Alexander. At the age of twenty-one, soon to be known as a principal interpreter of one of the period's most prominent composers, Alexander's star was brightening as a young virtuoso with an unusually wide-ranging and rapidly expanding repertoire. And then came complications, each one becoming an obstacle to be overcome with Fortuna's intervention and support.

Late in 1931, Lazare-Lévy was worried that Alexander had achieved stardom prematurely and was performing excessively at the expense of continued improvement. He insisted that his former pupil enter the Second International Chopin Piano Competition to take time to refine his skills and burnish his reputation as a mature artist. Alexander always added that he agreed only in deference to his maître. He suspended his performance schedule and, he recalled, hurriedly and insufficiently prepared for the competition. Even to a young listener, this was his way of emphasizing his bravado and talent and of acknowledging his debt to Lazare-Lévy. When he arrived in Warsaw in early March 1932, Nansen passport in hand, Soviet authorities challenged the Kyivan refugee's participation, arguing that as a Soviet citizen who had not been selected by his native country, he was ineligible to be a contestant. Alexander was certain this was done to prevent him from winning and he protested he was "stateless," as his Nansen passport confirmed, arguing he was eligible to perform as a person lacking the formal recognition of any country. In the matter of fact tone my father always used when he revealed incidents of timely support by the powerful, the French ambassador to Poland, Jules Laroche, a legendary civil servant and one of the main negotiators of the 1919 Treaty of Versailles, resolved the matter by announcing that Uninsky would represent France at the competition. Always indeterminant in my father's account was exactly what status he was accorded that permitted him to participate, whether the holder of an emergency provision of citizenship, a resident of France, or a person accorded French protection under special circumstances. Unfortunately, Laroche failed to mention this incident in his memoire of this period,[2] and in contemporary accounts of the 1932 Chopin Piano Competition, the young pianist remains forever a "stateless" participant, performing neither as French nor Soviet.

Although he was always by reputation one of the storied winners, Alexander in fact tied for first prize with the blind Hungarian pianist, Imré Ungár, a matter that was resolved by a coin toss.

Competitors and members of the jury in the 1932 Second International Chopin Piano Competition in Warsaw. In the middle row, fourth from the left, is Hungarian pianist, Imré Ungár. Fifth from the left is the "stateless" pianist, Alexander Uninsky. Photo courtesy of the author.

2 Jules Laroche, *La Pologne de Pilsudski: Souvenirs d'une ambassade: 1926-1933* (Paris: Flammarion, 1953).

My parents often added an unverified coda, that the jurors refused to accede to my father's request that the award be shared that year. In the family narrative, the Chopin competition served as a parable about talent, chance, excessive pride, and fame. Notwithstanding his lack of preparation, Alexander's gift and dedication to his art prevailed, confirmed with a special prize for his performance of Chopin's mazurkas. In her telling, Lucie would comment that when Alexander conceded he did not deserve to be the sole winner, it was a recognition that a moment of good luck should not be converted into winner's hubris. There was always another lesson embedded in this tale, that winning a competition, whether or not aided by good fortune, was not in itself a guarantee of musical success; widespread acceptance of musical virtuosity, a sustained career as a pianist, required much more, particularly the bottling of the ineffable, the ability to capture music's poetry and to express it compellingly and with individuality.

These conversations about Alexander's gift moved seamlessly from what seemed the mystical to the pragmatic. Artistic success came only through the hard work of constantly refining skills, risky experimentation, contemplation of how to express color, tone, and emotion through musicianship, and the creation of a worldwide reputation, which, by my parents' account, involved photo shoots, publicity events, recordings, and the seemingly eternal search for a manager who met with Alexander's approval. If Lazare-Lévy had hoped that the Chopin competition would remove his former pupil from the whirlwind of performances for a period, he must have been disappointed. What preceded Warsaw became an even more intense schedule afterward, as Alexander extended his performance venues from Europe and the Americas to include cities in the Middle East and Asia.

In the family narrative about Alexander's career from the 1930s through the 1950s, there was a fantastical consistency, when nothing seriously impinged on his ability to prepare and perform, not warfare, illness, or political persecution. His tour of duty in the French military was short-lived, and when he returned to Paris, even though he was sought as an undesirable by Nazis occupiers, he effortlessly escaped capture, moving through residences of sympathetic admirers, who offered him opportunities to continue practicing. Upon arriving in Latin America in 1941, Alexander claimed he toured as a humanitarian artist, raising funds to support the escapes of family and friends from Europe. In early 1942, less than a year after arriving in Argentina, he became dangerously ill from some unspecified stomach ailment, which necessitated an operation that proved to be spectacularly incompetent. This was the sole horrific tale of the narrative about the immutable gift, one involving failed stitches on a medical transport, resulting in a life of intestinal pain. Saved by army doctors in Galveston, Texas, he recovered enough in a matter of weeks to renew his incessant concertizing.

To a child, Alexander's wartime and postwar experience had an other-earthly, superhuman quality, and his artistry had an inexorability, arrested only in the 1950s by the return of another great nightmare that always seemed to nip at his heels. This time it took the form of McCarthyism, with its undertones and overtones of antisemitism and a highly personalized political persecution for being who he was, a progressive, unassimilated Jew born in Eastern Europe. Here again, survival and the perpetuation of his gift was supported by the unexpected intervention of a small group of prominent New York musicians, who helped financially until the family moved to Toronto.

When I think of these reminiscences, about talent adapting to what were often catastrophic obstacles of violence and loss, the persistence of innate talents aided by fortuitous interventions bordering on the magical, I feel exhausted on their behalf. Their gifts were inextinguishable, providing, guiding, and inciting distinctive paths for each of the three brothers who were, in their individual own ways, astonishing. Underlying this often incredible narrative were object lessons about survival in a dangerous world. Whether Lucie or Alexander knew it or not, the lessons were double edged. Being born with 'the gift' held the promise of survival and the possibility of achieving artistic virtuosity and success in a dangerous world, but it also could lead to destructiveness and a life of mundanity; how it turned out was in part a matter of chance. Clearly Alexander, Tola, and Choura were among a chosen few, but what did that mean for others who did not have the gift?

CHAPTER 12

Musical Humor, Mockery, and Flattery

Alexander's daily rehearsal sessions were undertaken with a solitary intensity that lasted for hours. He practiced in isolation because, he would explain, it took all his powers of concentration to extract poetry, wit, visceral excitement, and shades of color from a percussion instrument of strings and hammers. When performing in public, interpreting the intellectual and emotional content of great composers on a piano was a joyful experience, but preparing for an audience was a draining matter of utmost seriousness that could brook no interference. When anyone interrupted, we learned early on, it would result in colorfully expressed, temperamental soliloquies with a vocabulary that crossed many boundaries of normal discourse.

Yet this was a man with an irrepressible sense of humor, and in private, he allowed pianistic art and drollness to coincide at home, but only exceptionally, and it was always part of a curious blend of affection, laughter, and musical pedagogy. On my birthdays, before I became a teenager more interested in playing shortstop in Central Park than practicing my cello, my father would laughingly propose a family comedy in the form of a musical quiz. Because Alexander was always at home on my birthday in June, preparing for a tour, it was an anticipated ritual of childhood. He would begin by playing Mozart's twelve variations of "Ah! Vous dirai-je, Maman." This tune known in the Uninsky household by its French title, never as "Baa, Baa, Black Sheep" or "Twinkle, Twinkle, Little Star," always provoked laughter, performed with discordant notes and ridiculous exaggerations of tempo and volume. A version of this traditional ballad had long been sung by Lucie as part of nighttime routine with rhyming couplets about a rebellious child tormenting papa by insisting that candies (*bonbons*) were worth more than reason (*raison*), onions (*oignons*), and kidneys (*rognons*). After Mozart's variations came many other versions of the tune, increasingly complex over the years, in the style of Bach, Brahms, Beethoven, Chopin, Debussy, Tchaikovsky, Prokofiev, and others I can no longer recall. My sister and I were called on by an exhilarated Alexander to identify each composer. If we succeeded, the next variation might be less straightforward, as he would shift mid-tune between composers to create confusion.

This form of musical humor, a version of which Peter Schickele may have perfected with P. D. Q. Bach, was intended to playfully "train our ears," as he would put it, but it was also a joyful exercise in parental guidance and affection. On other occasions, the game "name that pianist on the radio" would become an opportunity for Alexander to drop obscure hints about the artist to aid in our identification. These were fragments from his extensive repertoire of musical anecdotes that were at times plainly witty and waggish, and sometimes a form of admiration, even if backhanded. Often there was little doubt he was also mocking some pianists to the point of cruelty, the effect of which he typically cushioned with loud laughter. After all these years, many of these hints still summon images of well-known pianists—"always a banger, may the piano survive"; "so much light between the notes my eyes hurt"; "at least someone likes a Tchaikovsky First covered in schmaltz"; "still playing after all these years, he's like a cow with two heads"; "that's why he is conducting now"; and "a pianist with great imagination and no ideas."

It was always clear that this pedagogical and often derisory humor was a private matter, never to be shared outside the family. Music, he believed, gave him meaning and even saved him from inhumanity, so to infuse it with comic jest in public would demean what he valued most. Only once did I see him play publicly for laughs. It was in the late 1960s, at a faculty recital at the Meadows School of the Arts at Southern Methodist University, where he was an artist in residence. Each year colleagues on the faculty would perform for the students with musical incongruities and other eccentricities intended to provoke laughter. Alexander refused to participate, with one exception. He had decided to appear, unannounced, in tails, and to everyone's surprise, sat at the piano quietly for what seemed an eternity, but which must have been all of two minutes, and then, with a dancer's flamboyance, pulled a banana from one pocket and an orange from the other. He flawlessly played a Chopin étude with fruits in hand, bowed, and departed without smiling. Alexander never explained why (or how) he performed this magic trick, but I sensed the presence of a mocking demeanor, as if he wanted to somehow embarrass his colleagues with his skill or express his impatience with a school of music that did not sufficiently revere artistry.

Only after Lucie died, forty years after Alexander, did I learn of another side of Alexander's artistic humor and mockery, using his uncanny gift of mimicry, perhaps tinged, in this case, with flattery, in the company of his peers. In a press clipping kept by Lucie, source unknown and probably dating from the early 1950s, was a review of an evening well spent:

> *Last Sunday evening I enjoyed a party at the home of Mr. and Mrs. Mischa Elman.*[1] *Among the guests were Mr. and Mrs. Alexander Uninsky, Mr. and Mrs. Isidor Achron (he was formerly Heifetz' accompanist), Mischel Cherniavsky, the famous 'cellist, and many other fine musicians.*
>
> *After supper, Mr. Uninsky sat at the piano and gave impersonations of Horowicz, Gieseking, Hofman, Brailowsky, and Rubinstein. It was a remarkably clever performance, and screamingly funny. Unfortunately, one can only see these things done when musicians get together for their "jam sessions."*

Most likely this exhibition of humor at the Elmans' was reserved for that exclusive, private audience, a type of

1 Mischa Elman, a legendary violinist, was a close friend of Alexander's and lived nearby on Central Park West in New York City. After his concerts, Elman would often entertain at his apartment and continue to perform for his friends.

preening before those who could readily recognize the artists impersonated and the skill required.

On other occasions, Alexander found some small measure amusement when he was inadvertently underappreciated. In Aspen one summer day, after a concert the evening before, Alexander remembered toying with a phrase repeatedly, searching for a phrasing and tonality that he preferred, when there was a knock at the window. "How is it possible," the stranger reportedly asked, "that you played so well last night and not today?" This story, and many like it, was accompanied by a shake of the head, a knowing smile, and then a burst of laughter. Artistry was the product of diligence and persistence, not just talent, and it never ceased to be a source of personal bemusement that its sources were not widely recognized.

Alexander's "jam session" at the Elmans' was someting I never witnessed, undoubtedly a rare occasion, when he was entirely comfortable in his own skin, surrounded by those who shared his relationship to music and obviously respected him and enjoyed his version of musical comedy. At that moment, in that closed circle of the gifted, Alexander was free to display all the elements of his gift that had bolstered his resilience throughout his life, a blending of intelligence, virtuosity, humor, and the conviction that he had attained the appreciation of an audience.

CHAPTER 13

On the Fringe

"I am a permanent alien," my mother Lucie often remarked, her voice laden with layers of sadness, regret, and recrimination. An eternal foreigner, she was detached from her community, country, and lineage, never belonging anywhere, always rootless. Hers was a history of extended exclusion, a sparsely detailed continuum of apartness. As a young woman, the France where she had lived since she was six months old was transformed into a cauldron of hatred, forcing her to flee all that she had known. She was emotionally distant from her parents, with a father displaced into anonymity and a living mother she ostracized and treated with barely concealed enmity. Lucie lived most of her adult life in America burdened by a profound sense of being out of place, sentiments nurtured by constant travel in the 1940s, Red Scare displacement, and an uneasy perch in Texas for forty years.

Alienated from the present, she also imposed an occluding veil over the family's past, never mentioning her grandparents by name, and alleging ignorance of her parents' birthplaces or residences before Paris. She balked at any discussion of her brief return to France from 1948 to 1952, other than her inability to suppress suspicions of living amongst hidden quislings. Lucie also harbored an unflagging wariness of the US, a land that spawned McCarthyism and fierce anti-immigrant sentiments and, which, at the age of forty-four, led to a life in Dallas, Texas, which for her was a culture-deprived flatland of artificial smiles, fleeting friendships, and ferocious intolerance. Rejection was close to her emotional surface. Lucie persistently but privately mourned for Monio, her brother lost in the war, the only member of her biological family for whom she professed affection, when she mentioned him at all. And she was married to a man who left her for months on end to perform for and with others, although such partnerships were never openly addressed.

Alexander too was a permanent alien, belonging in some unspecified elsewhere and chased from everywhere. He summed up his lifelong deracination with a bit of borscht belt psychoanalysis, claiming his paranoia was not delusional since he was actually persecuted. Like Lucie, chauvinism and expressions of attachment to any particular place were anathema; he only fully belonged to his ivory piano keys, his audiences, and his family. This was a life perilously balanced on a razor's edge, a persistent commitment to performance on one side, continual displacement to avoid physical and psychic destruction on the other. In the retelling, Alexander's musical triumphs could not forestall the dual obscenities of antipathy and violence, stripping him of the privilege of belonging wherever he lived, with one exception. He professed a cultural, even spiritual, anchoring to Kyiv, pronouncing himself as having a *українська душа* (*ukrainska dusha*), a Ukrainian soul. This was not an expression of a yearning to return, but an evocation of an emotional tie to competing memories of artistic beginnings and great suffering. For Alexander, his early years in Kyiv cultivated his nascent talent and began his lifelong sense of estrangement from the luxuries of safety and steady contentment. Alexander, no stranger to irony, was also undoubtedly aware that literally translated, "Ukraine" meant "on the fringe," as he seemed to accept he would always be. His Kyivan reminiscences reflected these competing emotions, invariably accompanied by a moment of dramaturgy when he intoned excerpts of Alexander Pushkin's poetry in Russian. These were always delivered in a dirge-like drone, perhaps in grief, but always intended to remind us of both the beauty of passages from *Ruslan and Lyudmila* and the musicality of the language.

Alexander and Lucie depicted our living aunts and uncles as an assemblage of personalities who also lived on the edge of society's norms, each distinctively anomalous. Elisabeth, Alexander's sister, existed on an alternate fringe, one empty of all that her siblings most valued. Unlike her brothers, she had no passion for reading and was never described as engaging in Paris's prewar life, being indifferent to the arts, rarely a denizen of the bustling brasseries, and not one to actively socialize. If she was born with any of the innate talents of the Uninsky brothers, it was never apparent; she was evidently exempted from that treasured family inheritance, the gift. Most strikingly, however, she persevered through wartime tragedy and postwar hardships seemingly untouched by trauma or travail, depicted in the family narrative as oblivious to the horrors of the world they experienced. Alexander would occasionally mutter, in an odd combination of condescending dismissal and wry admiration, that Elisabeth's rejection of the arts and life of the mind, along with her disinterest in world matters, insulated her, even protected her from the worst.

Lucie's sister Lola was banished to the closet of abhorrent memories, an outsider who entered the narrative on rare moments as a crystalline example of reprehensible conduct. Her postwar life in Buenos Aires was a charade, having disingenuously adopted the glittering status of old wealth and Catholicity. This deception made Lola a pariah in the eyes of my parents, a persona non grata whose life of leisure rested on the theft of her parents' fortune and whose religious identity, it seemed, was perfidy incarnate, accompanied by antisemitic beliefs. Dwelling in an unforgivable netherworld of dishonesty and duplicity, Lola was placed in arctic seclusion by Lucie and Alexander, never contacted and brought forward only as the quintessential object of contempt. In one limited sense, Lola inspired admiration because, like her male in-laws, she possessed a gift, one that was tethered to immorality, not artistic talent. Lucie always expressed a grim respect for her sister's feat after the war, when Lola convinced the guardians of reputedly impenetrable Swiss banks to open their vaults so she could retrieve the remains of the family fortune.

The fringe domains inhabited by Lola and Tola were, in some respects, diametrically opposed. What particularly distinguished them were the origin stories of their dishonesty and their relationship to Judaism. Tola after the war was a gambling-addicted grifter extraordinaire who had little regard for the possessions of others; he was by no means a Robin Hood. Even though Tola resided entirely outside society's norms about property and a life well lived, Lucie and Alexander expressed a tolerance, even forgiveness, for his waywardness. Tola was portrayed sympathetically, as a man understandably unmoored by the heroic Resistance struggle that firmly placed him on the fringe, but was also worthy of high regard, even forgiveness, for having waged the Just War. In stark contrast, Lola's daring raid on the family holdings in Swiss vaults may have inspired awe, but was unforgivable, greed shorn of any basis in sacrifice. And while Tola, as well as Choura, Lucie, and Alexander, rejected religious faith, a secular Judaism defined their cultural heritage. My parents said that it inhabited every fiber of their being; to it they attributed their love of arts and learning. By becoming a converso, Lola rejected that part of their heritage that my parents believed gave their lives meaning, and to do so during the war was the ultimate betrayal, siding with the long history of persecution that led to the Shoah.

Alexander's older brother, "poor" Choura, was destined, so my parents thought, to a lifelong marginality of deprived aspirations. As a young man in prewar Paris, he had adopted a solitary and penurious existence of visual experimentation, seeking a distinct voice that perhaps was submerged or overwhelmed in André Lhote's academy. By his own admission, his efforts at painterly distinction were disappointing and then disrupted by war. One form of fringe existence was then displaced by another, with years of lost autonomy in a prisoner-of-war camp. Alexander would occasionally ruminate about how a frail, sensitive Choura survived, creating an image of resilience fired by an unfulfilled passion, but upon his release, the earlier form of fringe existence was seamlessly replaced by another. Choura shifted into what Lucie and Alexander regarded as an unthinkable rural marginality. This was a lifelong voyage of fringe existences, from a bohemian struggle for artistic identity in the unconventional art world of Paris in the 1930s, through years in isolation from all that he had previously valued, to a form of hyper-normality in a remote bistro, seemingly as remote from his innate gift as could be. Instead of a solitary drive to express his artistic talent with originality, Choura was now a family man who carefully guarded his past, a tavern keeper thoroughly immersed in a world without galleries and museums. Art, and his unfulfilled gift, now served a different purpose, or so Alexander surmised after visiting his brother in the late 1960s. Choura had confided that in off moments he would withdraw to a storeroom in the back of his bistro, painting in privacy, ostensibly, my father concluded, to find solace from the hardship of the past and the hubbub of the present.

This constant and compelling theme, that all our family elders were fringe dwellers, distinct from the world around them, led to a lifelong belief by my sister, Eliane, and me that we also were not like others, not better, just fundamentally different and often on the outside looking in. The temptation is to link this family trait of thoroughgoing deracination to my sister's suicide at age fifty-eight. Eliane lived all her adult life in a fundamentally detached manner, although nothing coherently or convincingly explains her final act, her inability to persist. It could have been as much a sudden cataclysmic crisis as the long wearing away of a forceful, intelligent, and gifted woman by the loneliness of life on the fringe. It may have been an epigenetic transmission of trauma, but if the family history of serial trauma played a fundamental role intergenerationally, it was selective and without factual support, a theory without clear basis.

Suicide asks questions that most often cannot be answered by those left behind. My older sibling never felt compelled to act in accordance with clearly defined social norms, which seemed perfectly of a piece with the Uninsky/Biszkowicz way of being. This tendency toward fringeness may have deeply imprinted early on, and not just from family tales. She was seven when Alexander was blacklisted and had his passport seized by the US government. When we suddenly departed for Toronto, I was only three years old and generally satisfied to be wherever my family happened to call home, however temporarily. Eliane probably understood, or at least was aware of Alexander's intense frustration at being forced to relinquish international touring and Lucie's railing against the parochialism of their new home. Eliane would only say, in retrospect, that the move deepened her love of her father, whose artistry, she believed, transcended persecution. Eliane's musical talent marked her as a prodigy; like her father, she had perfect pitch, great musical expressiveness, and an other-worldly memory for musical scores. Even her name, Eliane, distinguished her, setting her apart. It caused phonic distress among English speakers in anglophone Canada and the US, and more often than not was misspelled as "Elaine", even on her medical diploma.

When I was seven or eight, it became apparent to me that she was restive around her classmates, uncomfortable forming friendships, insisting she was misunderstood. To see this as mental illness, worse yet as the onset of a fifty-year-long decline to suicidality, is too reductive, too facile an ascription of causation. What is clear is that belonging to a family whose narrative and self-identification were apart from readily identified norms placed my sister on that same distant plateau as her parents and often drove her to performative edges and an inability, sometimes a refusal, to conform. This was particularly apparent when she was an undergraduate at Southern Methodist University in Dallas, where Alexander was based at the School of Music. Eliane dated the first African American athlete to play football at the school, Jerry Levias. Her surprise was unfeigned when it led to her social isolation; unable to judge her peers and understand their biases, their racism had to be explained.

Later, every employment she had as a surgical ophthalmologist ended in friction and eventual dismissal. To guide her actions while she lived in isolation from her social and professional communities, and perhaps to reaffirm her identity in opposition to others, Eliane developed a stringent code of candor, honesty, and perfectionism that impelled her to make accusations about colleagues' misfeasance and malfeasance. No one met her strict, possibly unachievable standards of professionalism, and early in her career, she became an itinerant physician, banned from a series of practices by do-not-compete clauses. She often seemed to be taking the same, relentless path toward a virtuosic ideal she saw in her father. Eliane's demand for perfection led perhaps not to persecution, but certainly to isolation and a sense of being unwanted and unappreciated that intensified over time.

Eliane left only a handwritten will on her kitchen table that dispensed with property and pets but explained nothing. If there is a way of understanding her final act, albeit a proximal one, it may have been driven by an accretion of despair, the result of loneliness, chronic depression, and physical pain from arthritis, which she shared with her father. I still find this unconvincing, because until the end, her will to live had been palpable. She was highly active professionally and personally, helping patients to see, whether or not they could afford her services, working with vulnerable girls needing a mentor, traveling frequently, and filling her free moments by attending artistic performances. Perhaps, in the end, she decided that her lifelong struggle to subsist on the fringe, professionally and emotionally, was unsustainable. We will never know.

For others in the family, those who persisted, their resourcefulness and their ready ability to reinvent themselves did not result in comfortable assimilation to their new societies. It seems self-evident that there were direct connections between their traumatic experiences and their feelings of unbelonging, but those were never overtly expressed. The manifestations of an abiding sense of being unrooted characterized all members of this extended family, varying in its depth and forms of expression. With the exception of one member, Eliane, this pervasive sense of living on the fringe of society manifested itself in the form of a lifelong wariness, a sense that persistence would always be accompanied by the necessity of being apart from a world that had never assured safety or acceptance.

CHAPTER 14

The Manufacturer's Fault

Alexander was a polyglot profanitarian. Privately and publicly, he seamlessly introduced vulgar adjectives, nouns, verbs, and adverbs into his daily discourse. Gliding in and out of sentences without hesitation was his extensive vocabulary of ribaldry that many found difficult to square with his generally urbane and literate manner of discourse. In the midst of weighty conversations and humorous anecdotes alike, Alexander would unexpectedly shift languages to introduce his startling brand of earthiness. Alternating most often among Russian, Yiddish, French, Italian, English, Spanish, and German, his stock of profanities appeared inexhaustible, and he never paused to translate, seemingly indifferent to whether he was overwhelming the linguistic abilities of his listeners. In New York City, when Lucie and Alexander entertained friends and colleagues, the profane interludes of multilingual showmanship from the distinguished, literate, and immaculately dressed artist usually provoked either laughter or confused looks. Those who knew him well in those years probably expected it, even relished this discordant interplay of coarseness and refinement. Alexander's cursing in New York City was never, to my knowledge, met with anger or disgust. The opposite was true in Dallas in the 1960s and early 1970s, which in no way diminished his use of it.

Frequently a vulgarian, Alexander's swearing nonetheless had boundaries. His colorful vocabulary never appeared in the context of music, except in private and self-referentially, when he would, after exploring a passage intensively without arriving at a resolution that satisfied him, mumble in frustration, "this is life, you practice, practice, and practice again, but it's still *собачье гавно* [*sobach'e gavno*; dog shit]." While he undoubtedly meant to surprise, punctuate ideas, or shock with profanity, he was never, to my knowledge, trying to be hurtful or abusive. If he was feeling physical pain, as was often the case, he never swore about it; for Alexander, crudeness did not seem particularly cathartic. And while he admired most Brucean principles of profanity, Lenny's, that is, he never spoke, or left unchallenged, racist expletives. The comic often used them in performance, hoping that repetition would strip them of their hateful power and hurtfulness, but Alexander's axiom was that racist words were beyond crude, leading to the obscenity of persecution and murder.

As a profanitarian, my father generally limited his subject matter to body parts, secretions, and oaths about the unworldly and culturally ignorant. The stream of coarseness flowed vigorously, from *alter kaker* (ארצן פַּאלטַ; old fart) to *zhoppa* (жопа; ass), and his varied usage displayed the versatility of this choice vocabulary. These vulgarities appeared without warning, referring variously to fecal matter, urine, penises, gastric distress, dimwittedness, and the culturally uninformed. There were clear boundaries of inclusion and exclusion. The universe of the derided never involved race, women's bodies, religion, or ethnicity. Everything else was fair game. More than a stream of profanity, it was a linguistic maelstrom. In its incongruity with his normally elegant speech patterns, adding a linguistically discordant moment during a story, it was often a way to pause theatrically for levity, with Alexander gleefully laughing at its absurdity. Crudeness also expressed a particular sense of negativity, or the obverse, to provide support, even affection, including *petit emmerdeur* (little pain in the ass), schmuck (penis, although commonly meaning jerk in the US), and *дурак* (*durak*, fool), among many. Sometimes the purpose of the vulgarity was obvious, a way of shocking, provoking consternation, or showing disapproval. Alexander occasionally used befuddling expressions that he claimed, probably apocryphally, were commonly used in the prewar Paris of his youth; among them was the curious phrase *merde dans mon cul, ma chemise colle* (shit in my ass, my shirt sticks). In context, this oath seemed to describe something akin to confused awkwardness, but it was usually received with quizzical expressions that required translation for Francophones and non-Francophones alike, which Alexander never provided.

If there was an overarching purpose ascribed to this torrent of crudeness, it was derived from Lenny Bruce's routines that Alexander most admired, when the comic pushed the envelope of protected speech to include words censored by agents of puritanical mores. Alexander would paraphrase Bruce in his own defense, claiming that if there was something about the human body that caused disgust, it was the manufacturer's fault. Penis, whether a schmuck, prick, *bite, chota, pico, cazzo,* schlong, *khuy* (хуй), or schwanz, was not something to be embarrassed about or thought of as a dirty word, it was just part of the male anatomy.

Alexander, the great and practiced vulgarian, used this variegated salad of crassness as a weapon of free speech as well as a method for expressing humor, releasing tension, emphasizing assertions, or creating shock and confusion. But, as I learned as a young teenager, he had a pedagogical goal as well. He knew I wanted to roam, acknowledging, perhaps, his own wanderlust, and sharing my own sense of outrage that had spilled over into angry risk-taking after the assassinations of 1968, the escalating war in Vietnam, and what seemed like a Sisyphean struggle for equality in the US. To survive threatening environments, Alexander insisted, one needed to erect verbal barriers that offered avenues of escape. Humor and mental agility helped only so much; also important was the ability to defuse tensions with vulgarities. It could establish a cloud of confusion over my identity, which, from Alexander's point of view, was otherwise all too apparent from my uncut hair, scruffiness, and round gold-rimmed glasses. Protection from danger could come from creating a false sense of commonality. The clearly unfair, classist assumption was that reactionary, discriminatory, hateful, and violent people were coarse, *некультурные мужики* (*nekul'turnye muzhiki,* uncultured hicks or peasants) who could be held at bay by blurting out phrases in their lingua franca of insults. So my lessons in becoming a polyglot vulgarian began in 1968, preparing me for travel anywhere in Europe and the western hemisphere. The lessons intensified in the summer of 1970, when provoked by a low draft lottery number, I announced my intention to "understand" America by driving the circumference of the forty-eight states with another vaguely intentioned, hirsute Texan. My father added funding for a one-way plane ticket to Canada, just in case the Selective Service Board came calling. He knew, from a life of fleeing, that words alone would never suffice.

In Dallas, far more than in New York City, Alexander's flair for swift shifts from elegance to vulgarity startled many. When he returned from overseas tours, his alienation from all things Texan, and his profound sense of unbelonging, surfaced quickly, quite often adorned with profanity. He wore one incident of public coarseness proudly. After being blacklisted in the 1950s, Alexander rarely performed in the US, probably the combined result of his fraught relationship with North American managers and his own sense of pique. But one evening in the late 1960s he performed with the Dallas Symphony Orchestra. After the concert, one of the city's uber-wealthy, who lived in a pink mansion in the exclusive Turtle Creek neighborhood, held a post-concert cocktail party to honor the pianist. Alexander was ill-tempered about the affair, grumbling that the house was hideous robber baron rococo, paid for by a fortune immorally amassed from sales of life insurance policies to soldiers. No doubt he was in his cups when the host allegedly asked him that, while she had enjoyed his performance, whether she was right in thinking that Alexander's left hand was weaker than his right. According to Lucie, my father's eyes lit up and he responded, "My dear, you are full of shit." She was, feigned or not, horrified at his use of such a word in high society. Alexander launched into a lecture on the acceptability of profanity that reportedly went as follows:

> *It is not offensive anywhere I have been, except here in your house. The French say "merde" as an everyday matter, as do Spaniards, for whom "mierda" is commonly uttered without scandal. Italians do not hesitate to say "merda" in polite company, and Swedes say "skit" without problems. Germans know that "Scheisse" is hardly improper, Russians think "говно" (govno) cannot shock, and no Basque would be offended by "kaka." So my dear, please give "shit" a chance.*

And that last sentence became a family credo, a badge of honor, a sign of defiance, a reminder that only some words are truly dangerous. To Alexander's satisfaction, the encounter resulted in his deletion from the invitation lists of Dallas's high society in the late 1960s.

Alexander's profanity was emblematic of a personality forged during a lifetime of exposure to incidents of vile discrimination, violence, and loss of place and property. Vulgarity served multiple purposes. Often a provocative instrument of humor, it was also a mechanism for demanding notice, or of emphasizing a particular point. Expletives were also expressions of frustration, a perfectionist's unwillingness to tolerate human folly and ignorance. Using coarse language also was a tactic to protect himself from human folly and hate. Vulgarity was at once performance art and a method for maintaining a barrier against unwanted attention, creating confusion about his identity, and defusing tensions by the very idiosyncratic and unexpected way this language was used. It was also a distinct badge of linguistic talent that set him apart from most others, where he certainly preferred to be, and in the end served his perhaps quixotic goal of expanding the expressiveness of human discourse. Profanity was a Swiss Army Knife of persistence, a multipurpose tool of survival that worked everywhere.

CHAPTER 15

Dubitation Among the Playful Pantheists

While Alexander and Lucie spoke little of their forebears, they were resolute in their belief that both families had once stood at the apex of the Jewish hierarchy. Alexander asserted that the family tree was firmly rooted in the ancient priestly class, the *Cohanim,* who for many generations served as rabbis and cantors in Kyiv's synagogues. According to Lucie, Esther and Miron Uninsky were honoring the family's traditional role when they named their son after the brother of Moses, Aaron, from whom all *Cohanim* descended. Although I never heard Alexander use his birth name, he often remarked on his ancestry as a source of his artistic gift, using his quirky, unscientific version of genetic determinism involving skipped generations. His musical gift was thus inherited from a grandfather, one of many anonymous Uninskys in the family narrative who also happened to be a cantor. Inventive theories of genetic traits aside, by explaining the source of his talent in this way, my father was situating himself as an elite descendant of a religious tradition, even though he adamantly rejected any expression of faith.

Although violent political and religious turmoil and his musical training were the dominant elements in Alexander's recollections of his Kyivan childhood, he also briefly mentioned the strictures of his religious education, bemoaning the lengthy sessions of biblical studies and Jewish history. His formal introduction to the Jewish tradition apparently ended on arrival in Paris, but there was no doubting he was well versed, something he displayed during rarely attended Passover seders, and then primarily as performance among friends who also professed no religiosity.

The "Bracia Biszkowicz" (Biszkowicz Brothers), Lucie's father and uncle, were successful Łódź industrialists whose claims to an elevated ancestry were revealed to Lucie in the late 1930s. After the family left Poland and arrived in Paris in 1919, her father, Kleoman, purged himself of all commercial interests, aside from his reportedly vast wealth. When I was a child, Lucie described her father as withdrawn in his library, relentlessly tracing his Biszkowicz ancestors to Nevuah, the era of prophecy. That the task would have entailed following the family lineage across at least eighteen centuries apparently never stimulated any incredulity on the part of my mother. Perhaps this was Lucie's way of encapsulating a father too withdrawn to have been understood, or this could have been intended as a tale of paternal folly that Lucie knew her young listeners would never understand. The result of this ceaseless research in the 1920s and 1930s was to establish the clan's ties to one of the prophets or prophetesses of Judaism. It was never evident whether Lucie knew which grand figure in the Talmud was the ancestor Kleoman identified, but for her father, this apparently encyclopedic work crystallized an elevated family status in the Parisian Jewish community. In the family narrative, this life work of dogged genealogical and religious research disappeared during the war. If Kleoman's work enriched Lucie's understanding of Jewish theology, or if she went to *schul* or had a bat mitzvah, she never said, providing only a lightly drawn sketch of what was clearly an unhappy childhood. Her brother Monio, by contrast, underwent a rigorous preparation for his bar mitzvah with Kleoman, which included, in what was evidently a male dominion, a late-night yeshiva for two in his father's library. As described by Lucie, Monio must have disappointed Kleoman, who had high religious aspirations for his son. Instead, Monio restlessly pursued a secular life in the decade before the war. Studying with Henri Bergson at the Sorbonne may well have further estranged Monio from his father as Bergson, born of Jewish parents, began to openly edge closer to Christianity in the 1930s.

In our youth, my sister and I rarely saw the inside of a synagogue, only occasionally for Yom Kippur services, and only if the musical portion of the service met with parental approval. On the few occasions when I heard Alexander speak Hebrew and talk briefly about religion, it was during Passover seders occasionally hosted by families in our New York apartment building. On those occasions, any discussion of Jewish history and faith were eclipsed by the voluble activities of a very high holiday, more focused on wine liberally consumed, politics, and Yiddish shtick than the escape from Egypt. At home, Alexander only glancingly mentioned his formal religious training as a child in Kyiv, dwelling primarily on its tedium while regaling us with improbable pranks played on elderly rabbis.

Alexander's discussions of our Jewish heritage centered on the extent, persistence, and dangers of antisemitism. The pogroms that raged through Ukraine from 1918 to 1921 were a frequent backdrop to Alexander's reminiscences about his youth in Kyiv, serving as brief history lessons in inhumanity and the forms of persecution of Jews, but never on religious beliefs. My grandparents apparently had hoped that somehow the revolutionary changes launched in 1917 would temper the brutality directed at Jews, but it was soon clear that was not to be. With what in retrospect was told with uncommon accuracy and detail, Alexander would recount how Ukrainian Jews from shtetls to cities were endangered on all sides during the revolution and its aftermath. They were at grave risk from ordinary citizens and from soldiers of three different stripes, principally Petlura's Ukrainian nationalists, but also the White Volunteer Army, and, on occasion, the Red Army. Alexander never spoke about the effects of an increasingly strident and violent antisemitism on the religious beliefs of my paternal grandparents, other than insisting that it was a particularly crushing disappointment for them to realize that the egalitarian rhetoric of the revolution did not in practice apply to Jews.

Survival required excellent navigation skills in a world of unremitting hostility. Alexander marveled at his parents' ability to circumvent the implicit and explicit barriers of bigotry, although he never detailed their methods. Somehow, he recalled, they maintained a thriving haberdashery in Kyiv until they departed for France. Even as unassimilated and impoverished immigrants recently arrived in Paris, they quickly managed to arrange his admission to the elite Conservatoire de Paris that primarily served an elite, native-born, and Catholic student body.

In their limited recollections of prewar life, both Alexander and Lucie described antisemitism as a corrosive force eating away at the fabric of France. Somehow, at least until the late 1930s, they were personally unaffected in an increasingly diverse Paris of free thinkers and artistic visionaries. During this time, it seemed, they believed it was possible to be accepted as French, although they revealed little about how they overcame barriers of discrimination, which they acknowledged and no doubt encountered. Perhaps they managed to present themselves as assimilated, evidenced, at least in part, by changing their Hebrew names from Alisha (but written Alice) to Lucie and Aaron to Alexandre. But it was never clear whether they perceived themselves as French Jews or simply just French, or how others perceived them.

Much of their abbreviated account of life in prewar Paris focused on Léon Blum's brief ascendance as prime minister of the Popular Front government in 1936. They recalled their intense sense of identification with a France that could bring a socialist Jew to power, but they focused less on the accomplishments of this far-sighted government than on its short duration, quickly undone by a backlash that brought powerful undercurrents of antisemitism into the open. France, briefly an important obstacle to fascism, was now open to collaboration, resulting, as if inevitably for Alexander and Lucie, in the persecution of Jews during the war. These grim lessons in the irrepressibility of antisemitism did not dwell on traumatic moments they may have experienced before they left France, and certainly not on the Shoah. The stories of their life in Paris centered on the essential roles of art, language, education, persistence, humor, and cleverness in a life well lived, far more than on hostile and dangerous beliefs. And yet there was no forgetting that Jews were always at risk from bigotry and persecution.

When Lucie and Alexander recalled their own interests as young adults in Paris before the war, they described exclusively temporal pursuits, as if religious beliefs, rituals, and practices had no intrinsic value for them. Everything that interested them, from education to recreation, was placed in an entirely secular frame of reference. While they acknowledged living in a Catholic society beginning to seethe with religious intolerance, their memories summoned a Paris, no doubt idealized, that permitted them to be on their way to becoming assimilated French. The image they presented was of two young people adopting secular lives, or at least world views and identities far less framed by that strict adherence to Judaism found in Lucie's household and Alexander's Kyivan upbringing. Perhaps, even if my parents maintained strong elements of faith through the 1930s, the Holocaust crumbled any reservoir of religiosity, as it did for so many.

Throughout my childhood and beyond, Lucie and Alexander wore their lack of faith openly, a first principle of which was rejecting the existence of God. Their logic also was heard among the Shoah survivors and refugees in the Upper West Side of New York in the 1950s, that Judaism's deity could not be omniscient, omnipotent, and omnibenevolent and at the same time have permitted genocide. Those who maintained their Jewish faith through the horrors of the twentieth century were viewed by Alexander, Lucie, and many of their friends with indulgent benevolence, as having succumbed both to a critical blindness and a faith that demanded the unreasonable acceptance of a God who was unknowable, incomprehensible, and beyond questioning.

When asked about their Jewishness, Lucie and Alexander would claim inspiration from Baruch Spinoza. With no small dose of wryness, they asserted a kinship with the seventeenth-century philosopher, who was, like them, estranged from the community of religious Jews—although while Spinoza was expelled and shunned, my parents chose self-isolation. Spinoza's principal contributions, in the minds of Alexander and Lucie, were a matter of intellectual playfulness, reduced to a set of three guiding concepts—nothing existed outside of nature; all that needed to be understood about an ethical and fulfilling life resided in nature; and the principle of dubitation (handily the same word in French and English), which meant that what could be known with certainty about the world was the residue of everything that could reasonably be concluded to be false. This led inexorably to the conclusion that there was no immortal soul and no providential God who wrote laws binding on Jews. For Alexander and Lucie, given the world they had experienced, this seemed perfectly plausible, but more was needed to shape lives well lived. For this they looked elsewhere, to traditions which they asserted were long established and essential.

Lucie and Alexander identified as Jews, albeit secularly and culturally, which guided what they knew with certainty. To be Jewish was not a genetic inheritance, but it was clearly a binding force that shaped inclinations and perspectives across languages and nations. This all seemed to be incontrovertible, proven by centuries of consistent experience. From this perspective, Jews acquired a special understanding of the brutish nature of society, a preternatural sensitivity to injustice combined with a weary recognition that the world is infused with hatred, violence, and bigotry, often the result of religion itself. Borne from surviving generations of rejection and persecution, this grim awareness and wariness created a culture infused with pessimism and isolation. Survival from real dangers and abiding bleakness required commitments to those characteristics which nurtured resilience in a world of endless persecution. First and foremost, for my parents, being Jewish meant having a lifelong commitment to learning and awarding a special social value to intellectual achievement. Living in societies permeated with rejection required antidotes, especially by vigorously embracing humor and creating a central place in their lives for all forms of artistic creation, particularly music. For them, art was a critical component of existence, essential for spiritual and moral coherence. Pointing at the prominent role of Jews in advocating for social change, Lucie and Alexander were also convinced that historical continuity instilled a particularly intense sense of moral outrage among Jews about inequities of any sort. This was a dangerous cocktail of beliefs, at once outwardly embracing society performatively, playfully, and politically, while simultaneously suspicious and pessimistic, wondering when the next Bircher, Brownshirt, or McCarthyite would leap out from some dark shadow.

From an early age, it was evident that being Jewish, as Lucie and Alexander understood it, had clear consequences. In the late 1950s, New York City Cub Scouts tried to encourage the participation of urban boys by setting elusive paths to be tracked through the wilds of Olmsted's Central Park, learning how to set up tents on concrete floors, and discussing, with utter sincerity, badge accumulation for the likes of dentistry and truck transportation. Still, I went, and after only a few sessions was informed in no uncertain terms that a blue uniform was required to continue. What followed was a family discussion about paramilitary organizations, the use of rigid discipline to stifle creativity and impose false beliefs, and the slippery slope from such activities to mass murder. When it came to the blue-clad armies of scouting, they held nothing back.

Religious practice was never explicitly criticized or condemned; it was merely an established anathema. I asked once, only once, why some of my friends prepared for bar and bat mitzvahs and why the issue of my involvement never arose in our family. The next Sunday, I was offered a day of religious education at an Orthodox synagogue in the Upper West Side, dropped off in the morning, abandoned for a day of complete incomprehensibility. This form of deliberate immersion in a foreign world was a rather cruel, if unarticulated, expression of hostility to a religion that asked much of practicants, and for Lucie and Alexander, demanded belief in the unbelievable.

When the family moved to Texas to begin Alexander's tenure as professor and artist in residence, the entire family's sense of both being Jewish and of unbelonging was heightened. Driving into downtown Dallas in the summer of 1963, in giant faded black-and-red letters on the side of a large building, were the words "For Colored People Only." Apparently painting over the faded warning was far from a priority. Shudders and regrets about this move from New York were instant, reinforced soon after when we learned that Jews, along with those whose skin color was not "Caucasian," were barred from purchasing property near the University by restrictive covenants. Neither parent was tempted to challenge this obstacle, certainly unlawful and unenforceable since a 1948 decision of the US Supreme Court, but still on the books in University Park and many other communities.[1] Living in such a place was unthinkable anyway. Moving to the suburbs outside of Dallas, they concluded, was the best solution, to get as far from racist property restrictions as possible and hopefully, most likely with tongue in mocking cheek, to find a community of the individualistic and laconic Texans of lore, people who would leave us alone. What we found, instead, was a white Christian culture steeped in intolerance, accepting segregation as the natural order of things, and using the language of racial hostility with impunity. At recess, classmates found pleasure in dropping pennies and yelling "Jew!" when someone picked one up, and it was commonplace to hear the word "Jew" used as a verb.

We soon moved again, close to the community that attended Temple Emanu-El, which in true Texan humility, was known as the largest synagogue in the South. If neighbors asked about our religion, my sister and I were instructed to preserve our privacy with unreserved brusqueness. When the Welcome Wagon came bearing fruitcake from Corsicana, a confection with the consistency of drying adobe, I was congenially asked my faith and what church we attended; I responded as my father had instructed. It had the effect of creating an invisible Maginot Line around our house; we were, for a time, pariahs.

---

1 *Shelley v. Kraemer*, 334 US 1 (1948).

Welcome Wagons aside, insisting that our secular and cultural identity be a private matter in Texas was never a practicable solution to conflicts arising from the Uninsky cosmology. Enrollment in Dallas schools involved violations of core principles. First and foremost, was the theocratic chauvinism flogged at the beginning of the school day; Lucie and Alexander were stupefied at the pledge school children were required to recite in the morning, including "allegiance to thee, Texas, one state under God." When we learned that more than a decade after *Brown v. Board of Education of Topeka,* the Dallas public school district was still fighting against desegregation and for separate and unequal schools, stupefaction rose to chagrin and outrage. And then matters came to a rapid boil of unrestrained anger in 1966, when the high school in North Dallas required that I sign a loyalty oath as a requirement of enrollment, including a promise to forswear joining any organization dedicated to the overthrow of the US government. This was all too much for a family that denied the existence of God, linked organized religion to intolerance, saw racism as the Great Obscenity, experienced fascism, and was persecuted for their allegedly dangerous ideologies during the Red Scare of the 1950s. The politics of the "City of Hate" in the 1960s were insufferable. Upon reading the offending document, an outraged, immaculately dressed Ukrainian pianist, who probably deliberately pronounced the long "ee" as "yi" appeared at the principal's door waiving the unsigned loyalty oath and demanding, in a loud voice, to know what fool created this "shyit of paper." Somehow, I was not suspended.

After a few years of Texas life, religion slowly dropped away from family discussions, aside from occasional musings about

Spinoza. Only in late 1969 did it become clear that my playful pantheist parents had softened their positions about organized religion. Faith-based institutions, once only bastions of dangerous and fictitious beliefs to be avoided beyond the art forms they sponsored, were coming into their own as effective political actors in defense of just causes. Organized religion could be tolerated, not for its teachings, but for its capacity to rally ethical conduct, to promote moral responsibility.

Lucie and Alexander's call to action in a world they had rejected began with the Selective Service's first draft lottery drawing since 1942. Low numbers were a ticket to Vietnam, and mine was eight. Having declined an offer of a diagnosis of psychiatric impairment from family friends, rejected emigrating to Canada, and dismissed the notion of accepting imprisonment, I had decided on applying for status as a conscientious objector. In support of what I assumed was a futile quest in conservative Texas, Lucie and Alexander began organizing an ecumenical council of church leaders in defense of their son. At this time, the 1965 Supreme Court decision of *United States v. Seeger*[2] restricted conscientious objector status to those who opposed participation in the war by reason of their religious beliefs. In addition to continuing to insist on their fallback plan of purchasing me a one-way ticket to Canada, my parents called on four clerics, Congregationalist, Methodist, Jewish, and Catholic, all family acquaintances and admirers of my father, to speak with me about my religious faith as the foundation of my pacifism. The faith we agreed on was not associated with the teachings of a church or syna-

---

2 *United States v. Seeger*, 380 US 163 (1965).

gogue; instead, it was an idiosyncratic concoction drawn from a distinct upbringing and family history that borrowed the language of religiosity. That this was accomplished without mentioning a supreme being or referencing a religious tradition meant that antiwar sentiments coursed strongly through these four faith leaders. For Lucie and Alexander, this was never about asserting religious faith. Such conviction could justifiably be feigned; it was an expedient, to be used, sometimes even playfully, when necessity arose to navigate a traumatic world which they knew all too well to be unremittingly hostile and violent.

CHAPTER 16

They Might Return

The Uncle Choura portrayed in the family narrative was an enigma who inspired intense curiosity. I had long wanted to meet someone whose identity seemed so elastic, the war hero who foreswore painting for a bistro, a solitary existence for a large family, and a vibrant Paris for a quiet rural life in the Eure-et-Loir. Returning to France in early 1974, after seven months exploring the emigration of Jews from the USSR and their subsequent efforts to assimilate in wartime Israel, I drove to the village of Saint-Rémy-sur-Avre to meet Choura for the first time. The role religion played among emigrants starting life anew under great stress was uppermost in my mind. Of all my uncle's thoroughgoing transitions, one particularly intrigued me, his path from an urban youth immersed in Ashkenazi teachings to a rural life in a community which, like so many others in France, found its attachment to the Catholic Church waning dramatically after the war.

When émigré Soviet Jews made the move from a society where religion had little if any official role to a theocracy during the 1973 Yom Kippur War, it produced a spellbinding cacophony of diverse and unsettled reactions. Some found the religiosity of Israelis, which was particularly intense at this time, to be foreign, surprising, and even incomprehensible, as if all the friends they expected to meet had become strangers. For others, the prospect of finding solace by moving to Israel was quickly undermined by the widespread resentment expressed against newcomers who received generous government supports during a time of economic and military crisis. Some of the newly arrived rejected the idea of cultural and religious assimilation altogether and either joined insular, secular communities within Israel or decided to leave as quickly as possible for Western Europe or the United States. Choura's emigration to France in the 1920s, as portrayed by Alexander, followed a far different path, a straightforward adaptation to a new environment without, it seemed, much uncertainty or distress.

By all accounts, Evsey/Choura, born in 1908, the eldest Uninsky child, received a rigorous religious education in Kyiv for more than a decade, far more of a foundation in Judaism than any Soviet emigrant I encountered and far more than his siblings. In the early 1920s, the danger of pogroms and warfare necessitated a profound disjuncture in the life of this young teenager, a perilous flight of the Uninsky family to an unknown culture. With this radical shift from a rather self-contained Jewish community to an open-ended, diverse society where religion seemed an afterthought to many of his peers, Choura may well have felt unmoored from his past and certainly at great risk emotionally, socially, and religiously. But unlike Soviet Jews in the 1970s, who had great difficulty adjusting to their jarring emigration experiences, Choura allegedly made a rapid transition without tumult to his new iteration as a Parisian artist. According to Alexander, Choura easily assimilated to his new environs. As with so much in the family narrative, the key to Choura's resilience as a young man whose world had precipitously changed was recognizing his gift and finding a mentor who hopefully would properly nurture it.

In Paris, but inexplicably not in Kyiv, Choura was launched on an art-focused life by becoming comfortably ensconced in L'Académie André Lhote as an active member of an international community of young artistic talents. He was cocooned in a creative niche in Montparnasse and, like his peers, began searching for his muse. Art was the ultimate solvent, allowing the recent émigré to effortlessly shed his cultural and religious heritage. As portrayed by Alexander and Lucie, Paris was the gravitational center of the innovative universe, pulling talent from everywhere, helping elevate many of the gifted into paragons of inventiveness and creativity. This was a marriage of artistry and chauvinism, extending to a pride of place and a strong attachment to their adopted nation. For Alexander, his brother's decision in 1939 to enlist, even though he thought him physically unfit to be a soldier, was unsurprising; through art, Choura had fully embraced his new identity, French to the core.

According to Alexander, Choura had not only completed many more years of Torah studies than his siblings, he was also the most studious and religious of Esther and Miron's children. The rather simplistic picture of Choura's transformation into a secular artist may actually have occurred, or it may have been a role my uncle played to ease his transition into accepted membership in the Paris art community. Or this may have been one of Alexander's narrative devices, a way of foreshadowing the story of my uncle's capacity to change his identity. None of the authors of the family narrative provided any insight into Choura's religiosity once they emigrated. Choura himself never revealed any details about his faith, either in Kyiv or Paris, nor did he disclose whether he was perceived as Jewish by Parisians. It was never clear why Choura's faith was so thoroughly obscured or excised from the narrative once the Uninskys arrived in Paris. Perhaps this was a way of highlighting a rupture with religious beliefs that no longer had overt meaning for any of them in the cosmopolitan culture that seemed to be continuously renewing and constantly interesting. Or perhaps the claim of having adopted secular lives was to underline the persistent theme that antisemitism's reach knew no bounds, persecuting all Jews, no matter how strong their attachment to modern France.

The source of Choura's alleged embrace of secular life was particularly difficult to pinpoint when compared to the experiences of Alexander and Monio. Unlike them, his brief career as a painter was not marked by formal connections to elite, secular universities that would put him on a path of widespread recognition as a French intellectual or artist. Choura's intellectual experiences and aspirations were outside the bounds of government institutions of higher learning and focused entirely on securing an apprenticeship with a great painter who could help launch his career. This uncle, who I was about to meet in 1974, was indeed an enigma, religiously and intellectually.

There was one question in this story of secular assimilation that perplexed my father, as it came to perplex me—the unresolved mystery of how my uncle survived the war. Becoming

French had of course not entirely transformed Choura, and Alexander often expressed amazement that his older brother, with his eastern European accent and Slavic name, avoided being identified as a Jew by his Nazi captors. Somehow, Alexander mused, Choura had mastered the skills of masquerade and found a way to convincingly be a French goy in the eyes of his captors. That was difficult enough for Alexander to understand, but even more astonishing, this frail man also had the ability to survive years of maltreatment and total deprivation of everything he valued—his family and his painting.

In March 1974, I arrived unannounced in Saint-Rémy-sur-Avre, enthused about finally meeting my enigmatic uncle, the *tavernier*. A surprise visit, I somehow convinced myself, would be less of an imposition and would permit me to observe this branch of the family tribe as they were, a fatuous idea sprung from a youthful fascination with the work of Claude Lévi-Strauss. That it could be seen as impetuous and rude never occurred to me, and in fact, the diminutive Choura, barely visible behind the bar, had the one reaction I had not anticipated when he saw me, one of alarm. Entering the bistro, tall, long-haired, dressed head to toe in denim, having parked a battered red VW camping van in front, I was a discordant presence in this village, the epitome of a *soixante-huitard,* a rebellious youth who had participated in the events of May 1968, or worse. At the zinc-clad bar, several men, drinking their morning wine before heading to the fields, stared in my direction, puffing loudly, the Gallic sound of dismissiveness, and turned their backs. Once I identified myself, however, Choura bounded from behind the bar and embraced me.

The transition from outsider to inclusion by the family occurred in an instant, and it was certainly unexpected. In part this was a foreign sensation for me, whose prior connection to extended relatives was limited to a grandmother essentially shunned by Alexander and Lucie, an uncle on the run, and an aunt who had little to share. And these rural Uninskys, family members though they were, placed me quickly on unfamiliar ground by drawing me in as one of them.

From the outset of our quickly forged relationship, they showed neither signs of my parents' persistent wariness and estrangement, nor any sense that displacement was an ever-present risk in a world poisoned by bigotry. Choura's family was fundamentally different in so many regards. Conversations were apolitical, monolingual, and focused on school and food, where lunch offerings were discussed at breakfast and the dinner menu proposed at lunch. My ill-informed view of a stereotypical rural French family, shaped by films and family depictions, came to life. These Uninskys took daily trips to Saint-Rémy's only butcher and baker, raised chickens in the backyard, bathed in a metal tub in the kitchen, used an outhouse, and ended the day with boisterous dinner conversations lubricated with wine liberally poured. They were also well integrated into village life, active participants in village events, and, with the bistro attached to their home, tied, as if by an umbilical cord, to a steady flow of local news.

During this and other visits to Saint-Rémy, Choura never spoke of his life prior to arrival in the village. Even as I was getting to know him, he quietly withdrew from my efforts to engage in conversations about painting. With two adults and six children packed into three small bedrooms, and running a bistro, his life, he would say, with typical French food-centrism, was as "full as an egg." My sense that the family epitomized French, small-town normality was reinforced by my parents, who lived such a different life. Choura, after all, was married to Monique, who Alexander insisted on calling the baker's daughter. Alexander even took me to the Thalia to see Marcel Pagnol's *La femme du boulanger* (*The Baker's Wife*) so that I would fully appreciate their family joke, that Choura had truly become a French *goy*, accepted by a Catholic community. Much as the hapless baker in the film, he also ended up in a loving relationship. Choura the family man, stalwart member of the village, in no way seemed Jewish to me. He demurred when asked about his sense of being a Jew, saying only that it was in the past, and at least for a short while, it seemed that this part of his identity was fully obscured or submerged.

As I first came to know him, Choura's personality was in stark contrast to those of his brothers. Unlike Alexander and Tola, he seemed fully entwined in his community and content in his assimilation. His commitment to life in a village would have been unimaginable to his younger brothers. Tola passionately loved Paris, leaving only during the war, when the police were in pursuit, and at the end of his life, when his health failed and he returned to Brittany, the place of his Resistance heroics. And although he never mentioned religious faith, there was never any doubt how much Tola was marked by his defense of French Jews during World War II. Alexander, the resolutely urban pantheist, was never distant from a cultural heritage that was intertwined with his artistry and his socially progressive beliefs. As the Uninsky sibling most grounded in religion from his more than decade-long studies in Kyiv, Judaism, either as religious faith or cultural heritage, apparently became irrelevant to Choura. Getting to know this gentle, caring man, so focused on his nuclear family, it became rather easy to surmise that this outcome was the result of great suffering: five years of manual labor in Stalag X-A; the tragic death of his parents; a postliberation return to a Parisian life of great penury; and the loss of his attachment to Lhote's artistic community. In his rural life, I assumed early on, it appeared that Choura perceived no risks from bigotry.

But that was not at all the case. An initial sign was his quiet habit of reserving a supply of Jaffa orange juice imported from Israel to be served only to those he thought might harbor antisemitic beliefs, which, it turned out, meant anyone with a Germanic, Italian, or Belgian accent. His family seemed to be unaware of the jest, if that was what it was, but Choura included me after some time, winking occasionally and giving me a knowing smile when he served the juice. He alleged, when asked, that the people of Saint-Rémy knew him as a French veteran like so many. This Choura found truly risible, given his name and his accent. He was satisfied to maintain his religious anonymity, acknowledging, again in private, that it was best not to know what community members thought of Jews.

According to his spouse and children, Choura diligently maintained a silence about his past, never discussing his parents or any religious upbringing. After so many years of confinement as a prisoner of war, such silence certainly came easily. This was more than hiding in plain sight. Choura and Monique's children all had Christian names, such as Brigitte,

Frederic, and Christophe, as it took me some time to realize. When asked why this was the case, Choura only hinted that he had made even more preparations to protect his children. After some urging, he eventually showed me the white baptismal Bibles he had obtained for his children, although, he reassured me, they were never baptized, never went to church, and no discussions of religion occurred under his roof. Choura never made it clear whether anyone else in his family knew of this curious deceit, and it seemed evident I was not to ask. My uncle's intent was clear. His children would never be either Catholic or Jewish, but would be protected, impervious to anti-immigrant and antisemitic persecution. In name and religion, he said, they were everyday French people, like Monique. And when I asked why he went to such lengths, he said, simply and directly, "They might return."

CHAPTER 17

Platitudinous and Dangerous Stereotypes

When we lived in New York City, the subject of protecting the children from the ravages of bigotry rarely arose. When they spoke to Eliane and me about antisemitism, it was, my parents assured us, unlikely we would encounter it, and surely not on the Upper West Side of Manhattan. This safe world was a highly circumscribed one, and if we ranged a bit beyond it, there was little risk; such hatred had, in recent years, been submerged. Beginning soon after we arrived in Texas in 1962, Lucie and Alexander began to display a new sense of urgency about protecting their children from discrimination. They were now in a social borderland, the foreign territory of the Southwest, deprived of trustworthy friends and allies who had some understanding of their traumatic experiences and could offer them a safe haven of intellectual and artistic comradery. In Texas, there was only a nebulous and largely unavailable community of this sort, creating a deepening sense of isolation in our household, as if we were abandoned in a small boat on a turbulent sea of incomprehension. A fellow traveler would occasionally drift in, a Russian cellist who had escaped from Treblinka and eventually found himself uncomfortably anchored in Dallas. He unexpectedly would arrive late at night to share a bottle of vodka with my parents, all three laughing, weeping quietly, and murmuring in a bouillabaisse of Russian, Yiddish, and a little English, while my sister and I, assumed to be asleep, secretly listened around a corner, understanding just enough to recognize a rare moment of shared grief and comradery.

As a result of their lives of persistent precarity, now aggravated by an intensified feeling of isolation, Lucie and Alexander advised each of us to erect a wall of privacy. Be careful about revealing your Jewish identity, they would insist. The obscenity of vitriolic intolerance, whether overt or masked, was always nearby, they warned, particularly in Dallas. Unlike New York City, they cautioned, antisemitism was both closer to the surface in everyday interactions and yet, they believed, far harder for my sister and me to discern, buried deeply beneath a Texan culture of congeniality that hid so much. Intolerance of outsiders—a group broadly construed in early 1960s Texas—was encoded in ways we were only beginning to understand, including the continuing use of restrictive covenants and a frequently employed language of discrimination the likes of which we had never personally encountered before. In retrospect, we were all partly stunned by the shock of the new, and Lucie and Alexander were also idealizing New York, making the contrast between Northeast and Southwest seem even more extreme than it was. Nonetheless, we were all aware that racist epithets had certainly been part of our northern lives, and we were no strangers to illegal, exclusionary housing policies, which were used in several places we had lived and visited, including Fire Island, New York. Dallas seemed different, though, and it probably was. The far-right John Birch Society seemed comfortably settled and hyperactive in this part of Texas, contributing to antisemitism, attacking the civil rights movement, and spreading conspiracy theories about one-world governments and communist incursions into everyday life. To Alexander, this was all reasonably construed as an extension of McCarthyism. It was also hard to avoid the presence of the flamboyant retired General Edwin Walker in Dallas, who accused JFK of treason, opposed desegregation, and was, for Alexander, even madder than McCarthy.

Erecting a wall of privacy, however, was never seen as sufficient to protect the family from what Lucie and Alexander believed would surely come. This is why they began to include an informal, idiosyncratic survival manual as a component of our family conversations, one that was intended to make us more alert to the signs of antisemitism. They undoubtedly recognized that my sister Eliane and I were unprepared to wander harmlessly in this new environment, and that now we were adolescents, the time was right to inoculate us against the social illness of bigotry. Some of this seemed a casual form of linguistic banter, with antisemitic terms occasionally introduced in a rainbow of languages, particularly French, German, Italian, Russian, and English. In their anecdotes, these words were uttered by characters of all sorts, from bigoted cretins deserving of disdain to artists who had collaborated during the War and merited intense loathing. Not that such banter was an everyday occurrence, but it had a clear intent, to highlight the universality of the danger that antisemitism extended far beyond our current experience.

Lucie and Alexander were concerned not only about the language of hatred, but also about insidious forms of dehumanization, the efforts to typecast Jews with certain kinds of negative appearances and predilections. After we moved to Dallas, they summoned, for the first time and in detail, painful memories from their Parisian past, when stereotypical depictions had been intended to distinguish Jews from *les vrais français* (the real French). Never did they elaborate on the consequences of hateful stereotypes; they knew they did not have to. Their anecdotes detailing the forms taken by French antisemitism in both elite and popular culture were discordant with their typical conversational patterns. In this new theme of the family narrative, descriptions of *caricatures antisémites* stood out like a Bacon painting of a screaming pope in a room full of Rubens.

Understanding that ruminations about antisemitic depictions of Jews were unsettling, Lucie and Alexander used levity to defuse the sense of omnipresent danger they were creating. They elaborated their own stereotypes of Jews, mocking the obscene with silly platitudes and absurdities, creating an inverted world of typecasting, as if to provide a veneer of resilience by recognizing the foolishness of bigotry. Much of this centered on spoofing the claim that there were "Jewish looks," something which has long played a prominent role in antisemitic depictions. Until puberty, for example, my hair was blonde; it was proof, they claimed with mock sincerity, of the genius of Jewish genetic protection, an innate anti-Aryan defense mechanism. It was also always a sign that Alexander was entering comic territory when he would recall visiting synagogues in Asia and Latin America while on tour, to admire, he would say the cultural diversity of Judaism. Whether in Hong Kong, Bali, San José, or Caracas, somehow, in his accounts, there would be a moment of bewilderment and merriment, when hosts would gaze at Alexander and openly wonder if, given his appearance so different from their own, he could be Jewish.

In Dallas, both parents could never resist adopting false miens of wonderment that any Jew could have a Texan accent. "*L'chaim,*" they would say to each other with a bad Southwestern twang that had a French and Russian twist: "ya'll be sure to join us for Saturday services." Texan Jews were often depicted as living embodiments of alternate stereotypes. Where Jews were typically portrayed by Lucie and Alexander as natural progressives, moved by their experiences to lead the fight for social justice and comfortably residing in the intellectual and artistic avant-garde, here, in Texas, they were the antithesis: Republicans, Rotarians, wearing cowboy hats, and most mystifyingly, football fans. Perhaps, Alexander would say, as if to no one in particular, the state's myth of individual freedom created a powerful illusion of safety through Texanification, but whatever the reason, the reality of such whole hearted assimilation was undeniable, and to both Alexander and Lucie, hilarious.

While my parents never imagined the circumstances in which they would cease to be perpetual aliens, they accepted that others who had similar experiences to theirs might successfully assimilate. One winter day in 1965, we were on our way to Florida, for a few weeks in the sun and to meet Alexander's distant relatives, the Snyders, who, Alexander informed us, left Kyiv soon after the pogroms that began in

1903 and spent most of their lives in St. Augustine. There was an air of mystery about this visit. The Floridian branch of the family had never been mentioned before, and it was never clear in what way they were related. All Alexander could say about them, with insuppressible laughter, was that they were a ranching *mishpocha* (family) and, no doubt apocryphally, that his distant cousin, upon arriving in Florida in 1904, had changed his name from Schnaidermann to Snyder, thinking he had adopted a goyish name.

On the drive to Florida, stereotypes flew. Jews who migrated from Eastern Europe to the Southern states were peddlers, started dry goods stores, and some even became retail titans. In Dallas alone, there was Neiman-Marcus, Sanger-Harris, Volk, and Zales, among others, but ranchers? That image alone, of a relative from Kyiv lassoing cows, struck us all as inconceivable. What did he brand his steers with, a Star of David?

Saul Abraham and Sarah Snyder, eighty-five and eighty-four respectively, invited us for tea, served with Russo-Ukrainian trappings, samovar and all. We learned soon after we arrived at their modest house that the Saul was no mere cowboy. He had a huge herd of cattle and his wealth extended to commercial holdings, including a thriving grocery business, one of the largest in St. Augustine. The conversation that followed was a study in mutual incomprehension. Saul asked Alexander what he did, "But a pianist?" he quickly asked, "wasn't that someone who played in bars? You make a living doing that?" Alexander asked how he had come to ranching, and Saul replied, to our astonishment, that it was what he had done as a youth outside of Kyiv. Coming to Florida, he first shucked oysters in the fishing village of Ferandina, but soon left this work, so incongruous for an Orthodox Jew, and moved to St. Augustine, supported by someone who was short two men for a minyan and needed hands on his ranch. It must have agreed with Saul, who still rode a horse at eighty-five. His life beyond cattle and groceries, he said, centered around family and the synagogue. He was a Floridian to the tip of his boots, having founded the Florida Cattleman's Association, served as a charter member of the St. Augustine Kiwanis Club, and, he added, was an honorary member of the local Elks Lodge. Once tea was served, with Alexander sitting in rare stunned silence and Lucie stone-faced, the master rancher then turned to me and asked whether I had completed preparations for my bar mitzah. My blank look said everything, and he soon invited us to leave. We were related but not of the same tribe. We were neither practicing Jews nor authentic Americans. Saul and Sarah were both, and proud of it, and, it turned out, they branded Snyder cows with a Star of David.

CHAPTER 18

A Script for Heroic Death

The family narrative came with glaring omissions as well as obvious inventions. According to Gestapo records, my paternal grandparents, Esther and Miron Uninsky, were among a thousand on board the forty-sixth convoy that left for Auschwitz on February 10, 1943. They were listed among the many who died in the concentration camp on February 15, 1943. If their children, Elisabeth, Choura, Tola, and Alexander, knew even these meager, tragic details about their parents, they never divulged them as part of the family narrative. What may have been known, unknown, and unrevealed about the final days of Esther and Miron cast a dark, enveloping shadow on the family narrative.

Alexander's siblings maintained an unshakeable silence about this tragedy, offering no revelations about the events leading to deportation or ruminations about opportunities missed or wrong decisions made. Expressions of sadness, grief, guilt, or remorse never surfaced. My aunt and uncles never offered an opening to broach the subject. If they searched for news of their parents after the war, as one might have expected, if they asked friends about Esther and Miron, if they spoke with neighbors at their last known residence on the Rue Juliette Lamber in Paris, or demanded answers of postwar authorities, it was never mentioned, among the many subjects left unaddressed in the family narrative. Elisabeth, Choura, and Tola never revealed whether they learned anything about the arrest, deportation, and murder of Esther and Miron. Their determination was clear; that particular part of the past was not to be revisited, at least not with their nephew.

My father's revelations, such as they were, amounted to abbreviated and modulating versions of his last contact with his parents. Some are found in press reports during the war, which were followed by a wholesale revision in the 1950s as the parent of two children who were curious about grandparents they never knew. Alexander's accounts, however much he modified them, were all incomplete compositions, unexplored expositions that avoided any conclusion. What he knew or felt about his parents' death never emerged in his contributions to the family narrative. Probing for more information always seemed unnecessary, in part because the ending was obvious to young Jews in postwar New York. And in the Uninsky household, my sister and I were long accustomed to bumping into historical boundaries that we somehow knew could not be breached.

While our New York community of recent Jewish emigrants, survivors among them, depersonalized the Shoah, never speaking of deaths of family members or friends, they certainly made it an integral part of our upbringing. The scale of genocide was a matter of routine discourse. The number six million, a metonym for the Shoah, was iconic. While at home, the horror of genocide was merely intimated, many of us who saw parts or all of Alain Resnais's pathbreaking documentary *Nuit et Brouillard* (*Night and Fog*) in the late 1950s knew with grim certainty what happened to family members who had disappeared or were never mentioned. For many in my cohort, there was a commonplace duality about the Shoah, at once vast and horrifyingly present but never discussed in a manner that brought it close to home. It was, then, not entirely unexpected that my aunts and uncles, when we spoke years later, in the 1970s and '80s, also chose to place the last days of their parents in a terra incognita. Alexander, as we shall see, revealed slightly more, a dramatic account of his parents' arrest, but omitted any discussion of his parents' tragic end. What he knew or suspected of their placement in Drancy and deportation to Auschwitz was never clear. By introducing the arrest of his parents, however, he was indirectly acknowledging what must have happened to those who disappeared.

To me, nothing convincingly explains my paternal aunt's and uncles' collective silence about Esther and Miron, so all-encompassing and shorn of even the slightest detail. Mementos were not in evidence, nothing recounted about attempts to learn of their last days, no efforts to commemorate them. Perhaps their deaths were so profoundly disturbing they resulted in a collective act of complete sublimation, voluntary or involuntary. Esther and Miron had persevered in the face of serial, life-threatening traumas, successfully bringing their four children across Europe at a time of great turbulence. It could have been that, more than loving parents, they became saviors in the eyes of their children, making their fate all the more shocking. Perhaps this was a deep cognitive burial, the pain of loss amplified by guilt over the inability to save their saviors. Having, by all appearances, rejected religious faith after the war, the death of their parents may have been even more inexplicable and shocking to Elisabeth, Choura, and Tola, now stripped of even the cold comfort of attributing it to the will of a greater being. These explanations for their collective excision, though, seem insufficient. My aunt and uncles not only refused to speak about the death of their parents; they had decided to cleanse their postwar accounts of prewar recollections of family life. They resided in a world where their parents were not formative influences, as if their past with Esther and Miron had no bearing on their present.

Among Alexander's three siblings, only Choura actively did more than merely refuse to acknowledge much of his upbringing. He walled it off from his children, creating an alternate identity for them as assimilated, rural Catholics that he hoped, if need be, would insulate them from his past and its implications for their future. Perhaps excluding any open consideration of their parents' death by my aunt and uncles had a very simple explanation. It is reasonable to assume that shortly after the war ended, they learned about the deportation of tens of thousands of French Jews to Auschwitz. That was common knowledge long before Klarsfeld's work appeared. Elisabeth, Choura, and Tola all had children, none of whom, when I met them in the 1970s, could recall their parents talking about Esther and Miron. My aunt and uncles may have individually made the decision to spare their children exposure to their own trauma by avoiding discussions of missing grandparents altogether, hoping to sidestep conversations that would inevitably lead to the horrific, incomprehensible fates of Esther and Miron. Or it could be that the three siblings, Elisabeth, Choura, and Tola, were unable to summon the emotional strength to speak of the horrifying fates of their parents with anyone, not only with their children. Or just maybe, ask as I might, it was none of my business. I will never know. And then there was my father.

During a tour in the United States and Canada in 1942, Alexander's reputation, now firmly in place, engendered reporters' questions about his recent past. His biography started to emerge, dwelling, just as in the family narrative, on his flight from Paris to Spain and his eventual arrival in Argentina in 1941. But when asked about his parents, Alexander initially refused to respond. In several articles published in early 1942 he was portrayed as suddenly becoming silent at the mention of his parents, his eyes "darkening," unwillingly betraying signs of internal turmoil, revealing strong emotions barely submerged beneath his buoyant and congenial personality. Whether or not this was dramatic projection by reporters, an imposition of a turbulent moment on a young, vibrant pianist, it is clear that Alexander, typically loquacious, was adopting the silence that his siblings would display in later years. He was also, distant from his parents and out of touch with his siblings, unable to adopt a demeanor that disguised his worst fears.

But by late 1943, Alexander began to respond to questions about Esther and Miron, perhaps due to persistent inquiries. Word of the mass murder of Jews was now appearing regularly in the press; in New York and elsewhere, organizations such as Peter Bergson's Emergency Committee to Save the Jewish

People of Europe were engaged in well-publicized efforts to pressure the Roosevelt administration to end its inaction. Alexander's public remarks about his parents, who were never named in the press, suggested a frustrated son whose repeated entreaties to leave Europe had been rejected. The dutiful son now reported he regularly contacted his parents, who claimed they felt safe in Paris, a place they loved, a city so important that it could be safely assumed the Germans would spare it as a jewel of the Third Reich rather than daring to destroy it. Perhaps this was an expression of Alexander's guilt or regret, thinly veiled, at not having done more to insist they emigrate again to a place of greater safety. Or this may have been avoidance, playing on an image of Paris the irresistible, a place like no other, a haven for dreamers of all stripes.

In retrospect, reading these wartime interviews, there was a glaring inconsistency in Alexander's portrayals of his parents as reluctant emigrants. Alexander had already made it clear in several interviews that he left France in 1940 under duress, a celebrity artist from the Soviet Union, a Jew who fled his new homeland for his life and artistic freedom. It seems inconceivable that the perilous situation of the son would not have extended to his parents, but this was never mentioned in interviews that generally lionized the young artist.

Later, Alexander would provide us with a brief, emotionally fraught account of his last encounter with Esther and Miron that left little doubt about its meaning, albeit unstated. His version of events bore no resemblance to the ones provided to the press during the war. Instead of a story of a misplaced sense of security, Alexander presented a heroic script that had Esther and Miron, always nameless, courageously facing death's inevitability without explicitly acknowledging the manner in which they died. I can remember hearing this story only twice during my childhood. At some unspecified time after returning from the front lines, Alexander, now reunited with his younger brother, Tola, went to see their parents. When they arrived at rue Juliette Lamber, the two sons saw Esther and Miron being pulled from the building by Paris police. Alexander recalled this as part of the first wave of arrests of Polish and Soviet Jews. Before either son could say a word, their parents began to speak loudly to each other in Russian, addressing their sons without looking at them, calmly directing them to "pretend you do not know us." The brothers did as they were told. This was Alexander's heroic script of death, a dramatic moment that Tola neither acknowledged nor denied. In this account, Esther and Miron adopted two distinct forms of heroism, at once stoically confronting their mortality at the hands of an implacable, overwhelming enemy, while also saving their children one last time, an act of courage and sacrifice in the face of fearsome adversity. Implicit in this story was that Alexander and Tola were being liberated, free to carry on, one to perform, the other to join the Resistance.

Upon reflection, this beautiful homage to his parents, their heroic reckoning with death, was most likely a confabulation. Alexander was already on his way to Spain in late 1940, where he was, so he claimed, arrested. Upon his release, he made his way to Cadiz, where he somehow arranged for an exit visa, and, according to the ship's passenger list, boarded the *Cabo de Hornos* with at least seventy-five other Jewish refugees, arriving in Buenos Aires on May 17, 1941.[1] It is highly improbable that Alexander was in Paris the day his parents were seized. The first wave of arrests of French Jews began in May 1941, targeting men between the ages of eighteen and forty. It is only a remote possibility that their arrest occurred earlier than mid-1941. If so, the implication is that they were subsequently released and rearrested two years later, an event which rarely occurred, particularly for former Soviet Jews. Drancy, where Esther and Miron were placed awaiting deportation, only became operational as an assembly and internment camp in June 1942, more than a year after Alexander had arrived in the New World.

Why provide this probably fictional heroic script of death? Alexander could well have been wrestling with submerged grief and guilt, that far more should have been done to save Esther and Miron, who had undoubtedly sacrificed so much to pave the way for his artistic success. Or perhaps his interviews in the mid-1940s were candid, and his beloved parents did insist on remaining in Paris, even though the risk must have been palpable, with their son a marked man. What we do know is that Alexander was inventing an indelible image of parents heroically protecting their sons while facing certain death. This was as close as Alexander ever came to explicitly acknowledging the extent of his parents' strength and loving sacrifice. At the same time, he was perhaps narrowly and

---

1 "List of Passengers of the Ship Cabo de Hornos to Argentina," Jewish Genealogy in Argentina, accessed March 9, 2025, https://www.hebrewsurnames.com/arrival_CABO%20DE%20HORNOS_1941-05-17.

fleetingly opening a door to an understanding of his own sense of responsibility for not having done more to help them avoid their fate. If so, a burden such as this could only have been unendurable.

CHAPTER 19

Language of Memories

Recollections of Choura before the war were suffused with the recurrent family motifs, the presence of a gift, a commitment to refining artistic skills, and persistent search for an audience to appreciate his work. Choura's path as a painter was distinct from Alexander's pianistic success and Tola's abandonment of authorial talent. Before the war Choura lived for his art with an unquestioned diligence and dedication, but he remained, in the estimation of his family, an artist manqué, never developing a distinct, praiseworthy visual language. His talent was evident but his originality was not, constrained, or even suffocated, by working as a studio painter for André Lhote. Tola, when viewing Choura's work, would urge him to use his gift of pastiche painting, a well-developed skill at mimicry, for forgery, but Choura never considered it. Alexander repeated this perhaps apocryphal anecdote often, delivering it as a comic revelation of character where Choura displayed honesty and a singular commitment to art, while Tola saw it only as a missed opportunity.

Not only marked by his probity and persistence, Choura was also a luckless man, immediately captured at the outbreak of hostilities in 1940. Confinement to hard labor was particularly difficult, or so my parents imagined, depriving him of the tools of creativity so central to his being. His long pursuit of a singular expressiveness on canvas may have been fractured by this experience, the loss of his parents, postwar poverty, and the dispersion of the artistic community he had admired. Lucie and Alexander saw Choura seeking the solace of family, which pulled him even further away from painting and toward achieving financial stability through the daily drudgery of a bistro. Memories of former creative interests and aspirations were now either suppressed or permanently obscured, as if they were paintings obliterated with a heavy coat of white paint.

And initially it seemed just so to me, this bittersweet tale of traumatic, serial misfortune that derailed the promise of a gift and initiated a journey away from creativity into a settled acceptance of conventionality. When we first met in Saint-Rémy-sur-Avre in 1974, nearly thirty years after Choura was liberated by Allied troops, there were no evident signs of an appreciation for artistic expression, the governing passions of Lucie and Alexander. In this Uninsky household, attached to a nondescript bistro, the art of living took precedence over fine art. Conviviality, work, education, and food held center stage. When Choura mentioned art at all, it was offhandedly diminished, an avocation, not a profession. My efforts to steer conversations toward the windows of Chartres or museums recently visited were deflated by seeming indifference. Even though, as I learned later, a few of Choura's paintings had survived the war, they were nowhere in sight, hidden in a back room. A living space brimming with art, essential to my parents, was at best an after-thought in Saint-Rémy, where decoration was a servant of the practical and the popular, consisting mainly of calendars and posters. This was practically an art-free zone, until several years later, when Choura began, gradually, to reveal an enduring interest in painting.

The first glimmer of Choura's abiding interest in painting came in 1975, when I mentioned that the painter Jean Hélion had invited me to visit him in his chateau in Bigeonnette. Hélion and my father were close friends before the war, enlisted at the same time, and by a happy coincidence, found each other in New York City in 1942. Elated to see his old friend, the painter gave Alexander an assemblage of several of his recent works that he had pinned on his studio walls; inspirational totems, my father called them. This gift held a prominent place wherever we lived, a memory of a shared past and the two friends' common appreciation for the innovative. In his long career, Hélion had proved a restless creator, beginning as an abstract painter, moving onto a period of cubism, which was replaced after the war, by a more naturalistic and figurative style, and this collection of totems had embodied all three stages of his art, his languages of visual expression past and present.

Bigeonnette was near Saint-Rémy-sur-Avre, and I hoped the impromptu addition of my uncle to Hélion's invitation would be irresistible. They were close in age, and the art world in prewar Paris was small enough that they may have known each other. Choura agreed to accompany me, hardly with alacrity, more with what seemed a sigh of resignation, but which was, it later became clear, a dismissive recognition tinged with a slight, perhaps reluctant, curiosity. On the road, Choura acknowledged a passing acquaintance with Hélion and his work, but he had no idea what to expect now. What in particular piqued my uncle's interest in the visit he would not say, whether the large estate in nearby Bigeonnette, which he said was known to be beautiful, or the artist's current paintings.

We were greeted with warmth, and it was clear that Choura was someone Hélion had known fairly well. The painter immediately steered us to his studio, a cavernous, unadorned space that was dominated by several large canvases commemorating the events of May 1968 in Paris and a triptych devoted to the nearby market of Châteauneuf-en-Thymerais. Hélion was engaging, speaking passionately about his forthcoming projects, asking if the emotions he sought to portray, both about political discord and daily life rang true. My still emerging command of French probably rendered me nearly incoherent, although the artist managed to ignore it, even inviting me to join him in a few weeks at his Paris studio to meet recent Chilean political refugees. Choura, throughout, remained silent about the art, preferring only to speak briefly about his recently deceased brother. During the short drive back from chateau to bistro, Choura at first avoided discussing the artist and his art, despite my urgings, but finally rendered his verdict, saying only, "He was more interesting before."

The next day, Choura, without discussion, pulled from a closet that 1937 portrait of his two brothers, with Tola and Alexander gazing outward, as if uninterested in the misshapen, nearly surreal chessboard before them. Choura, laconic as usual, was quietly bemused by my elation when he offered me the painting, saying only it was an early effort, playful but unsatisfactory. And there the conversation ended, with no discussion of later efforts, of André Lhote's influence on his approach to painting, or of what he had preferred about Hélion's earlier work. Access to the past was firmly shut once again. His memories of a painter's life, of the visual language with which he once strove to communicate, again were sequestered, at least for a time.

Three years later, in 1978, again in France and now living in Normandy, I was spending my days in the departmental archives collecting information about criminality, policing, and the courts in the eighteenth century. Friends found my fixation with historical criminology abstruse, or trivial, and began teasingly to predict my dissolution by historical association, with my inevitable decline into becoming the "roué of Rouen". To break up the archival tedium, I began visiting Choura again. On one of my trips to Saint-Rémy, I noticed a new ebullience in his demeanor. Particularly when we were alone together, he displayed unmistakable signs of congeniality and a nervous energy that had not marked this normally laconic and reserved man. He pulled me aside during a quiet moment in the bistro and announced his artistic epiphany, a style of painting that he could claim was his own. Why had he started painting again? What was the visual language he had finally found satisfying? Questions about motivations and strategy of artistic expression were waved away, the paintings would evidently speak for themselves. Entering a storeroom, Choura pulled me into a makeshift gallery of more than a dozen paintings, all examples of an approach developed by Pablo Picasso and Georges Braque from 1910 to 1912. Each canvas was a direct descendant in style, color, and perspective of that pathbreaking moment in art history, with ordinary objects fractured into new geometric forms using a limited pallet of greys, light browns, and black. Umbrellas, pianos, tables, and other subjects were deconstructed and given new life and altered form. Choura had discovered analytic cubism. My first reactions were that this was a prank or that my sweet uncle of unfailing probity had become a forger. But it soon became clear that pride, a sense of authenticity, and a belief in a lifelong quest achieved were held with great conviction and without artifice. Somehow, he found a visual language for his memories, once forgotten and now recalled in a fulfilling discovery. He was no longer an artist manqué. He had a distinctive voice; he had advanced his gift and was proud of his achievement.

In all other respects, Choura was the same person I had known for several years, an attentive and affectionate parent and spouse, a competent business owner who was attached to the quotidian, content with his quiet village life. His memory seemed perfectly normal in all other respects. These paintings, however they arose, remained a private conversation with himself and, apparently, with me. They were never, to my knowledge, revealed to the public, leaving his identity as a *tavernier* intact. The works also disappeared without a trace.

As Choura aged, he no longer could maintain his bistro and retired to a cottage near the ocean with Monique. In the summer of 1990, Kira and I called to see if we could visit. Monique responded, inviting us in with a warning that Choura had withdrawn completely and was not communicating coherently. When we sat with my eighty-two-year-old uncle, he spoke without hesitation and with perfect clarity, in Russian. He seemed content, even happy, speaking another language, that of his youth and, quite clearly, from a time he chose to remember, perhaps relishing moments before great hardship had so reshaped his persona.

Language bears rich, personal, and nearly unfathomable associations with the past. Twenty-two years late, Lucie, dying in an ICU, looked me in the eye and began to speak French to me, something she had done all my life. But this time, with a difference, asking me what I was going to play that night. She was smiling, and I imagined she could hear Alexander at his keyboard. I began describing a program, starting with Chopin, a Mazurka in F-sharp minor and the Sonata no. 2, thinking of the *Marche Funèbre,* followed by the Liszt *Rhapsodie Espagnole,* and ending with two Prokofiev Gavottes. "They do not fit together well," she said, smiling even more broadly, "but you will make it work." And then one of the last things she ever said, "Why aren't you wearing your tails?"

CHAPTER 20

Dislodging Memories and Verifying Deceit

Alexander died in his sleep on December 19, 1972, and Lucie outwardly grieved for a brief period. She then quickly returned to her stoic, equilibrated self, generally impassive, refined, but suddenly impoverished. There were house payments to be made, no life insurance or savings, a daughter in medical school, a son in college, and Alexander's retirement fund was several months short of vesting. A lifetime of alternating wealth and poverty in historical whirlwinds led Alexander and Lucie to dismiss preparations for the future as a fruitless endeavor. If this was the result of a life of preternatural presentness focused on the creative arts, Lucie never said, nor did she express any regrets. The uncontrollable forces that had disrupted her life and Alexander's made planning for financial security beyond the next season of performances a pointless task. A safe future, after all, had proven chimerical.

Quickly putting outward signs of grief on a hold that endured for the rest of her life, Lucie sought employment. She instructed her children to go back to their educations, and for the first time since 1942, Lucie declared, she was putting her "hands in motion." This was a ruefully comic reference to her first paid activity during the war, when she assembled watches in a New York City basement. In the weeks after my father's death, we spoke regularly. Efforts to inquire about her emotions or to encourage reflections about her life in music with Alexander were met with silence, occasionally forcefully rejected. Lucie seemed thoroughly enmeshed in the moment, teaching French to children in a Montessori program and to Texans needing refresher courses before traveling to Paris. Questions about these activities were brushed aside, everyday mundanities that were accepted as necessities and nothing more. Occasionally, when she betrayed a bitterness, edging on anger, it was directed at family acquaintances in Dallas, who she believed were distancing themselves from her now that Alexander was gone. Language, beyond her work as an instructor, became an additional source of isolation in the alien Texan world where she found herself. Lucie, who had once only occasionally used English in our private conversations, now exclusively used French. She also began to direct her social attention to the small Francophone community of women in Dallas. This reinforced her longstanding sense of estrangement as an alien in a strange land. Her English became more accented, sometimes incomprehensible to Texans, and, she readily acknowledged, her new social community was in all ways profoundly different, now composed nearly entirely of women and without the musicians and patrons of the arts who had included her in their social gatherings when Alexander was alive.

In occasional moments of candor, Lucie bemoaned her lack of commonality with her new acquaintances, uncharitably characterizing them as lonely, nouveau riche widows. All had recently emigrated to Texas, and some, Lucie claimed, were casually antisemitic. Lucie never acknowledged exploring the obvious, asking that question, "and what did you do during the war?" What they shared, and what Lucie clearly sought, was an appreciation for lunches of quality and amicable, polite conversations in French that maintained an old-fashioned sense of formality, never moving from *vouvoyer* to the informal *tutoyer*. Withdrawing to the language of her youth may have been a confirmation of Lucie's deepening sense of deracination after Alexander's death, and, it seemed, part of her effort to wall off unwanted contact in the very foreign and threatening heart of Texas. Linguistic isolation may also have provided comfort to the fifty-three-year-old widow, as might equally have been the case with Choura at the end of his life. Perhaps it allowed her to live more easily with memories of her youth and of Alexander, with whom she had usually communicated in French. But if it did, those memories were never revealed, and the present, more than ever, obscured the past. In the months following Alexander's death, Lucie lived on a singularly remote edge of her community, alienated and isolated but without outward signs of grief. When she expressed any enthusiasm and pleasure it was only with reference to exhibits, concerts, and literature. This was Lucie confined and refined, decidedly remote from her past, largely maintaining her rock-like identity, isolated by language from an environment she found unwelcoming and even threatening, and still enmeshed in the arts, her principal source of inspiration and satisfaction.

Several weeks after Alexander's death, Lucie's self-containment ended briefly, compelled by an urgent circumstance, the arrival in the person of a niece, daughter of her estranged sister Lola, the author of deceptions and betrayals. The need to correct lifelong deceit was the mother of revelation. Alexander's obituaries, published widely in the American press, stirred the curiosity of someone never mentioned by my family, Lola's eldest child, who then resolved to travel to Dallas and meet her aunt. Until then, the Argentinian converso branch of the family had lived enshrouded in the perpetual state of ignominy imposed by Lucie and Alexander. Glimpses into Lola's behavior during the war were occasional fare in the family narrative, offered as grim evidence that consanguinity was not a guarantor of any affinity. Lola was the Great Antithesis of everything held dear by my family. She was presented as rapacious and dishonorable, having stolen the family fortune, adopted a religion whose spiritual leader, my family believed, abetted the persecution of Jews during the war, and married a figure of repression, a police psychiatrist. And, if that were not enough, she was uncultured.

This nearly feverish litany of the horrible was more comprehensive than believable until Lucie's niece appeared. She contacted my mother using a Latina first name that Lucie insisted could not be her given name, and offered to make the long journey from the upper Midwest to support her aunt in Texas. Lucie, understandably suspicious, first confirmed to her satisfaction that the thirty-one-year-old woman was in fact her niece. Her age aligned with Lucie's memory, and the description of her sister was beyond dispute. The reason offered for this sudden appearance, after more than fifteen years in the US, seemed credible enough. Alexander's obituary in the Chicago press awakened distant memories of Lola's infrequent mentions of her French sister who had emigrated to the United States during the war and married a pianist. This vagueness notwithstanding, Lucie was satisfied this was indeed her niece and invited her to Dallas.

The night before she arrived, one month after Alexander's death, Lucie called, alternately apprehensive that her niece might be a version of Lola and pleased about the prospect of meeting the woman she had known only as a newborn and who now suddenly appeared, concerned about her aunt's welfare. Several days later, Lucie proudly informed me she had worked a radical transformation. Her niece was no longer, as she put it, a *femme profondément égarée* (a profoundly misguided woman), thanks to her own timely intervention. Lucie, for a moment, shed her somber demeanor and sounded relieved. From a product of the Great Antithesis as Lola's progeny, her niece had moved, in a matter of days, from what she acknowledged were offensive beliefs to remorse and a greater understanding of who she might be. These were, to put it mildly, stunning claims and were the result, so both aunt and niece agreed, of Lucie's intervention, remedying her sister's misguidance.

Having traveled to Dallas to care for a grieving aunt she had never met, the niece's intentions were soon transformed by the law of inverse consequences. Lucie was not grieving, and her niece soon discovered that her aunt had far greater personal knowledge of her than she could have imagined.

The great wall retaining the past was suddenly breached when Lucie's niece, unbidden, spoke of her upbringing as a devout Catholic. She expressed her own indifference to religion, which momentarily assuaged Lucie, until, unprompted, there was a slide down the banister of intolerance toward a dangerous landing, splinters and all, with seemingly off-handed, loathsome, and derogatory depictions of Jews. Lucie abruptly halted her niece and said, beginning with that telltale term of affection: "Dear, I have two things to tell you, neither of which you will like. First, you yourself are a Jew, and second, you are also a bastard." And then the details of both of their lives during a time of extreme duress came pouring forth, all of which Lucie had never previously disclosed. In early 1940, Lola, Lucie's unmarried sister, gave birth to a daughter. The father, a prominent member of Paris's Jewish elite in the 16th arrondissement, refused to acknowledge the child as his own. Perhaps to exaggerate her niece's fall from a state of grace, my mother's primitive version of shock therapy, Lucie added that the father was "*peut-être un comte*" (perhaps a count), at least a notable.

By late May of 1940, Lucie and Lola decided to flee approaching Nazi troops and commandeered one of the family cars, driving south across the Spanish border to Portugal, where their mother had taken up residence. The elder sister, Lola, drove, while Lucie cared for the newborn. "I held you all the way," Lucie insisted on telling her niece. They were wealthy travelers but without French passports or visas, and yet they managed to circumvent all the obstacles by paying bribes, traveling at night, and hoping the baby would help elicit sympathy. Eventually they arrived in Porto and rejoined their mother, who, Lucie divulged to me for the first time, had taken on a new identity as a Catholic. Lola followed suit, and soon after married the man her niece had understood to be her biological father throughout her life. Lucie described her own reaction to these events in muted tones, saying only that religious conversion had quickly led her to separate from her sibling and mother. She added that her late brother, Monio, reacted even more viscerally at the news of these conversions, without mentioning his suicide.

Some of Lucie's recollections may have been pure inventions, perhaps spoken for shock value. Not that I knew Grandmaman Bisco well, but it was never clear she had any religious faith. Or perhaps her wartime conversion was a convenience that she later shed. Invented memories or not, my cousin's reaction was surprising. She never contested the veracity of this tale of origin and danger. Saying nothing about her father, she confided to Lucie that these revelations finally explained what she had always thought was a problematic claim by her mother. Having lived in the US for years, she had hoped to become a citizen, but that path was blocked by the absence of a birth certificate. Lola always explained her failure to document her child's birth as consequence of war, that the paperwork was destroyed and copies were irretrievable, an explanation that, for her daughter, never rang true. This relatively small deceit somehow verified the rest, that she was not a Catholic, that her father was someone else, and that she was a Jew. Perhaps it was the power of Lucie's dislodged memories that confirmed, and in some way, remedied the deceit.

A door to Lucie's traumatic past was opened, for a brief period, and then it closed, abruptly and permanently.

Subsequent efforts to encourage my mother to elaborate upon her life in Paris and during the war were ignored, as if unheard, or they were deflected. Perhaps this moment of open reflection was an instrument of assuagement, a way of redressing some of the pain she had experienced as a result her sister's betrayal and depredation. Lucie's niece was now more kin than disquieting stranger; prevarications from a painful past were at least in part resolved. Memories revealed possibly had served their purpose.

CHAPTER 21

Memento Mori and Memento Vivere

Days after he won the International Chopin Piano Competition in 1932, the twenty-two-year-old Alexander Uninsky decided to plan for the financial well-being of his family and purchased a life insurance policy. This occurred eight years after the Uninsky family had arrived in Paris penniless, and in that short time it was evident that the young pianist was doing well. He had been performing incessantly for five years, and his address listed on the policy was on rue de Babylone in the 7th arrondissement, at the heart of one of Paris's poshest neighborhoods. Like so much else in the city center, the address has maintained its allure. At that moment Alexander could afford to invest a portion of his prize award of five thousand złoty in an insurance policy to benefit his parents. What stands out is that this purposeful step toward diminishing his family's financial insecurity in the event of his death was not something Alexander would ever repeat, either by accumulating wealth or investing in other insurance policies. Perhaps the repeated cycles of prosperity and penury that marked his life from 1940 on served to discourage any belief that financial security could be ensured. There was never any doubt that this part of my father's unspoken credo was forged in the context of incessant turmoil, and it was one that my mother shared. It was consistently *memento vivere,* remember to live in the moment, and certainly not the classical Christian notion of *memento mori,* remember that you shall die and must, in life, act accordingly.

And yet, on that day in 1932, the young pianist, now assured of an even greater success as the prize winner of the most prominent piano competition of his time, walked into the Warsaw offices of the Prudential Assurance Company Limited and purchased some measure of financial protection. Later, through the whirlwind years of multiple resettlements caused by war, McCarthyism, and career choices, evidence of that life insurance policy had disappeared, and perhaps any recollection of it as well. By then, Alexander had long since placed memories of his parents, Esther and Miron, in a virtuous and transcendental haze, nameless, but loving and resourceful in successfully navigating a hostile world. With one exception, in Alexander's heroic script of their death, Esther and Miron's lives were placed beyond explicit recall, his efforts to provide them financial security included.

There proved to be many surprises about that Prudential policy, most particularly that it resurfaced. The company's Polish offices were closed by Nazi occupying forces in 1939, and all its records were destroyed during the Warsaw Uprising of 1944. Prudential's London office, beginning in 1955, undertook the task of reviewing its prewar files to identify possible claimants living outside Poland, while the Polish government settled its own citizens' outstanding claims. In 2015, all this activity came to the attention of an enterprising filmmaker based in Warsaw, who offered to help open a line to this part of my father's past. Serendipity provided a glimpse to an event eighty-three years old, and Prudential, in its own cautious manner, settled the claim.

This insurance apparition of my father, appearing long after his death, marked what must have been a rare moment of *memento mori* in his life. The Alexander I knew never acknowledged a responsibility to plan for death; the territory of life's ending was otherwise only exceptionally conceded, and any concept of afterlife was derided, dismissed as foolishness. When discussions of mortality arose at all, they were never about immediate family or close friends. The possibility of imminent death only appeared in one odd vignette. It was the only time I remember when the Shoah impinged on his storytelling, in an oblique reference both to that horror he no doubt imagined on many occasions and, perhaps, to the proximity of death while he was in the army and during his flight from occupied Paris. Arriving in New York City in 1942, he saw himself facing nearly insuperable risks, readying himself for his Carnegie debut while exhausted by his travels, ill from a bungled operation, and only beginning to speak English. A knock on the door awakened him, and when he groggily asked who was there, the unexpected visitor responded "I am the exterminator," and Alexander fainted. The visitor was not the Grim Reaper, my father would add unnecessarily. This was as close to his own mortality and the Shoah as he would ever go. The anecdote was intentionally offensive humor, serving as a warning that certain subjects were barred against trespass, but also of a piece with the dominant themes of his family narrative. Resilience, physical and mental, was front and center, as was preservation of the gift, and there was no doubt that this performance at Carnegie, enthusiastically reviewed in the "Old Gray Lady," went as planned. The possibility of death was leavened with linguistic playfulness, and his thoughts about the genocide of exterminators elided. Not for the first time, humor served both as a shield, used to deflect traumatic experiences with laughter, and as a ready pathway to a completely unrelated subject.

Once my relationship to Alexander was confirmed to Prudential's satisfaction, I learned of Alexander's Parisian apartment on rue Babylone. Alexander had rarely mentioned its existence, saying only that when he bicycled to Spain, all he took with him were a few jewels, which he hoped would be valuable enough to pay for his release from any arrest or for passage to Latin America, among other uses he recalled in differing accounts. Lucie knew some details about the apartment on rue Babylone, but never mentioned them in Alexander's presence. It was an artist's sanctuary, she occasionally mused, alive with paintings by contemporaries, great art that surrounded a Pleyel, the type of piano Chopin had played. Beyond its proximity to the Jardin Chatherine-Labouré, which still exists, and La Pagode, which in the 1930s was a temple of cinema, and beyond its rehearsal space, the prominent address, the art, and the piano, I suspect that Alexander also savored the particular irony of living on rue Babylone. Having attended *shul* from an early age until the family left Ukraine, he was well-versed in Jewish history and certainly knew that when Nebuchadnezzar II took inhabitants of Jerusalem to Babylonia, it was viewed by many Jews as the first permanent diaspora. Perhaps my father's silence about the apartment was part of an unwillingness to dwell on what may have been a strong attachment to this special place, his first of great comfort and independence, a symbol of his early success as a pianist, and his lair of creativity. Why, I once asked, had my father not set about retrieving what had been taken during the war. He scoffed, saying only that it was a naïve suggestion, and in any event, all of that was *de la merde,* referring both to the question and the possessions; what the French stole during the war would never be found, nor did he want it to be. Those objects, which he never detailed, were defiled and unwanted, their memories erased. And what about applying for reparations? His response was indignant, adamantly so, implying that some money was inherently unclean; those payments would have blood on them. Unstated, but clearly implied, was the sense that there could never be recompense. *Memento vivere.* Those personal objects, no matter their importance, belonged to the past and summoned memories best left alone.

Some objects, but not all. Present near the piano, wherever we lived, was the bronze bust of Chopin by the Polish sculptor Stansilaus Roman Lewandowski, awarded Alexander in 1932 for the best Mazurka performance during the competition.

The bronze bust of Chopin awarded Alexander Uninsky on March 23, 1932 for his performance of Mazurkas. Photo courtesy of the author.

Its presence was unexplained, perhaps inexplicable. It did not evoke unspoken memories, never openly serving as a mnemonic device introducing past events previously undiscussed, but it was always in place, clearly emblematic of a moment of pianistic virtuosity and my father's lifelong embrace of Chopin's enigmatic genius. Alexander also had a score of Prokofiev's Third Piano Concerto, ostensibly marked by the composer himself in the early 1930s. The penciled notations were obscure, only understood, Alexander would explain, in the context of their conversations when the two spent occasional evenings together, playing the composer's two piano compositions and chess. The score, like the sculpture, was an expression of pride, but it also had special significance, serving not only as evidence of achievement but of the requirement that artistic gifts needed nurturing by others of exceptional talent. Neither Lucie nor Alexander ever divulged how the fragile score and the unwieldy sculpture were the only objects to survive the seizure of his prewar apartment. One imagines they were left in the care of friends and later retrieved. They were treasured as links to certain highpoints of Alexander's prewar life, to the richness of past experiences. But these objects probably served other critical purposes. They were reminders that no prior success could be maintained without striving in the present, *memento vivere*. Artistic achievement was intrinsically tenuous and demanded constant attention, and it served as a critical element of persistence in even the worst of times. Ensuring that Alexander's gift had every opportunity to find its full voice was a strenuous, ongoing commitment made in the present, one that involved maintaining a continual state of wariness about the enduring risks and that rejected expectations of a secure future.

CHAPTER 22

In the End

The five members of the Uninsky and Biszkowicz families who survived the Second World War and spoke to me about their lives, invented and otherwise, were paragons of diversity and atypicality. They were an undeniably odd assortment of personalities, a great pianist and raconteur, a stoic grande dame, a hustler extraordinaire, a village tavern keeper, and a denizen of an unflaggingly cheerful present. Two others had cameo roles, appearing only in rarely expressed parental memories, but were also strikingly distinctive. One was a converso aunt remembered by my parents as a consummate betrayer and malevolence incarnate, the other Lucie's ostracized, laconic mother whose past was veiled and who was anything but a doting grandmother. Those I knew well, Lucie, Alexander, Choura, Tola, and Elisabeth, each had their own particular relationship with the past, ranging from Alexander's colorful canvas of high art, resilience, and ribaldry to his sister's silence. None had a "gift" like his, some seemingly no gift at all, and their senses of humor, interests in art, intellectual curiosity, and reliance on ribaldry and polyglotism in daily conversation ran every which way.

Highlighting the glaring distinctions among my parents and their siblings should not obscure some notable similarities. Aside from Lola, whose wartime conversion to Catholicism may have been a matter of either faith or expediency, or both, the others were not religiously observant. Alexander and Lucie regarded Judaism, like all organized religions, with a suspicion often bordering on hostility. They embraced instead a roughly sketched version of a secular and cultural Judaism, occasionally bracketed with hints of pantheism that may have been more about identification with Spinoza, an outcast Jew, than an assertion of spiritual belief. Other religions could be acknowledged, but at a very stiff arm's distance, and only if they had a certain utility, such as helping their son avoid military service in an unjust war. Choura, who deflected all discussions of what seems to have been an Orthodox upbringing in Kyiv, adopted an entirely secular public presence, hinting at his Jewish identity only in wry asides. He had a purely instrumental sense of religion when it came to his children, using Catholicism as a protective pretense. Aside from Elisabeth, who refrained from disclosing anything of her past or acknowledging any present disquiet or religiosity, Lucie and the three Uninsky brothers harbored lifelong concerns about the persistent threat of religious persecution. They took it for granted that the savagery of antisemitism was permanently entrenched, ineradicable, bubbling barely beneath the social surface and ever ready to emerge in full-throated form. While the danger was imminent, none revealed the details of their shared history of proximity to violence, terror, and genocide. It was treated as understood, to be revealed only through oblique hints and shadowed expressions, but neither denied nor affirmed with any specificity.

With notable variations, my parents, Choura and Tola, famous or not, treated any semblance of belonging, of feeling settled, as a charade. Alexander and Lucie framed their lives with an understanding that the here and now lacked any possibility of permanence, easily swept away by any of the recurring hazards that had marked their lives. Tola's pretense as an entrepreneur was always begun as a prologue to its deconstruction, forcing him to be on a continual ramble outside society's norms. Choura perfected a stable, multidimensional identity on the margins, minimizing his community to what seemed the smallest possible, ensuring that his own heritage was never transferred to his children, and hiding his passion for art with silence within the privacy of a locked room. And if names impart identity, Lucie, Alexander, Choura, and Tola seemed quite able, from a young age, to replace one persona with another.

The family narratives were marked by parallel, glaring absences about my maternal grandfather and paternal grandparents. None were ever named, and their disappearances during the war were never directly addressed. Esther and Miron Uninsky existed by inference, facilitators of their son's pianistic gifts in ways barely enumerated. Only once did Alexander give voice to his parents, in what was clearly an invented heroic script of selflessness. Lucie's father was depicted as a distant figure, wholly immersed in his efforts to trace the family's ancestry to the period of prophecy, when Jews returned from their exile in Babylon. An anonymous parent, Kleoman, stood as an antithesis to Esther and Miron, unwilling to prepare his daughter to pursue her talents, lacking in fatherly affection, and, by implication, ready to abandon her. And yet, despite the many differences in narrative and behavior that distinguished my relatives, their experiences of trauma followed by consistencies in recollection (their secularism, avoidance of discussions of past traumas, persistent wariness, and highly constrained reflections about their parents) helped to frame the family history for my generation.

Considering the commonalities of their narratives, one might ask, was there a direct throughline from having lived through successions of horrific ordeals to a threatened capacity for resilience and a shared fragility in their ability to persist? Such a shared through line offers a well-traveled view, a common, if not dominant one. Much of the discourse about severe trauma finds that it persistently and negatively results in a rather wide spectrum of frailty among survivors, including occluded memory, loss of agency, chronic sadness, depression, survivor's guilt, and suicidality. Survivors of trauma become living embodiments of their experiences, which indelibly, uncontrollably, and negatively mark their lives. As credible as this discourse about trauma may be, it often overexplains and has a flattening effect that is at odds with both the individuality and ebullience that clearly marked the lives of Lucie, Alexander, Choura, Elisabeth, and Tola. The cumulative effect of pogroms, revolution, the Shoah, imprisonment, and political persecution did not leave them with failing memories, lacking in resilience, persistence, distinctiveness, adaptability, or expressiveness, or at least not discernibly so. The evident cause had no signal effects. These architects of a family narrative rarely betrayed any of the telltale markers predicted by trauma discourse. Each of them, in their own way, succeeded in managing the present, inventing lives that often seemed shorn of many constraints, rebuilding from one catastrophe after another, pursuing forms of secular satisfaction. Their particular and often widely divergent personalities and behaviors emerge as a canvas of extremes, the eccentric and conventional, the self-effacing and the triumphantly comic, the conscientious citizen and the wayward criminal. If they were disguising or suppressing the negative consequences of trauma, they did so brilliantly, each in their own way, rarely showing signs of sadness and loss, perhaps guilt, but never feelings of hopelessness.

In all my conversations with Lucie and the Uninsky siblings, only Elisabeth draped a uniformly opaque cloak over the past, creating a blank slate. The others maintained verbal screens dotted with small openings that permitted carefully curated information about trauma to emerge, much of which was impossible to verify and some of which was likely part of the creative reimaginings they used to reinvent lives. These were hints that their memories of trauma were probably intact, but no details were offered. Grandparents disappeared, but the camps were never mentioned. At least in my family and those of my French cousins, we, their children, were left to imagine the worst. Our parents who survived did so by flight, combat, heroic endurance, or consummate obliviousness, but their closeness to disaster or how much they may have suffered never played a central role in their accounts. Children of survivors, we were left to decipher much of the past at school and from mass media.

Family reminiscences occasionally led my parents and their European siblings to observe that sudden emigration and war had deprived them of tangible connections to the past and any semblance of economic security. Such important outcomes of preceding events were only vaguely recalled and their loss rarely openly regretted, seemingly unimportant and consigned to an historical dustheap. Limiting discussion of the past in this way might well have been a strategy of emotional self-preservation, but it was also an instrument of creative reinvention. It fit well with their determined presentness, their thoroughgoing immersion in the moment, and their astonishing capacity to persist without blaming setbacks in their pasts. And perhaps their uncanny malleability, their startling capacity to adapt as circumstances seemed to dictate, was also partly due to conscious disassociation from earlier events.

The refusal, or unwillingness, to have the present affected by prior traumatic experiences also plausibly influenced the way they exercised their primary responsibilities as parents. Aside from Tola, whose anarchistic grifting and sudden departures left him distanced from his daughter, Lucie, Alexander, Choura, and Elisabeth were determined to nurture the next generation, particularly to foster resilience. For Lucie, with a surviving mother she could not tolerate and a father who seems to have ignored her emotionally and educationally, it was probably unsurprising that she chose to select a different maternal model and leave Kleoman an ungraspable ghost. It was likely for far different reasons that Alexander and his siblings left Esther and Miron nameless, grandparents who never emerged from the war and yet were unmentioned or who lived a faintly detailed, nearly two-dimensional existence. This may have been out of a reticence to engage in discussions that remained too emotionally fraught for them, tantamount to a conspiracy of silence, but there are other explanations equally in keeping with their postwar personalities. Perhaps this was partly a positive act of memory amber, an effort to preserve their parents enshrined in the time before the Shoah, idealized, loving, and protective. At least for Lucie and Alexander, circumventing trauma seemed in keeping with their commitment to creating a humane and creative environment, one that refused to countenance, as much as they could, its antithesis.

During my fifty-year quest to interpret the memories and behaviors of these extraordinary relatives, I expected to find, hiding behind these dense thickets obscuring major portions of their past, that deep roots of despair about human nature would emerge and that thorny vestiges of well-hidden hatreds of their tormentors would also somehow show through. As they aged, I wondered if memories of trauma would intrude upon the invented lives of these survivors, perhaps emerging from long years of diligent and intentional confinement. My aunt and uncles showed few indications that any such thing was occurring. Over time, what little new information about the past that emerged continued to bank away from past horrors and grief. Tola winked at his time in the Resistance and his earlier aspirations to be a playwright; Choura reminisced briefly about Alexander's early artistic career but suppressed any remembrances about his own, and Elisabeth revealed nothing at all. No tell-tale signs emerged that the past was exacting negative emotional consequences and forcing horror to the surface. And why this was so can only be surmised. In their own ways, excepting Tola, they all strove to promote the resilience of their children, and protecting them from the worst may have strengthened their armor against the past. Particularly in my household, humor, bawdy and refined, may have helped not only to deflect, but also to sweeten, as it were, helping to suppress pain and replace it with self-induced laughter. Perhaps all the silly jokes and arcane polyglot wit cushioned dreadfulness. Lucie, Alexander, and his brothers also found ways to vault past the worst with magical thinking propelling them through adversity and terror. A baron located the destitute Uninsky family among the masses of impoverished; a young pianist without a state performed at a critical juncture in Warsaw with the timely intervention of an ambassador and won in a coin toss; a young Ukrainian Jew was plucked from obscurity by de Gaulle's niece to lead a rearguard action against invaders in Brittany; an imprisoned fraudster had his sentence commuted at the death of a president he detested. The improbable pushed memories along, making the impossible seem plausible.

I kept in touch with Elisabeth over the years, and from what I could tell, she still kept her memories well confined to a mental safe deposit box, along with any signs of emotional tribulations. Elisabeth's distinctive quality in youth, as remembered by her siblings and Lucie, was her unflagging good will and optimism; unlike her siblings, she lacked ambition and was not endowed with a "gift." From the time we first met in 1973, it was clear her alleged prewar demeanor persisted in a form that her brothers might have recognized. For Alexander, his sister, the *papillon*, was a remote sibling who represented a nearly alien duality. Happiness, contentment, and a life so lightly engaged protected her from harm and insulated her from conflict and notoriety, but without a gift or any intention to discover one, she was deprived of so much that gave life meaning. To the end, she lived fully in the present, never openly recalling past atrocities, and, for all that I could tell, excluded from any downward spiral predicted by trauma discourse.

Tola's recounted memories and his grifting ways changed little during the years that I knew him. While others spoke of his youthful literary ambitions and playful nature, followed by Resistance heroics, my uncle provided only slight glimpses to his own past. On a few occasions he casually pointed toward a manuscript he identified as an unfinished play, one he never let me read. Until his final months, Tola rarely responded to questions about the war, offering instead either a brief criticism of de Gaulle's wartime inefficacy or a quick change of subject. From the time I first met him, Tola was already fully formed, a quirky denizen of the present, a charming fraudster, an economic anarchist who derided private property and who seemingly operated without regrets. For a quarter of a century after the war, he could, in large part, sustain this way of life because he was constantly forgiven, supported, beloved, and bailed out, primarily by Alexander, whom Tola indebted innumerable times during his life of habitual gambling. After my father's death, others occasionally came to his rescue, including his former wife and her partner, from whom he reportedly embezzled. From family, rejection was never a consequence for one who had given so much during the war. If Tola had darker thoughts or inclinations stemming from his violent and traumatic past, they were never evident, and certainly not close to the surface. Perhaps he suppressed them through incessant risk-taking, which kept him on a knife's edge, between prison and freedom. It seemed a life of joyful indeterminacy, moving happily forward, from one fleecing to another.

If Tola changed at all in his demeanor and memories, it was during his last year or so, when he began to mention the Resistance. These were unembroidered tales alluding to heroism—escapes, acts of sabotage, and tricksterism in a time of war—but never involving violence. These late-in-life memories may have emerged as instruments of safety. Frail, unable to scam and scheme, Tola reverted near the end to his nom de guerre, Robert, and returned to Brittany in the belief that some there still remembered him as a hero. Perhaps to assure his welcome, he appended the military rank of colonel, a curious addition for one who so openly disdained hierarchy. His Resistance status, he claimed with a charm and certainty that had long bolstered his credibility and melted the caution of many marks, resulted in admission without charge to a retirement center in Plouguernével in central Brittany. Once someone who refused to say much of his years in battle, Tola now lived partly in his version of the past, a source of pride and a guarantee of some security. Soon after my last visit, a few months before he died in December of 1992, I called Lucie, worried about my charismatic, ailing uncle. Might he be better off in the States, where he could be near his sister-in-law, who had always professed deep affection for her Tolichka? "Please do," she replied, "but only if you want all our bank accounts emptied."

Meanwhile, throughout his postwar years, Choura appeared to inhabit a life of perfect equilibrium. His new identity as a small businessman in a rural village afforded him a measure of personal and financial safety and, it always seemed, contentment. According to his wife, Monique, and in my presence, Choura's placid demeanor never gave way to mood swings, depressive episodes, or bouts of self-pity or despondency. Aside from glimpses into his rather secretive commitment to his palette and brushes, Choura managed to treat most of his past as if it was no one's affair. It was never clear if he had created any sort of coherent narrative for his family. His children seemed unaware of their father's religious upbringing or what he experienced from 1940 to 1945. Choura had created a façade of permanence, as if he had always been part of Saint-Rémy-sur-Avre. He belonged there, and no information to the contrary was available. This thoroughgoing state of presentness, and a lifetime of living in the Uninsky family historical haze, quickly tamped down my temptation to intervene with disruptive questions. Choura eventually offered a few openings past the façade of his adopted personality, perhaps because he recognized his nephew's need for some explanation. Unlike many in France in the 1970s, he once surprisingly announced, without any instigation, he was not anti-American. Their armies might be needed again to subdue the fascism that had so recently overcome France. He was vigilant about past dangers becoming present, even to the point of inventing Catholic identities for his children. Most of this alertness to danger played out covertly. If Choura suspected others of harboring antisemitic thoughts, he engaged in what seemed like a nonconfrontational theater of the absurd in his bistro, serving them Israeli orange juice or falsely pretending to be out of items they requested.

Although reinvented in his small village, what Choura had yearned to be before the war never entirely left him. At some point he returned to painting, but there was no apparent dissonance with his adopted identity as a *tavernier*. He painted in private and closely guarded his dream of painterly success, adopting the character of a dabbler with his family. But to his nephew, the son of a successful pianist, he made it clear that he had never relinquished his dream of a perfected gift. Why he settled on cubism remains unresolved. Perhaps it was a memory lapse, but it would have been curiously selective for someone who was so capable, when prompted and away from his family, of speaking knowledgeably about twentieth-century art. It could be that this one-time studio painter for André Lhote occasionally lapsed into his earlier role, following the footsteps of others. But his excitement and pleasure at his stylistic turn seemed to point elsewhere. When I asked why he chose this approach to his art, Choura, so often quizzical, laughed and teasingly asked if I could see the innovations in form, how he met the challenge of using a restricted palette, and the ways he gave new perspectives on common objects. There was no possible response but the affirmative. Choura had finally succeeded in acquiring an essential sense of satisfaction from his painting, deciding, it seemed, that the promise of the analytical cubism of Braque and Picasso had not yet been fulfilled. He was convinced that he had moved beyond the imitative to extend the work of giants past. What at first appeared to be a sign of a distorted memory, perhaps finally succumbing to tragic hardships endured, eventually struck me as a satisfying resolution to lost opportunities and persistent setbacks. This was more than an academic exercise in technique. Choura found a satisfying link between past and present in a private artistic conversation with himself, much as he did in his last months, in retirement, when he found a certain repose and satisfaction behind a linguistic wall of Russian. In his last months, Choura decided, after years of living in his invented persona, to become a cheerful recluse within his loving family. As death approached, this wry and resilient man was happily and coherently reminiscing about his youth in Kyiv, even if those around him, failing to understand the language, believed he was babbling in senile incoherence.

In the end, only two of the Biszkowicz and Uninsky survivors, Alexander and Lucie, eventually displayed behaviors that were a marked departure from their former demeanors. Beginning with our relocation to Dallas, signs of emotional discomfort began to break through. It is impossible to know if this change was a product of traumatic experiences finally wearing away some of their equanimity and ability to persevere. Memories of the past did not change noticeably, largely remaining focused on appreciation of artistry and artists, humor, cleverness, and bravery, but never on horror, grief, or loss. Only once, the year before he died, worried about Tola's determination to exact late-in-life revenge against a collaborator, did Alexander reveal a specific horror, the death in Auschwitz of a branch of the family never before mentioned. For both Lucie and Alexander, the intrusion of these new emotions that co-existed with their postwar lives were displayed largely at home, with their urbane public personae intact, aside from occasional risk-taking by Alexander, perhaps an expression of his increasing impatience with his environment. Even though I knew them far better than my aunts and uncles, there was never any clear disclosure about what precipitated these changes. The lifelong habit of deflection and invention never ceased. What distinguished Lucie and Alexander from others in the family was the extent to which they were beleaguered by invidious circumstances that Elisabeth and Choura managed to avoid. And as for Tola, often on the run from law enforcement, it seemed that what kept him intact and seemingly inoculated him against emotional fragility was, perversely, his enjoyment of living with risk, a pleasure he clearly derived from his anarchic ways. But Lucie and Alexander, after moving to Texas, were exposed, far more than in New York, to an unrelenting wear and tear that made life on the fringe seem ever more tenuous. While it was never evident that banked emotions of a traumatic past had now begun to pay painful dividends, there was no question that after moving to Texas, they found that much of what they held dear was repeatedly exposed to new tensions, insults, and injuries.

Although neither Alexander nor Lucie believed a secure future was attainable for their family, in 1963 they attempted to attain a small measure of it by moving from New York City to Dallas, where Alexander would become an academic artist. If financial stability was the goal, the compensation was too modest, but it came with the freedom to continue touring and the possibility of tuition-free college education for my sister, Eliane, and me. But thereafter the signs of disquiet, attenuated at first, began to appear. Lucie's stoicism, her rock-like demeanor, would occasionally slip away, replaced with brief episodes of incommunicative melancholy. Irritated wrangling between mother and daughter began more often to escalate into angry disputes. In retrospect, this was likely a collision of distinct problems, Lucie's dissatisfaction with life in Texas and Eliane's increasingly erratic and tempestuous outbursts, at that point an undiagnosed mental illness that would intensify as she aged. Alexander also gradually changed, drinking more, his stories more laden with vulgarities, and engaging in new behaviors where he took uncharacteristic risks. Despite these emerging fissures in their armors of resilience, both Alexander and Lucie were able to hold the two sides of their personalities in a tenuous balance. Even though signs of a darker side emerged in Texas, what had always been in evidence in their personalities remained—an inexhaustible dedication to art, a formidable will to persist, an ability to leaven the worst with their brand of polyglot humor, and a wariness that kept them on the fringe.

From the moment we arrived in Dallas in 1963, there were adverse circumstances, unpredictable stressors, that undermined hopes of a relatively smooth transition from New York City and unsettled Lucie and Alexander. An unremitting deluge of alienating incidents placed them on a more remote fringe than they had expected. The very existence of exclusionary residential areas confirmed their worst suspicions about the persistence of segregation. Living in outer suburban Dallas jangled all our nerves with a local dialect infused with common interjections of casually expressed racism. Some of our reaction to something we all expected was rooted in a sense of cultural superiority, partly feigned and certainly defensive. Slurs spoken in the streets of Manhattan were often muffled, we assured each other, somehow less offensive, spoken in the many languages of our neighborhood. Now we were far more firmly identified as outsiders, by diction and, for Lucie and Alexander, by accent. The murders of JFK and Oswald were an exclamation point on their growing estrangement from Dallas. For weeks, Alexander could be heard exclaiming to anyone who might listen that the city was "now on the map of malevolence."

Then came the obsession that often accompanies persecution. We initially took up residence on the edge of Dallas, close to White Rock Lake, near where H. L. Hunt, the oil tycoon lived in a copy of Mount Vernon. He was known to start the day on his front lawn with cannon blasts as the US flag was raised, accompanied by a highly amplified recording of the "Star-Bangled Banner." This, both Lucie and Alexander insisted on witnessing, an opportunity to mock the McCarthyite white supremacist and the ludicrous right-wing publications and radio programs that he funded. Returning to the car afterwards, a recent copy of *Lifelines,* a Hunt publication, had been slipped through an open window. The main story was about Alexander; it lamented the arrival in Dallas of a notorious socialist, a once blacklisted participant in the international Jewish conspiracy. This was not a coincidence, Alexander proclaimed theatrically. Perhaps his response was an act of playful dramaturgy, but it was also an expression of alarm. The intensified feeling of being unwanted and dangerous outsiders soon led Lucie and Alexander to cast their net of suspicion more widely, reducing sociability and deepening their isolation. Alexander continued to find solace in music, but now, more often, in drinking. "How can you say I drink too much," he would protest when his children expressed concern, "when my glass is always empty?"

Being singled out as a danger to the community by a buffoonish, antisemitic billionaire also led to planned resistance using the instrument of defiance my parents most prized, humor. Soon after the incident at White Rock Lake, Alexander, assisted by a group of music students and laughingly supported by Lucie, placed a papier-mâché globe in a fountain on the SMU campus with a banner that read "In Your Heart You Know It's Flat." The university's leadership was not amused by this mockery of Goldwater's presidential campaign, and the family's sense of alienation and vulnerability escalated with the threat to discontinue Alexander's contract.

By the late 1960s, Alexander's occasional forays into uncharacteristic behaviors began to worry Lucie. They quibbled about his drinking and risk-taking. My mother soon reverted to her more stolid role, the family rock, apparently to dilute the impact on Eliane and me and, it appeared, to place some boundaries on her mercurial spouse. It did not work. Alexander had begun adopting identities that he thought others would find off-putting and dangerous. When annoyed by someone's curiosity about his speech, for example, he would, uncannily, identify the source of their accent, hinting darkly, his form of ironic and personal humor, that it was part of his work for the government, inducing someone to ask if he worked for an agency like the CIA, to which he would only respond with a serious glare. He detested country clubs, bastions of undeserved privilege and racism, but in Dallas and on vacations, he entered their bridge tournaments, where he was unknown. Pretending to be a novice, Alexander would mercilessly fleece the unwitting. And when he drank it was certainly not just to temper his deep sense that he had erred horribly by moving to Dallas, but also because of arthritic pain in his hands. His existence as an artist was threatened, and medical care was ineffective. His solution, true to form, was to make sure all around him appreciated the humor of his mock solution. He was treating himself with "whiskerin, an opiate for pain." It was his special blend of Bufferin, which he claimed would protect his fragile stomach, and the whisky he insisted was the pope's number at the Vatican: not really an opiate and certainly not for the masses, he would slowly intone.

In December 1972, Alexander Uninsky died in his sleep, months before he was to begin a tour long in the planning to celebrate his career. Lucie lived on for forty years, with the past rarely coming to the fore. She only spoke of Alexander if prompted, and then only on those rare instances when inaccurate biographical details about her husband were mentioned or written. Then she would respond with a brief, pinpoint correction, without emotion or sentimentality. If she lived with Alexander's music, it was only as a memory. She never played his records. To the end, she insisted on living in an art-infused present, frequently attending concerts and museum exhibitions, expressing her well-informed judgments about artists without framing her comments by referring to those luminaries she had known when she was a grande dame. For forty years, she lived alone, reminding everyone who asked if she would prefer to be in a more supportive environment, that those were places to die, not to live.

They and those like them deserve to be remembered, these survivors of unimaginable trauma, who managed through their inventiveness, tenaciousness, humor, and more, to be resilient, vibrant, and humane throughout their lives.

Index

www.ingramcontent.com/pod-product-compliance
Lightning Source LLC
Chambersburg PA
CBHW071008140426
42814CB00004BA/159

* 9 7 9 8 8 8 7 1 9 8 4 7 7 *